T0275257

CAMPESINO A CAMPESINO

CAMPESINO A CAMPESINO

Voices from Latin America's
FARMER TO FARMER MOVEMENT
for Sustainable Agriculture

Eric Holt-Giménez

FOOD FIRST BOOKS
OAKLAND, CALIFORNIA

Copyright © 2006 by Eric Holt-Giménez

All rights reserved. No part of this book may be reproduced or transmitted in any form or by any means, electronic or mechanical, including photocopying, recording, or by any information storage retrieval system, without written permission from the publisher, except for brief review.

Food First Books
398 60th Street
Oakland, CA 94618
510-654-4400
www.foodfirst.org

Cover and text design by Amy Evans McClure
Cover photograph by Eric Holt-Giménez
Copy editor: Kelly E. Burch
Proofreader: Hope Steele
Indexer: Ken DellaPenta
All photographs by Eric Holt-Giménez unless otherwise indicated

LIBRARY OF CONGRESS CATALOGING-IN-PUBLICATION DATA
Holt-Giménez, Eric.
    Campesino a campesino : voices from Latin
    America's Farmer to Farmer Movement for
    Sustainable Agriculture / Eric Holt-Giménez.
        p. cm.
        Includes bibliographical references and index.
        ISBN-13: 978-0-935028-27-0 (pbk.)
        ISBN-10: 0-935028-27-7 (pbk.)
    1. Movimiento Campesino a Campesino.
    2. Sustainable agriculture—Central America.
    3. Soil conservation—Central America.
    4. Farmers—Training of—Central America.
    5. Agricultural innovations—Central America. I. Title.
        S476.A1.H65   2006
        333.76'160972—dc22   2005033767

Food First Books are distributed by:
Client Distribution Services (CDS)
387 Park Avenue South, New York, NY 10016
800-343-4499
www.cdsbooks.com

Printed in Canada

5 4 3 2 1 – 06 07 08 09 10

Contents

Preface

TWENTY-FIVE YEARS AGO, on the parched Meseta Central of Mexico, I sat under a tree with a small group of *campesinos* as we shared our thoughts during a break in a soil conservation workshop. The workshop, like many others before it, addressed the pressing problems of soil erosion, drought, and low crop yields. Unlike the other courses, however, this one was not taught by professional extensionists; it was given by farmers for other farmers. The campesino teachers were indigenous visitors from Guatemala who still wore the richly embroidered, handwoven clothes typical of the Kaqchikel Mayans. Speaking in slow, broken Spanish, they repeated themselves frequently as they dug their hands into the soil feeling its tilth. They carefully inspected roots, observed leaves, and counted insects. Sometimes, they unsheathed their machetes from their belts and drew figures in the dirt to illustrate their points. Their manner was warm and unassuming, their curiosity infectious. These teachers were a far cry from the government extension agents I knew who gave formal lessons in classrooms, read from coveted books, and used unintelligible technical words to teach about modern agriculture. In the minds of the Mexican farmers, however, schools were for learning and fields were for working. They were still skeptical of the knowledge brought by these strange, yet somehow familiar, outsiders . . . and I was nervous.

I had organized the course months earlier as one of the last activities of the alternative agriculture project I was concluding with my partner in the village of Vicente Guerrero, Tlaxcala. Crowded onto a small communal *ejido*, the seventy campesino families eked out their livelihoods on one- to two-hectare plots of hilly, drought-ridden, largely treeless land. Everywhere, *tepetate* (lifeless, weathered dirt the color and consistency of brick) pushed through the thin brown layer of receding topsoil, making the ground impenetrable.[1] Work was hard, and agriculture, a mixture of traditional cultivation methods laced with a bit of chemical fertilizer and inordinate amounts of questionable pesticide, was risky. Though yields were low, farmers depended on them, and were generally unwilling to risk losing their meager harvests by introducing new techniques. If a crop failed, they migrated to Mexico City to work as day laborers.

Our project, sponsored by the Mexican Friends Service Committee (MFSC), was supposed to improve rural livelihoods by introducing "appropriate" agricultural technologies. Villagers, gracious and genuinely entertained by the presence of a North American couple among them, had provided us with a small plot of land for an integrated "model" farm that we stocked with rabbits, goats, ducks, a solar shower, a composting toilet, and a lush biointensive garden fortified by a sturdy (if exotic) chicken wire fence. The campesinos viewed the farm with a mixture of curiosity and amusement (the gringos *shit* in a barrel!). We were learning as we went along, and most of our techniques had been dismal failures: the neighbors' dogs ate our rabbits, the milk goats came down with mastitis, and the ducks mysteriously died off one by one. . . . We ate reasonably well from our garden, but often what our integrated model farm had in fact modeled was what *not* to do. While a few families planted biodynamic beds in their patios, for the most part, villagers politely ignored our suggestions for composting, crop rotations, organic farming, and reforesting on the ejido land where they grew the family's corn and beans. As volunteers, our two-year appointment was coming to an end, and except for the vegetables in our own garden, we had little to show for our efforts at agricultural development.

Guillermo Corado, the Guatemalan sociologist evaluating our project, suggested I contact Marcos Orozco, a retired agronomist from the highlands of Chimaltenango, Guatemala. Don Marcos worked with Kaqchikel farmer-extensionists and gave inspirational classes in soil and water conservation. Since they were touring Mexico with the help of World Neighbors, I had nothing to lose by organizing a course—nothing but my own hubris —I still believed in our model farm. My last hope was that perhaps Don Marcos and the Kaqchikeles would convince the campesinos of Vicente Guerrero of what I had been telling them all along.

I announced the soil and water conservation workshop at a Sunday village meeting. After some cajoling, twenty farmers reluctantly signed up. A week later, I picked up the Guatemalans at dawn in a crowded bus station in Mexico City. With their bright clothing, woven handbags, and machetes strapped to their waists, the Kaqchikeles were easy to spot. (Of course, light haired and blue eyed, so was I.) We set off for Vicente Guerrero where, I assured them, a sizable group would be waiting. We bounced to a halt in front of the treeless village square three hours later. Only two men were waiting, Roque and Paz.

"Where is everyone?" I asked, too flustered for introductions. Roque and Paz just shrugged. I ran from house to house looking for the other eighteen participants. Everyone was either attending to an "urgent matter," or busy working. Some assured me they would be along later. When I got back, Paz had already left. I was devastated, embarrassed by my failure as an organizer, and ready to call the whole thing off.

Don Marcos said calmly, "As long as there is one person interested, we will stay to share the little that we know."

It looked hopeless to me. "But we have more teachers than *students!*"

One of the farmer-extensionists, José Cupertino, smiled and shook his head politely. "No," he said, "we too, are students."

Poor attendance notwithstanding, the course was excellent. Don Marcos was an agronomist, conservationist, and master storyteller. The Kaqchikeles were artists. Relying on few words, their machetes, and a tape measure, they marked off square meter demonstration plots on the sloping ground. Leaving one plot bare, on the other they built small terraces with pebbles, then protected the soil with leafy ground cover. They poured water from cans on both plots to show how erosion started then pointed to the terraces to explain how conservation worked. Then they measured the differences in runoff, soil loss, and moisture retention between the two plots. Working slowly, they took pencils and notebooks from their handbags and patiently estimated the tons of soil conserved on a protected hectare of land. Of course, this was also an estimate of the hundreds of tons of topsoil soil being *lost* from the village's fields every year. Soil, Don Marcos reminded us, that had taken hundreds of years to form.

For three days the Kaqchikeles mounted brilliantly simple demonstrations that communicated abstract ecological and agronomic concepts. Paz returned intermittently and learned, along with Roque and me, how to make a rustic transit to lay out contour lines. Then we built terraces. We collected mulch and made compost. Our teachers found organic matter and moisture everywhere. Unlike the poorly trained, frankly haughty extensionists I had encountered previously in Mexico, these men were *sencillo*—humble and respectful—despite their impressive knowledge. Don Marcos joked frequently about making mistakes in the field, about embarrassing lessons he'd been given by clever campesinos. He didn't appear to be bothered by farmers' reticence about changing their practices but saw their behavior as a logical reaction of someone who was not yet convinced of new ways of doing things. To him, this resistance was an important attribute.

"Better for a person to accept things after great resistance," he said, "Those that adopt new ideas quickly, drop them just as quickly."

The team carefully introduced us to new farming and conservation techniques by introducing new ways of thinking. Somehow, they always based this new thinking on the timeless values of dignity, fairness, mutual aid, and common sense. Speaking from their own experience, they appealed to the strength and wisdom of campesino culture and invited Roque and Paz to modify, not abandon, their way of life to make it better. Using parables, stories, and humor, they presented agricultural improvement as a logical outcome of clear thinking and compassion: love of farming, of family, of nature and of community. Rather than try to convince us of their innovations, they insisted we experiment with new things on a small scale first to see how well they worked.

If only more campesinos had taken the workshop! I had seen them sit uncomfortably for hours in the small desks of the local grammar school as they were subjected to boring, dense monologues from government extensionists. On the off chance that the visit from a government employee might result in some "favor" (materials, supplies, credit), they listened to recipe after unworkable recipe of expensive seed, fertilizer, and pesticide packages, to irrigation and machinery schemes they would never implement, and to long harangues criticizing the backwardness of peasant agriculture. Yet they had missed *this* workshop that was practical, interesting, respectful, and applicable. I felt strangely fulfilled and defeated. I was happy with my new knowledge, yet frustrated with the villagers' poor attendance.

When the course was over, we evaluated our work. Because so few people had participated, it had lasted only four days rather than the customary six. However, the team had covered all the basic material and was satisfied that we had learned enough to begin working on our own. José Cupertino reminded us of the basic principles of starting small, going slowly, experimenting with everything first, and sharing our knowledge with others only after we had something concrete to share. The Guatemalans passed each of us a hand-lettered "diploma" they had made, indicating that we had all graduated from our first course in soil and water conservation. Don Marcos thanked each of us for our hard work and mentioned several things he had learned from us during the workshop.

"I don't care if you try new ideas out on a one-meter-square test plot," he said, "and if you only tell a neighbor. But do *something* and show *someone*. You have worked hard, and now have something precious that no one can take away from you."

José Cupertino continued, "This knowledge has not been easy to attain for any of us. *Nos ha costado a todos.* We have given it to you willingly because you showed interest, and now you have the *compromiso moral* (moral obligation) to use it wisely for the benefit of your family, your village, and others."

The team invited us to say whatever we wanted about the workshop but to also indicate what we were going to do. Roque spoke first.

"*Bueno, compañeros,*" he said rising formally, removing his sombrero and bowing slightly toward us. "We are poor campesinos and didn't know anything about these things before you came." Then his voice cracked. His hat shook in his hands. Tears welled up in his eyes and streamed shamelessly down his face. I looked on in astonishment.

"What you have given us . . . I can't thank you with words." He put his hand on the diploma in front of him. "We never went to school. We are *ignorantes.* This is the first time we ever learned anything so good, *tan bueno.* I can never repay you. I only hope that you did not come here in vain. I don't know if anyone will listen to me, but I will put soil conservation on my lot in town in front of everyone. I will teach anyone who asks. Bueno, compañeros, that is all I have to say."

I was speechless. I remember looking around dumbly with a lump in my throat. Whatever I said I was going to do must have been inconsequential because soon thereafter I abandoned all pretensions of teaching farmers to farm. Roque, true to his word, went on to put all of his land under sustainable farming processes. Hundreds of campesinos have visited him over the years. Further, he was instrumental in organizing the first Campesino a Campesino team in Mexico. As for me, helping farmers teach farmers became my *compromiso moral,* an activity I have pursued for over twenty-five years.

The "story" of el Movimiento Campesino a Campesino (MCAC) is really many stories, all intimately personal and profoundly political, all woven deep in the cultural fabric of the Mesoamerican countryside. The stories are transformative, deeply social, and highly individual: a painfully shy farmer who, responding to the irrepressible desire to share the results of his innovations, receives group after group of visitors in his field; a teenage girl braves the dangers of a war-torn region to learn the power of women in agriculture; an elderly campesina with a passion for experimenting leads her cooperative to national recognition as a nursery of agrobiodiversity; the conventional agronomist who, after seeing the power of farmer-led approaches to agroecology, abandons the role of expert and dedicates herself to knowledge sharing between smallholders. There are political stories as well, such as the reorganization of a Mexican *municipio* to support farmer-to-farmer development; the field schools for sustainable agriculture organized and run by farmers; the transformation of government agricultural services; and the regional gatherings where campesinos cultivate their collective wisdom by sharing seeds, techniques, information, songs, poems, and many, many stories.

Because of the plurality of experiences and voices within the movement, telling the definitive Campesino a Campesino story is impossible. However, the lives of the *promotores, agrónomos,* and *profesionales* in the Movimiento are all stitched together by daily livelihood struggles and by the shared visions of sustainable futures in which campesinos are the protagonists.

Contrary to conventional wisdom, today's campesinos are not culturally static or politically passive. Nor are they disappearing as a social class. Campesino families across Mesoamerica and the Caribbean (and around the world) are constantly adapting to global, regional, and local forces. The stories of Campesino a Campesino are embedded in a political framework that is itself a story of unflagging resistance to decades of a "development" that sought to eliminate peasants from the countryside and, more recently, to neoliberal economic policies that prioritize corporate profit margins over environment, food security, and rural livelihoods.

This book, the result of a decades-long relationship with the men and women of the MCAC, is made up of stories chosen to relate a narrative of cultural resistance. I present these stories in this way primarily because of the effect that the movement has had on me. I have campesinos to thank for disabusing me of my (not very) original notions regarding sustainable agriculture, rural development, politics, and social change. In their place, I have begun to see sustainability as an emergent property that springs from autonomy and food sovereignty; development as an interface for political negotiation; and social change as an open, undetermined process where peoples' collective agency clashes with the hierarchical structures that oppress them.

I relate the story of Campesino a Campesino as a struggle for cultural resistance because campesino culture has withstood both socialist and capitalist versions of progress. Indeed, while both systems worked to industrialize agriculture and eliminate the peasantry, both depended on the massive labor subsidies supplied directly and indirectly by smallholders. Even today, campesinos across the Mesoamerican isthmus resist the devastating economic effects of globalization both from their home communities and from the fields, factories, and service sectors of the United States, to which they supply an inexhaustible army of cheap, expendable labor. In the first instance they are the main supply of basic grains for the poor of Mesoamerica, in the second, the mainstay for food and services for the affluent North. In Cuba campesinos were instrumental in saving the country from starvation after the fall of the Soviet bloc.

I employ the term *cultural resistance* in a deep sense that includes campesino expressions of "agri-culture," that is, the ways farmer innovation, free association, mutual aid, food production, and environmental protection work through tools, organization, and language to fashion autonomous paths to equitable, sustainable futures.

Finally, I have decided to narrate the story of Campesino a Campesino as a resistance struggle because this is consistent with the way campesinos in the movement tell stories to each other, sharing their knowledge and wisdom, helping each other to help themselves in the face of the abuses of government and capital. The tales from Campesino a Campesino are grounded in peoples' will to feed themselves and others in fair, environmentally sustainable ways; to develop their own agriculture; and to provide for dignified livelihoods based on mutual respect and self-determination.

Given the obstacles to sustainable agriculture in the industrialized North and given that our futures are inextricably tied to the South, we may all learn something from this resistance. Reaching toward Campesino a Campesino's rich body of experience can help us identify allies and opportunities for collaboration with our own, related struggles. By sharing in the "wisdom of resistance," we also share in its inspiration.

Acknowledgments

I want to thank all of the professionals and nongovernmental institutions that supported this work over the years, and all of the technicians and agronomists who accompanied me as we changed our relationship with farmers from one of outside experts to that of facilitators and allies.

Gracias a mi compadre Manolo, who taught me how to travel deeply through cultures; to the late Rogelio Cova, who infected me with optimism; and to the Programa de Campesino a Campesino (PCAC) technicians of the Nicaraguan Farmers and Ranchers Union, who adapted and improved upon my work far beyond anything I ever imagined. Thank you to the many *compañeros y compañeras internacionalistas* who unflinchingly put their lives on the line and their careers at the service of the *campesinado*, especially Roberto Vega, Anasonia Recinos, and Pascal Chaput.

Thanks to Margaret Fitzsimmons and David Goodman who taught me to use political economy, and to Jonathan Fox who showed me how to combine activism and academia. Thanks to Steve Gliessman, who shared his extensive knowledge of agroecology; and to Miguel Altieri, who along with Peter Rosset helped me apply it politically. Thanks to my students at UC Santa Cruz and Boston University's International Honors Program for keeping the personal and the political refreshingly confused. *Gracias a mi madre* who always believed in me, and to my late father, who eventually did. Thanks to my brother Miguel, whose faith in me is unconditional. *Gracias a mis hijos Gabriel y Evarosa*, who insisted I write down the stories, and to their mother, Kaki Rusmore, who was instrumental in having many of them happen in the first place. *Gracias a La Ceiba por compartir mis pasiones y a la Urraca por su pasión por compartir.*

Finally, to the many campesino *promotores* and *promotoras* of the Movement, who took me into their fields, their homes, and their communities, and who gave freely of their food, time, wisdom, and good humor; your stories, linked as they are to mine, are a constant source of hope and inspiration. Thank you, I can never repay you.

Introduction

Agricultural transformation in the world's developing regions will require
a thrice green revolution: green for productivity, green for environmental
sustainability, and green for increased income as the entry
point to improved living conditions.
—*Ismail Serageldin, Executive Director, CGIAR, 1997*

Sustainable development is a process of progressive change in the quality
of life of human beings, that situates them in the center as primary
subjects of development, through economic growth with social equity and
[through] the transformation of the methods of production and the
patterns of consumption, and that sustains ecological equilibrium and the
vital support of the region. This process implies respect of the ethnic,
cultural, regional, national and local diversity, as well as the strengthening
of full citizen participation, in peaceful coexistence and in harmony
with nature, without compromising and guaranteeing the
quality of life of future generations.
—*The presidents of Costa Rica, El Salvador, Guatemala, Honduras,
Nicaragua, and Panama (CCAD 1994)*

I just want to know, why is it big farmers are always getting services, credit
and subsidies, and all we campesinos ever get are projects for
sustainable agriculture?
—*Peasant farmer, Campesino a Campesino movement, Nicaragua,1998*

Sustainable Agricultural Development

FEW PEOPLE ON THE PLANET argue against the importance of sustainable agriculture. Everyone, from the World Bank to the Zapatistas, is in favor of some form of agricultural development that "meets the needs of present generations without compromising the needs of future generations to meet their needs. . . ." However, many argue about just *what* sustainable agriculture is; who should develop it, and how, and for whom; and about who should pay the costs of transforming unsustainable agricultural practices into sustainable ones. While it may be informed by ecology, economics, sociology, and other disciplines, *sustainability* in and of itself is primarily a political and social concept—a normative framework within which to make decisions (Lélé 1991; Hynnemeyer et al. 1997).

This means that sustainability is *decided* upon. So who gets to decide what it is? Environmentalists? Scientists? Politicians? Corporations? Villagers? Behind the apparent social consensus for "sustainability" lies a conflictive arena of struggle in which different business interests, political institutions, cultures, countries, states, municipalities, towns and villages, families, and individuals sort out the costs and benefits of environment and development.

Some institutions, such as the World Trade Organization (WTO), the Food and Agriculture Organization of the United Nations (FAO), the World Bank, the International Monetary Fund (IMF), the Consultative Group on International Agricultural Research (CGIAR), and the United Nations Development Programme (UNDP) are particularly well equipped to generate and disseminate their arguments. But ironically, the primary actors actually practicing sustainable agriculture in Mesoamerica today do not belong to any of these institutions. The cutting edges of sustainable agricultural development are not found in the international agricultural research facilities or in the air-conditioned offices of the world's food and agriculture experts. Neither are they found on the mechanized, irrigated farms and corporate plantations occupying the region's rich valleys and bottomlands. They are found on the shares of ox-drawn plows, and on the blades of the shovels, hoes, and machetes of hundreds of thousands of innovative but resource-poor smallholders who work the fragile hillsides, drought-ridden plains, and remote forest perimeters of the agricultural frontier. The people actually producing food and protecting the environment are too busy surviving to engage in institutional debates. They live far from the centers of power and are simply not able to sit around hammering out project proposals, policy papers, or op-eds. They don't have the time or resources to lobby politicians and multilateral decision makers. For them, sustainable agriculture means sustaining their livelihoods. It is a full-time job, and a way of life.

Luckily, hundreds of farmer's organizations, nongovernmental organizations (NGOs), development professionals, and individual researchers work with and support these smallholders—putting on workshops, arranging gatherings, carrying out action research, and studying and writing about farmer-led development and sustainable agriculture. This book is part of this supportive effort. It is an attempt to bring the voices of the men and women presently developing sustainable agriculture on the ground in Mesoamerica and the Caribbean into the debate about the region's future. It is not an attempt to speak for them, but to amplify their voices in an effort to make their experiences more visible.

Movimiento Campesino a Campesino:
Peasant Roads to Sustainable Agriculture

The following chapters follow the MCAC (Farmer to Farmer Movement) in its thirty-year effort to improve smallholder livelihoods and rural environments through farmer-led, sustainable agricultural development. As this book will illustrate, the MCAC is actually a nascent movement for social change. Based on principles of agroecology, solidarity, and innovation, the movement resists the ecologically degrading and socially destructive commodification of soil, water, and genetic diversity and asserts the rights of smallholders to determine an equitable, sustainable course for agricultural development.[1]

The stories from the MCAC provide an insight into decades of campesino struggles in the face of the First World's project to "develop" the Third World. Despite government rhetoric and with the possible exception of Cuba, in Latin America sustainable agriculture does not form a structural part of any national agricultural policies for development, trade, or food security. Sustainable agricultural development is primarily practiced in village-level development projects run by a diverse, loosely associated array of nongovernmental agencies and community-based organizations. Working with poor, politically disenfranchised villagers, projects for sustainable agriculture tend to focus on farm-level technological change rather than national-level policy change. The actual, on-the-ground experiences of farmers trying to farm sustainably almost never inform, much less influence, formal agricultural research agendas or government agricultural development policy. They are not reflected in the policies of the WTO, in regional trade agreements, or in the lending policies and practices of the IMF or the World Bank.

The reasons behind the marginalization of farmer-driven sustainable agricultural development have to do with the dominant political and economic structures that prioritize the free movement of international finance capital, economic growth in gross national product (GNP), and conventionally grown agricultural exports rather than food and livelihood security or sustainable production. To be viable at a national level, and to compete with conventional agriculture, sustainable agriculture *practices* require *policies* and institutions that ensure timely and appropriate services (credit, marketing, research, etc.) much like those enjoyed by large-scale, conventional agriculture since the beginning of the Green Revolution in the 1960s. Really developing sustainable agriculture will require fundamental changes in the political and economic structure of agriculture itself. This would itself require a major social and economic transformation. As such, sustainable agricultural development cannot be viewed as just a collection of projects and techniques, but as part of a larger process of *social change*. With hundreds of thousands of members and over a hundred grassroots organizations, the MCAC provides us with a view from the actors on the ground involved in this change.

The Development Context: A Quick Summary

Sustainable agricultural development is largely a response to the social and environmental shortcomings of agricultural modernization. It first appeared in Latin America when the agricultural development strategies of the Green Revolution of the 1960s and 1970s failed to solve the problems of rural poverty.[2] This led a handful of progressive rural development agencies to introduce "alternative" agricultural practices. By the 1980s it was clear that not only had the Green Revolution actually exacerbated socioeconomic disparity in the countryside, its indiscriminate use of agrochemicals, irrigation, and heavy machinery had also resulted in widespread environmental damage to rural ecosystems. In response, the UNDP and a few other development agencies began to talk about "sustainable agricultural development."[3] Some NGOs actually tried to put it into practice.

The 1980s also ushered in the now-chronic Third World debt crisis. The World Bank and the IMF responded to the problem by conditioning their development loans on neoliberal "structural adjustment programs," or SAPs, which were to be carried out by the governments of debtor countries. In order to obtain fresh loans, governments were obliged to sell off state-owned industries to private investors, devaluate their currency, open their markets to foreign goods and investment, deregulate their economy, and drastically reduce the size of government. These programs were extremely lucrative for northern corporations. The people of the global South fared less well.

In Latin America, these neoliberal economic policies had devastating effects on the countryside. State-sponsored production credit and agricultural extension services disappeared. Subsidies for agricultural inputs dried up. Unregulated international trade led to the dumping of cheap, subsidized grains from the United States into the South, driving southern farmers out of business and concentrating land in fewer and fewer hands. Dispossessed of land and abandoned by their governments, the rural poor retreated onto fragile hillsides and pushed deeper into the region's shrinking tropical forests. This exacerbated their geographic and economic marginality. Environmental problems such as deforestation, soil erosion, and water scarcity got worse, not better. This reinforced the widely invoked but tautological belief of a "vicious cycle of poverty and environmental degradation": the poor are poor because they scratch out a living in degraded environments, and because they are poor, they have no choice but to destroy the environment to survive. This circular argument ignores the causes of both poverty and environmental degradation.

Nonetheless, "sustainable agricultural and rural development," or SARD, was tasked with breaking this vicious cycle. But the concept of SARD was introduced *after* structural adjustment had wreaked its economic and social havoc. In its wake there was no institutional capacity and little human capital in affected countries for *any* development programs, sustainable or otherwise. Thus, from its inception, sustainable agricultural development was marginal to global economic trends, entering the development mainstream precisely when the classical notion of development itself had already been abandoned for all practical purposes.

At the same time, the world was shrinking. Southern deforestation and burning contributed to global warming, and though the role of northern economies in producing global warming (and southern poverty) was not always analyzed, there was a growing awareness that consumption patterns in the North put a strain on people and resources in the South. The situation was globally unsustainable, and it began to be perceived that it was in the interests of the rich and the poor of both northern and southern nations to work together to solve the world's environmental problems.

The challenge of sustainability as outlined by the Brundtland Commission's *Our Common Future* (WCED 1987) is on the surface a global environmental issue, to be taken up locally by all those interested in a sustainable future—that is, everyone. If we are all to live well now and in our "common future," both the natural resources of the planet and economic growth must be sustained and somewhat equitably distributed.

But just as earlier notions of development often ignored the causes of poverty, these ideas of sustainability did not look very deeply into the causes of unsustainability. The drive to sustain concentrated economic growth continued unabated in the face of the growing need to redistribute wealth, guarantee food security, and conserve natural resources. Reconciling the powerful forces of economic expansion and capital accumulation with the need for conservation and equity under the single rubric of "sustainability" was difficult and frequently led to political confusion. In this sense, while the call for sustainability has been discursively heroic, it has not been structurally transformative.

Clearly, invoking "sustainability" or "common futures" in global, regional, or local scenarios between actors of inequitable levels of political and economic power and with vastly different levels of control over resources is problematic—or worse, dishonest. If the possibilities for agricultural sustainability are to be understood at all, the power struggles operating *behind* the sustainability discourse must also be revealed. Otherwise, framing sustainable agriculture as a solution simply elides the issue of sustainability as a problem. This means that sustainable agriculture has to be understood as more than just a set of environmentally sound practices; as we will see in the story of Campesino a Campesino, sustainable agricultural development must also address the causes of unsustainable agriculture as well. It must speak to the struggles of people actually putting sustainability into practice.

Mesoamerica's Peasantry: The Plight and the Promise

Modern-day peasant agriculture is a baffling mix of market and subsistence strategies, international capital flows, global and local institutions, complex environmental interactions, and contested resource use. Marginalized by modernization and abandoned to globalization, smallholders in the Mesoamerican countryside have had few lasting rural alternatives to improve their livelihoods. Many of the rural benefits of economic development have been eclipsed by war, debt, and structural adjustment. Literally millions of campesinos have been forced into the historic escape of last resort: migration to the cities, the United States, and the agricultural frontier. Smallholders who have managed to stay on the land have often done so in spite of, not because of, mainstream strategies for agricultural development. On the ground, smallholder agriculture is battered by global and local push-pull factors, away from and back to the farm. On one hand, the lack of services and capital for the rural sector, combined with low grain prices, have driven campesinos to the cities in search of work. On the other hand, chronic urban underemployment has reinforced the importance of the family farm as a fallback livelihood strategy. Migration to the United States has drained the smallholder sector of labor, but steady flows of remittances from family members working abroad maintain those still at home.

Under these circumstances, new agricultural practices, sustainable or otherwise, are adopted as much for reasons of family survival as for environmental health or economic growth. Alternatives that protect smallholders' livelihoods from risk, build farm capital, and are flexible enough to accommodate the extended family's multiple survival strategies are frequently preferred to those that offer promises of direct but risky financial gain.

International NGOs introduced village-level projects for sustainable agriculture to Mesoamerica in the late 1970s and early 1980s. While the techniques advanced were not linked to formal research at mainstream agricultural research institutions, and although the science of agroecology had yet to inform their practices, these techniques were incorporated by many smallholders scattered across the region's hillsides. Working empirically, over time these innovators produced a diverse, low-risk mix of traditional, modern, and alternative farming techniques designed to increase productivity and strengthen agroecological resilience. Sharing knowledge and information, smallholders worked in loosely organized networks of *intercambios de campesino a campesino* (farmer-to-farmer exchanges). They gradually translated simple collections of "sustainable" techniques into complex agroecological farming styles.

Much, if not most, of the actual, existing sustainable agriculture in Central America and Mexico during this period was pioneered by campesinos whose agroecosystems had experienced declining yields and severe environmental degradation *after* the farmers adopted conventional, Green Revolution techniques (i.e., chemicals, high external inputs, high-yielding varieties). Basically, neither the older traditional methods nor the new conventional methods were capable of providing viable livelihoods. As the economic and institutional effects of structural adjustment policies reverberated across the countryside, both traditional and conventional agriculture became unsustainable, and more and more smallholders were drawn to sustainable agriculture. As NGOs expanded their influence, farmer-oriented, participatory methodologies and extensive, informal knowledge networks began to appear, challenging both the technologies and the centralized, expert-driven extension practices of the Green Revolution.

Thus, in the second instance, sustainable agriculture may also be viewed as a hybrid form of "everyday peasant resistance" to the forces of development and globalization (Colburn 1989; Scott 1989). Under extreme economic uncertainty and historic political disadvantage, campesinos, unable to affect agricultural or economic policies, defend their livelihoods not through confrontation but by improving their agroecosystems. Because most smallholdings function at extremely low levels of productivity and because production is frequently limited by environmental degradation (e.g., erosion, deforestation, loss of biodiversity), the ecological recovery of the agroecosystem can often result in dramatic increases in productivity of 100 to 200 percent or more. In these cases, smallholders benefit materially by investing in sustainable practices such as soil and water conservation and cover cropping.

The reduction of chemical inputs is often the first step in a process of agroecological autonomy. External inputs are later replaced by on-farm, organic inputs. In turn, as production is reorganized to enhance and depend more directly upon basic ecological functions and cycles, these organic inputs are often phased out. The transition from production dependent on high levels of external inputs to production based on the efficient management of the agroecosystem itself can result in a higher degree of control over one's own labor process and in a greater degree of rural autonomy. This management of production factors gives farmers more options and more "room to maneuver" in the face of powerful, volatile economic forces (van der Ploeg 1986).

The MCAC has given hundreds of thousands of smallholders in Mesoamerica and the Caribbean more room to maneuver. While it has not affected the structural rules of the game, it has had a profound influence on the way sustainable agriculture projects are carried out. It has also created a vast, "thick" network of farmers, professionals, and NGOs with cultural legitimacy, proven technical capability, and tremendous social potential. Could these capabilities and potentials ultimately affect the political and economic structures currently *holding back* sustainable agricultural development? To answer this question, we need an understanding of the farmers, the context in which they struggle, and the movement.

Synopsis

The organization of this book follows a loose chronological order. In the first chapter, "Emergence: Mayan Roots, Mexican Branches, Nicaraguan Fruit," I describe the emergence of Campesino a Campesino in the Mayan highlands of Guatemala. The fundamental role of culture in indigenous resistance and the horizontal methods developed for learning and leadership are explored through the experiences of Kaqchikel farmer-extensionists. I use Roland Bunch's principles for people-centered development to describe the early expressions of innovation, mutual aid, and self-reliance that characterized the Kaqchikel's ingenious resistance to the cycles of blinding economic oppression and agroecological degradation. This chapter chronicles the swift reaction of the agrarian elites to the Kaqchikel innovation and resistance and the campesinos' flight from the brutal military repression that ensued. I follow Kaqchikel extensionists to Mexico where the support of World Neighbors, Oxfam, and the Mexican Friends Service Committee helped the Guatemalans link with the Mexican *ejidatarios*[4] of Vicente Guerrero, Tlaxcala. It was here that the first international campesino teams for soil and water conservation were formed, where *promotores*[5] started a soil conservation school, developed a municipal farmer-to-farmer development program, and received farmers from the Sandinista cooperatives of Nicaragua. These farmers organized the first farmer-to-farmer workshops in revolutionary Nicaragua at the height of the civil war and coined the term *Campesino a Campesino* to describe themselves as a smallholders' movement for sustainable agriculture. Using revolutionary and postrevolutionary Nicaragua as a case study, I explore in depth the agrarian conditions that led to the explosion of Campesino a Campesino as a method and as a movement. The chapter ends with the introduction of Campesino a Campesino to Cuba, where it was adopted by the ANAP, the National Association of Small Farmers, during the "Special Period" in which the country began its profound transformation toward sustainable agriculture.

Chapter Two, "Tales from Campesino a Campesino," brings the voices of the movement directly to the reader through testimonies that reflect the struggles and negotiations between villagers and outside institutions (state, market, NGOs) in Mexico, Guatemala, and Nicaragua. I introduce the reader to longtime campesino promotores whose stories describe the evolution of the movement. These sections, largely transcriptions, relate experiences, insights, wisdom, and hope from Campesino a Campesino. They are a conscious attempt by the movement's promotores to share their experiences with the rest of the world. This is their first chapter.

The third chapter, "Campesino Pedagogy," takes an epistemological approach to Campesino a Campesino. I describe how campesino promotores, technicians, and professionals build the networks for agroecological knowledge that form the movement's learning communities. The learning methods and key innovations of the Campesino a Campesino approach are introduced in their original context and then followed through their transformations. As an agricultural development worker, I rely on stories from my own experience as case studies in popular development, campesino experimentation, action research, and farmer-to-farmer training. Examples are given of the tensions between culturally grounded campesino ways of learning, formal learning, and the "participatory" approaches advanced by NGOs and development institutions.

Chapter Four returns to campesino voices for "Campesino Politics of Development." In this chapter the promotores from the movement address a wide array of agricultural and rural development issues, including sustainable and organic agriculture, environmental justice, agricultural innovation and diffusion of practices, gender, globalization, genetically modified seeds, land reform and agricultural policies, local organization, education and learning, and their vision for the future.

Rather than a lengthy background at the beginning of the book, I have chosen to contextualize MCAC in the fifth chapter. In "The Political Economy of Campesino a Campesino," I relate the political and economic forces that dominated the countryside during the development decades of the 1960s and 1970s, the politicomilitary conflicts of the "Lost Decade" of the 1980s, and the neoliberal assault on Latin American economies of the 1990s. Using basic analytical tools from political economy to describe the changing structural context, I analyze the emergence of Campesino a Campesino in light of the search for alternatives to mainstream agricultural development. I also describe the rise of social movements in Latin America and how the popular education movement dovetailed with the explosion of NGOs, the turn toward sustainable agriculture, and the development of agroecology.

In "Movimento Campesino a Campesino: From Cultural Resistance to Social Change," the sixth and final chapter of this book, I address the issues of "going to scale" in sustainable agriculture. A review of the strengths and weaknesses of NGOs, mainstream development institutions, farmers' unions, and agricultural research institutions leads into an assessment of MCAC and the prospects for sustainable agriculture in the face of globalization. I discuss the potential of MCAC as a catalyst for transforming sustainable agricultural development into a movement for social change and suggest that a key component is the development of *structural literacy* within the network. The notion of integrating transnational advocacy networks with sustainable development work on the ground is introduced as way of overcoming the divide between politics and the struggles of everyday resistance in the Mesoamerican countryside. I end with a challenge to activists and professionals working with MCAC to build broad-based, integrated social movements for farmer-led, sustainable agriculture.

ONE

Emergence

Mayan Roots, Mexican Branches,
Nicaraguan Fruit

Farmers helping their brothers, so that they can help themselves . . .
to find solutions and not be dependent on a technician or
on the bank. That is Campesino a Campesino.

—*Argelio González, Santa Lucía, Nicaragua, 1991*

Farmer-Led Alternative Agriculture and Popular Education

IN 1961, TWO YEARS AFTER the Cuban Revolution, U.S. president John
F. Kennedy announced the "Alliance for Progress" in an effort to counter
the rising revolutionary tide in Latin America (1961).[1] Under U.S. leadership, economic development was to lift the region from poverty and backwardness, forming a bulwark of democracy against communism. Though
not completely as a result of the Alliance for Progress, the 1960s did usher
in an era of unprecedented economic growth in Latin America, but it was
growth without significant social reform. The newly generated wealth was
concentrated in the hands of elites. It widened the gap between the rich and
the poor and led to explosive political unrest. In response, many Latin
American regimes unleashed a wave of military repression upon their own
civilian populations. The United States frequently provided counterinsurgency training and economic support to repressive governments. While
Marxist politicomilitary organizations waged guerrilla war and focused on
the overthrow of the state, so-called Popular Movements mobilized hundreds of thousands of campesinos and poor urban dwellers for social change
(Sinclair and Nash 1995; Winn 1997).

During this convulsive period, the Second Vatican Council of Medellín,
Colombia, in 1971 took a "preferential option for the poor" grounded in

1

liberation theology. Progressive sectors in the Catholic Church organized vast networks of Christian-based communities—groups that reflected on social justice messages in the New Testament and worked for social change. "Popular education" grew out of these networks, first as a means for developing political consciousness while teaching adults to read, then as an action-research methodology for reflecting, analyzing, organizing, and mobilizing for community action (a process known as *autogestión*). Built on the extensive theoretical and practical work of the Brazilian educator Paulo Freire, popular education uses horizontal communication between "learner and teacher," combined with a praxis of "reflection-action-reflection" for political consciousness and social transformation (Freire 1968, 1970a, 1970b, 1973a; Freire er al. 1975).[2] The combination of liberation theology and popular education produced a highly motivated, broad-based cadre of social activists and local leaders, as well as some of the first local NGOs.

Though theorized by Freire in *Extension or Communication?* (1973), agricultural development was not the forte of popular education. Activist-professionals tended to come from urban backgrounds, and those with formal higher education (often from Jesuit universities) studied political science, history, sociology, economics, or law. Agronomists from the technical schools and the agricultural colleges tended to work for large plantations or for fertilizer, machinery, and seed companies. Those working in the state agricultural extension services were primarily involved with distributing credit and fertilizers but did very little actual training and had limited contact with campesinos.

In the early 1970s in Mesoamerica, appropriate technology advocates found some receptiveness for their alternatives among campesinos living in fragile ecosystems, such as on hillsides and in the dry tropics, where modern agricultural technologies worked poorly and where a combination of displacement and population pressures had disrupted the ecological balance of traditional methods.[3] Adoption of alternative agriculture technologies among this forgotten sector was slow. In part this was because many poor farmers could not risk change. Others were unwilling to adopt techniques—such as composting—that added to farming's drudgery. Because of the northern bias of the appropriate technology movement, many of the alternatives extended were ill suited to, or simply did not address the limiting factors of campesino production, the ecological functions of tropical agroecosystems, or basic peasant economy.[4] Diffusion of "appropriate" technologies was negligible.

Then, in 1972, a small NGO program in Chimaltenango, Guatemala, and a group of Kaqchikel Mayan campesinos hit upon a methodology appropriate to developing agroecological alternatives for local farming systems (Bunch, 1995).

Kato-Ki: People-Centered Agriculture

Don Marcos Orozco, a retired soil conservationist employed by World Neighbors, a U.S.-based NGO, had a problem. He had successfully demonstrated the effectiveness of contour ditches and organic soil amendments on his small, backyard plot. The corn plants in his experimental plot were visibly higher and the ears bigger than the ones in the control plot he had planted alongside. An extensionist with over forty years experience, he would have used this demonstration to convince farmers in surrounding communities to adopt the new techniques, but he spoke no Kaqchikel, and the Mayan farmers of Chimaltenango, wary of outsiders, spoke little Spanish.

The Mayan farmers certainly needed new techniques. The steep hillsides of Chimaltenango were severely eroded and maize and bean yields were at an all-time low. Grain production had initially increased with the application of chemical fertilizers but had dropped again, despite heavy increases in fertilizer application.

Most farmers had difficulty paying back credit for hybrid seeds and fertilizers and were forced to work off their debts as laborers, either on local coffee plantations or on the dreaded banana plantations of the Pacific coast. The vicious credit-debt cycle was held in place by loan sharks, labor contractors, and extension agents working for the big plantations and the fertilizer companies.

Taking a cue from the "barefoot doctors" of the Berhorst Clinic in Guatemala, World Neighbors encouraged Don Marcos to train a few Spanish-speaking, Kaqchikel campesinos as farmer-extensionists. By his own account, Don Marcos initially found this very difficult. Farmers were not willing to change their own practices, much less those of others. The Kaqchikeles did not trust expert advice or outsiders' intentions. Only after several farmers agreed to try a few small experiments on their own land did things begin to change. When their own experiments on small plots demonstrated the value of the alternatives, the farmers implemented them on the whole field. Enthusiastic with their success, they taught their neighbors in the same manner they had learned: through demonstration and small-scale experimentation. While it is not clear that World Neighbors had consciously attempted to make it so, the method was consistent with Freire's "teacher-learner/learner-teacher" model of horizontal adult education.

Because soil and water were the major limiting factors to production in the highlands of Chimaltenango, contour ditches, bunds, terraces, and heavy applications of compost tended to provide quick and visible results. The heavy labor requirements were assimilated by the Mayan *kuchubal*, the mutual assistance groups traditionally used by the Kaqchikeles. Groups of

Don Marcos Orozco speaking in the field.   Mayan farmers working in a kuchubal—a mutual
"Better one good idea in a hundred heads   assistance group. *Photograph by Roland Bunch*
than a hundred ideas in one good head."

three to ten men took turns working together on each other's land until all
had implemented the basic conservation and fertility practices.

A machete, a tape measure, and the *aparato-A* (a simple A-frame made
of three poles and a carpenter's level) were the basic tools of the Mayan conservation strategy. These tools allowed campesinos to measure the slopes on
their land and lay out contour lines for conservation work. Tape measures
allowed for measurement and comparisons of soil depth and the design of
experimental plots and conservation structures and reinforced the principles of precision, quantification, and fair comparisons. These tape measures
were incorporated into the typical campesino toolkit of shovels, hoes, and
so forth and applied to the theory and practice of farmer-led agricultural
experimentation.

Since yields on the Mayan farmers' lands were extremely low to begin
with (less than one ton per hectare) and because the factors limiting production were basically soil and water, increases of 100 to 200 percent within
a year or two of implementing the conservation and fertility practices were
not uncommon.[5] Enthusiasm and interest spread rapidly. Soon, the knowledge and skills of the small group working with Don Marcos were in high
demand.

Requests soon outstripped the capacity of the innovators to respond
through the traditional Kaqchikel systems for mutual assistance. Farmers

Campesinos using aparato–A
to measure slope

Building a compost heap in a farmer-led
workshop. *Photograph by Roland Bunch.*

who experimented were encouraged to share their knowledge as soon as
they were sure of their innovation. As the farming systems became more
complex, so did the small-scale experimentation. The knowledge and skills
employed also became more sophisticated and required the ability to understand abstract agroecological concepts. The transfer of knowledge from
farmer to farmer required consistent, sustained effort. The Kaqchikel promotores worked with Don Marcos to put on village workshops. Workshop
activities focused on a bit of theory and a lot of hands-on practice. New
teaching techniques using simple, physical demonstrations to illustrate
basic agroecological principles were developed for understanding what
much later came to be called "sustainable agriculture."

A steady combination of hands-on technical training, farmer-led workshops, cross visits, field days, and soil conservation fairs spread the Kaqchikeles' new knowledge throughout the area. Subsequent training in
cooperative administration, product industrialization, and commercializa-
tion allowed them to develop new forms of marketing. Oxfam and World
Neighbors helped the Kaqchikeles take advantage of the government's agricultural cooperative program to establish Kato-Ki, a 900-member cooperative that bought supplies, sold the farmers' basic grains, and provided
farmer-to-farmer training in basic conservation and fertility techniques.

The Kaqchikeles of Chimaltenango appeared to have unleashed a virtuous cycle of autonomous, farmer-led agricultural development that broke the vicious cycle of dependency and land degradation that had held them in the grip of poverty for so long. Oxfam and World Neighbors brought other campesino groups in to learn from the experience. The NGOs were keen to spread the experience to other parts of Guatemala and Mesoamerica as a means of combating rural poverty.

Unfortunately, structural reforms needed to address the political roots of poverty in Guatemala were not forthcoming, with disastrous consequences for the Kaqchikeles.

As campesinos of the Kato-Ki gained more and more economic autonomy, they began to arouse the ire of the large landowners. Farmer-led agri-

THE AGRARIAN DILEMMA OF GRASSROOTS DEVELOPMENT

The Kato-Ki debacle was only one of many acts of institutional violence committed against the peasantry during the decades of politicomilitary upheaval in Central America. The episode is symptomatic of the contradictions in the type of development advanced by the Alliance for Progress in Central America. Agricultural modernization actually concentrated wealth within agrarian elites and drove the peasantry from the land. Because they were not absorbed into the industrial sector, most peasants were forced to work for starvation wages on existing *latifundia* (plantations). These plantations captured both agricultural and labor surpluses from the impoverished peasant sector. The net effect was an expansion of the traditional export sector (coffee, cattle, cotton, and bananas) and a strengthening of the reactionary agrarian oligarchies and rural bourgeoisie. Their economic power allowed them to solidify their control over the government and the military.

The problem for development programs that focused on basic needs or institutional reform was not only how to reform the state while bypassing it, but also how to evade the power of the oligarchy in the countryside. Under these conditions, development projects were incapable of addressing the magnitude of rural poverty and were no match for the entrenched rural bourgeoisie, who were capable of mobilizing state violence. Rural NGOs were caught in the clash between grassroots development approaches and the violence of economic growth without social reform. Their development dilemma consisted in the fact that the more successful their projects were, without corresponding changes in agrarian structure, the more the participants in those projects risked reaction from the rural oligarchies.

cultural development meant higher yields and higher incomes for poor campesino families, and subsequently fewer agricultural laborers willing to work at starvation wages on the plantations. Co-ops meant local organization and freedom from debt peonage. But the crowning blow to local elites came when World Neighbors and the Kato-Ki began to buy up eroded coffee plantations and redistribute land among their members. These farmers not only implemented conservation practices and grew their traditional basic grains, they also grew coffee and sold it through their own cooperative. The coffee oligarchy realized that the Kaqchikeles were, in effect, organizing, financing, and providing technical assistance for their own land reform. They were no longer employees but competitors. Action was swift and brutal. According to its members, the Kato-Ki and its campesino-extensionists were accused of being communists. The Guatemalan army was called in to "disappear" the co-op. Those co-op leaders who could, fled Chimaltenango. The co-op and much of the land was abandoned. After over a decade of patient training, painstaking organization, and backbreaking work, the Chimaltenango experience appeared to have been aborted.[6]

The political events of the early 1980s in Guatemala led to the unfortunate disbanding of the cooperative and the diaspora of its best farmer-extensionists. But Kato-Ki had trained visiting campesinos from Mexico, Honduras, Panama, and Costa Rica, and these had returned home to start conservation work in their own villages. With help from NGOs, a handful of promotores from the Kato-Ki found jobs with sustainable agriculture projects in Mexico, Honduras, and Nicaragua. They were instrumental in starting dozens of farmer-led agricultural development projects. One man started his own technical school. Far from their homes and culture, they perfected their Spanish, became familiar with a wide range of dry to humid tropical agroecosystems, and integrated themselves into the social and cultural life of the Mesoamerican campesino. Several of the Kaqchikeles formed an agricultural consulting firm with Roland Bunch, author of *Two Ears of Corn: A Guide to People-Centered Agricultural Improvement*. This organization, COSECHA (Association of Consultants for a Sustainable, Ecological and People-Centered Agriculture), offered international consulting services worldwide.

The people-centered agricultural development pioneered in Chimaltenango became a farmer-led approach that found fertile if uneven ground as it spread throughout the Mesoamerican isthmus. The approach was compatible with the "basic needs" approach to development assistance pursued by the United Nations and was easily adapted to the village-scale projects run by NGOs that had begun to proliferate in Central America.[7] For rural advocates of social change, the methodology fit nicely with popular education's praxis, bringing together dialogical consciousness raising with agricultural problem solving. The philosophy and social practices of the Kaqchikeles found deep cultural affinity with campesinos throughout the isthmus.

While neither Oxfam nor World Neighbors could prevent the destruction of the Kato-Ki, they helped many campesino-extensionists and their families relocate safely. But just as important was the solidarity of the Mexican and Honduran campesinos who opened their homes to their Guatemalan compañeros and compañeras.[8]

Grupo Vicente Guerrero:
Promotores and Sustainable Agriculture

With the help of the MFSC, a group of five farmers from Vicente Guerrero, Tlaxcala, a small ejido in the dry central plateau of Mexico, traveled to Chimaltenango in 1978 for a short course in soil conservation. Upon returning, they put their new knowledge to work, holding several workshops for other villagers. The MFSC continued to support the Tlaxcalan farmers' extension work in several other villages in the municipality of Españita. Three years later, when the MFSC helped relocate two Kaqchikeles to Vicente Guerrero, the extension work was given a critical boost. The MFSC's support was later continued by SEDEPAC (Servicio de Desarrollo y Paz, A.C.) a Mexican NGO founded by the ex-director of the MFSC program.

As the Kaqchikel and Mexican farmers shared ideas and practices, they produced a number of technical and methodological variations on Bunch's original "people-centered" approach to agricultural development. Technically, for example, animal traction, biodynamic gardening, and orchard care were added to the farmer workshops that until that time had usually just addressed contour terraces, the incorporation of organic material, precision fertilizing, and seed selection. Methodologically, the incorporation of the Guatemalan kuchubal into the Mexican ejido system gave rise to campesino teams that worked to establish school gardens, communal orchards, and community agricultural development projects throughout the municipality.

Socially, the Mexican farmers viewed themselves as distinct from the government's agricultural extensionists. Extensionists were viewed with suspicion by the ejidatarios because they spoke an unintelligible technical language, generally gave bad or irrelevant advice, and were often more interested in helping the rural bank recover its production credit than they were in helping farmers solve agricultural problems. Above all, they were outsiders and, for the most part, had little or no farming experience. In the tradition of community health and literacy advocates, the farmers working

Farmers of Vicente Guerrero, Mexico, measuring a slope

with SEDEPAC called themselves *promotores* to identify with their neighbors and distance themselves from the extensionists.

Working two and three days a week as volunteers, a team of six to eight promotores ran school orchard and garden programs, provided technical assistance in alternative agriculture to local ejidatarios, and helped households establish biointensive gardens. The use of teams allowed for greater diversity. Some promotores were good at experimenting, others better at teaching. Each had a slightly different kind of technical expertise to share.

Results of composting, legume rotations, and new crop associations on the hard clay soils of Españita's one- to two-hectare farms were rapid and recognizable. Maize yields jumped from one-half ton per hectare to three or even five tons. One farmer from Vicente Guerrero won the state competition for the highest yield in rain-fed corn. Crops diversified, and production and small service co-ops were formed. Demand for the promotores' technical assistance spread to other villages. SEDEPAC supported the work with further technical information and travel for promotores, tools, and methodological training.

The experience of Vicente Guerrero led to several unprecedented developments. First, because the promotor base was well organized and highly experienced at the time of the project's transition from the MFSC to SEDEPAC, under the new NGO the Vicente Guerrero project was run directly by the campesinos, without the usual outside coordinator. This led to the formation of a local development organization called Grupo Vicente

Guerrero. Within a few years, "El Grupo" left SEDEPAC, continuing the work on its own. The popularity and autonomy of their work in the municipio of Españita led to the election of one of the promotores as *agente municipal* (county supervisor), a move that further strengthened the group's autonomous development work (Holt-Giménez 1996; Ramos Sánchez 1998).

Two particularly interesting perspectives emerged from El Grupo's experiences:

1. The importance of civic organization for sustainable agriculture, and
2. The need for campesino families to assume the responsibilities of agricultural training and education.

In the first case, years of patient community work by a team of promotores built a solid network of intervillage relationships. These relationships were based on practical, problem-solving actions and training in sustainable agriculture. When the political opportunity arrived, villagers were able to gain control over municipal resources despite the opposition of the dominant political party (Holt-Giménez 1996).

In the second case, while work had first concentrated on a single village, it spread from village to village on the basis of the extended family ties that are characteristic of campesino culture. Further, the work was organized around an "ejido-school-patio" strategy that integrated the whole family in learning activities (to say nothing of the local mayors, *comisario ejidales* or land commissioners, and school principals). Thus, entire families were involved in the instruction of sustainable agriculture. Culturally, this was not novel. Farming is highly knowledge intensive, requiring years of apprenticeship. In peasant systems the use of natural and human resources reduces economic risk (Scott 1976). Family learning is key to developing the skill, judgment, and coordination necessary to manage the myriad of social, technical, and ecological aspects of farming (Netting 1993). Insertion into the market does not necessarily simplify these relationships. On the contrary, they may become more complex by introducing more economic risk and more decisions (Long et al. 1986).

As a municipal group for agricultural development, the Grupo Vicente Guerrero was instrumental in advancing the farmer-led agricultural development process initiated by the Kaqchikeles in Chimaltenango. Later, they transferred the farmer-led approach to Nicaragua. Ironically, war-torn Nicaragua provided farmer-led agricultural development with its most spectacular qualitative and quantitative leap.

Campesino a Campesino:
Movement Led Sustainable Agricultural Development

The Sandinista Revolution (1979 to 1990) attempted to implement a non-capitalist approach to development. The Sandinista state took over farms held by the Somoza dynasty, thus assuming control of 20 to 25 percent of the most productive and highly capitalized agricultural land in the nation (Faber 1993; Baumeister 1998). Foreign engineers were brought in to manage the state sector and set the course for agriculture. The objective was to develop state capitalism for the transition to socialism. However, medium and large private holdings in cotton, bananas, coffee, sugar cane, basic grains, and beef ranching still controlled over half of Nicaragua's agricultural production, giving the rural bourgeoisie considerable political influence (Maldidier and Marchetti 1996). Through absolute control over commodity prices, finance, and import-export flows, the Ministry of Agriculture and Agrarian *reform* (MIDINRA) attempted to maintain the productive capacity of the rural bourgeoisie while at the same time limiting their political power. This resulted in a shaky alliance with the private sector and a pragmatic, if dubious, development model the Sandinistas called a "mixed economy."

MIDINRA considered the peasantry to be a social anachronism and was, as an institution, reluctant to develop its economic potential. In the ministry's view, an economically active middle peasantry would compete with the state farms. A successful peasantry would absorb rural labor, thus driving up wages state farms had to pay to available workers. Family farms would undercut state farms, producing commodities at lower cost through family "self-exploitation." They also believed that, in the long run, a class of small commodity producers would ally themselves with the rural bourgeoisie against the socialist project of the Revolution. The dominant ideology within the ministry embraced the Soviet-Cuban collectivist road to modernization. Discursively, the peasantry was equated with poverty and backwardness and was thus destined to be transformed:

> As far as the campesinado as a productive unit able to secure a dynamic expansion within the existing structural conditions in our countryside . . . it's not a viable alternative, and instead [they] should be seen as an entity to be transformed. . . . Basically, they should integrate into the cooperative movement or in forms of production for special products in special conditions that will surely occur, but I don't see them as important. (Manuel Coronel Kautz, vice minister of agriculture, Baumeister 1998)

These hard-line, technocratic positions, characterized as *desarrollista* (developmentalist), pinned their agrarian hopes on the development of state farms: large, mechanized, capital-intensive agroindustrial complexes. The *desarrollistas* were tempered by the *colectivistas* who, subordinate to the former, were concerned with the development of "superior" forms of peasant production through cooperatives. A third, institutionally weak tendency known as *campesinista* argued for strengthening individual middle-peasant producers and for alternative technology approaches to agricultural development (Baumeister 1998).[9] This latter tendency was considered romantic on the part of the Sandinista leadership. Referring to sustainable agriculture, Minister of Agriculture Comandante Jaime Wheelock stated flatly, "We are a poor country. Unlike the [North] Americans, we do not have the luxury of programming our underdevelopment."[10]

Productively, the peasantry was considered marginal. Conceptually, it tended to be conflated into the rural "semiproletariat" and was considered an impediment to the full development of the forces of production (Maldidier and Marchetti 1996). However, in 1982 this perspective changed as the internal struggle with the rural bourgeoisie led to selective expropriations of large landholdings and extensive land distribution under the 1981 Agrarian Reform Law (Faber 1993). The violent breakup of the latifundia quickly exploded into a full-blown civil war whose "contra" opposition was financed by the United States and fought (on both sides) by the peasantry.[11] While most agrarian analysts agree that the Sandinistas never recognized the economic or productive potential of the peasantry, the counterrevolution was a painful reminder of the existence, persistence, and critical politicomilitary importance of this sector. In an effort to hold on to the campesinado, the Sandinistas distributed more land in the form of cooperatives (the Sandinista Agricultural Cooperatives, or CAS). By 1984, 45,000 campesino beneficiaries controlled some 2.4 million acres, one-fifth of the productive land in Nicaragua (Faber 1993). At first, in an effort to modernize and incorporate the peasant sector into the Revolution, the CAS were flooded with subsidies of cheap credit, agrochemicals, and Belarus tractors. But the economy stumbled under the weight of the war, inflation, and heavy-handed, centralized mismanagement. Services for the co-op sector became thin and inconsistent and in many cases simply dried up. The state-as-patron proved incapable of providing the basic conditions for minimum income during the agrarian transformation, leading to further disaffection on the part of campesinos, many of whom considered themselves to have been better off under the feudal conditions of the latifundias.[12]

Ironically, land reform became both the central agrarian instrument for incorporating the campesinado into the Revolution and the main engine driving them toward the counterrevolution. By smashing the latifundia without consistently replacing it with anything better, the Sandinista agrarian reform unwittingly split the peasantry down the middle. Half defended the patronage system of their old hacienda owners, the other half, the new patronage system of the Sandinista state.[13]

The land reform itself, an internally contested process between the different tendencies within MIDINRA, went through several fundamental shifts as the Revolution struggled to respond to the economic crisis and political and military events on the ground. Put simply, as capital and human resources became scarce and as more and more campesinos became disaffected, the desarrollistas' bureaucratic approach ceded ground to the colectivistas' cooperative approach, which in turn opened space for the campesinistas' demands for individual forms of land titling (Baumeister 1998). These shifts were highly uneven: some state farms were turned into co-ops, some co-ops worked individual plots or divided some or all of the land among members, and some campesinos received individual titles directly. The Agrarian Reform Law of 1981 was reformulated in 1986 to allow for this flexibility, reflected in the subsequent increase of individual titles (Baumeister 1998). By 1988 the Sandinistas had redistributed some 2.3 million acres to 77,430 families—over a quarter of the peasant population (Enriquez 1991). Meanwhile, the rural bourgeoisie and many medium-sized producers lost approximately 1.73 million acres to expropriation (Maldidier and Marchetti 1996), and tens of thousands of campesinos filled the ranks of the U.S.-financed counterrevolution (Bendaña 1991).

The problem of the peasantry in Sandinista agrarian politics required new forms of political organization within the revolutionary state. The Unión Nacional de Agricultores y Ganaderos (National Farmers and Ranchers Union, or UNAG) was established in 1981 by the Sandinista National Liberation Front (FSLN, Frente Sandinista de Liberación Nacional) as a broad-based mass organization to forge a pro-Revolution "agrarian front" of large, medium, and small producers (in particular, the beneficiaries of the land reform). Controlled primarily by large producers, UNAG was nonetheless the only institution to represent campesino interests within the Revolution. According to Baumeister (1998), UNAG was able to distance itself from the desarrollista thrust of MIDINRA over time. He describes their position on development as a loose mixture of the three development strategies.[14] Because of the desire of the large- and medium-scale farmers within UNAG for modern production factors and capital goods, UNAG never formulated a clear alternative to the state's development project. Instead, UNAG lobbied for cheap credit, machinery, chemical inputs, guaranteed prices, and market access. UNAG was instrumental in pressuring the government to broaden and loosen the land reform in response to peasant demands. However, since the board of directors of

UNAG was dominated by large- and medium-scale cattle ranchers and coffee producers, these products usually took precedence over the maize, beans, plantains, and root crops grown by campesinos. Put another way, as far as agricultural policy was concerned, large farmer demands in UNAG eclipsed smallholder peasant demands. Nonetheless, UNAG produced a patronage system that attempted, with varying degrees of success, to channel resources to the campesinado through a series of development projects. The Programa Campesino a Campesino (PCAC) became the most enduring and arguably one of the most successful of these projects.

UNAG and the Soil and Water Conservation Project

In 1986, with the support of Oxfam, the Catholic agency CODEL, and the Ford Foundation, Grupo Vicente Guerrero of Mexico began a soil and water conservation project with UNAG that lasted for two years. The result of the project was the transformation of the "farmer-led" approach to the campesino-a-campesino (farmer-to-farmer) approach that eventually led to the Campesino a Campesino movement for sustainable agriculture (Holt-Giménez 1989, 1996; Ramos Sánchez 1998).

The soil and water conservation project administered by SEDEPAC and implemented through UNAG aimed to establish a farmer-run conservation program in Nicaragua. After an initial training visit to Tlaxcala by Nicaraguan campesinos, the first Mexican promotores arrived in Nicaragua in 1987 and stayed in the villages of their "pupils" for several weeks. Along with the volunteer who originally started the conservation project in Vicente Guerrero,[15] Roberto Vega, a Mexican adult education specialist in the campesino training section of UNAG, arranged a series of two-week training sessions on two different UNAG-affiliated production cooperatives (CAS) and with a group of individual producers loosely associated with a credit and services cooperative (CCS).

UNAG's board of directors gave the project political permission to operate but did not consider it a program priority. They were more interested in using the project to establish political links to Mexican farm organizations than in "people-centered" or "farmer-led" development. It was not even administered from UNAG's production section but through the international relations section. UNAG's modernization vision, a mixture of expert-driven Green Revolution and Cuban-Soviet technology, was considered superior to SEDEPAC's small-scale, farmer-led, sustainable agriculture approach.

Initially, the project's effect on cooperatives was minimal. In most cases, while coffee, cattle, or bananas were worked collectively, basic grains were farmed individually. Cooperatives rotated plots among the membership every year in order to give each farmer a chance to farm the best patches of land. The soil and water conservation and fertility techniques offered by the Mexicans were not readily applicable to the co-op's cash crops, and farmers were reluctant to invest their labor on the plots they farmed only for a year at a time before turning them over to another member. Another factor for low adoption of the techniques was the relatively good access that co-op members had to cheap credit and external inputs. Furthermore, co-ops tended to be land rich and labor poor. If farmers exhausted a plot, rather than invest in restoring fertility, they simply moved on to another. Finally,

Mexican promotor Rogelio Sánchez recalls, "In the first workshops . . . it was difficult because we didn't see any results. Fortunately we met people like Don Chepe Chu who worked hard on his own farm and made it a demonstration plot. Don Chepe Chu was able to increase his bean production in a short time, from one agricultural cycle to the next. This was very convincing and the people . . . started to follow his example." (Ramos Sánchez 1998, 70). Don Chepe Chu (José Jesús Mendoza) of Santa Lucía, Boaco, was an individual, CCS-affiliated farmer and Sandinista sympathizer. He later successfully spread Campesino a Campesino to nearby Asiento Viejo, a primarily "contra" community.

Don José Jesús Mendoza (Don Chepe Chu) of Nicaragua (background) working with Rogelio Sánchez of Mexico (foreground)

those cooperatives based on extensive beef production rather than agriculture had little interest in the Mexicans' techniques.

The war also prevented the spread of SEDEPAC's farmer-led soil and water conservation approach. Members of production cooperatives had many political responsibilities, not the least of which was to give three to six months military service each year to protect the agrarian reform from the counterrevolution. On one hand, many promotores were deeply motivated members of their cooperatives and volunteered for duty. One of the first Nicaraguan promotores, Luis Mejía, was killed in combat shortly after he had been trained. On the other hand, some farmers joined cooperatives for a season or two until their tour of duty was imminent then left, sometimes for another cooperative. The instability of the co-op membership made it very difficult to establish the experiential knowledge base for the farmer-led approach.

These pilot efforts by SEDEPAC and UNAG tended to be successful among the small, individual producers grouped around the credit and service cooperatives (CCS) than among independent smallholders or among farmers flatly opposed to the Sandinistas.

Irrespective of their impact on farming, the Mexicans had a profound cultural and ideological influence on the Nicaraguans, who pressured UNAG to expand the program. Not only did the Mexicans have two generations of land reform under their belts, they also had several years of farmer-to-farmer training experience and had learned how to present themselves in front of large groups. They knew how to deal with the onerous problem of professional jealousy from agronomists and technicians. Further, they did not limit themselves to project "goals and objectives" but taught and shared as they saw opportunities arise and enthusiasm increase.[16] Echoing the sentiments of many Nicaraguan campesinos, one wizened president of a cooperative in Pochocuape said, "When we first met the Mexicans, we were shocked just by the way they stood! And they knew how to talk about what they knew. They showed us to only preach what we practice. We [campesinos] understand each other. The Mexicans are campesinos just like us. We understand each other. They have shown us what we can become. Those Mexicans! We love them!"[17]

The Mexicans lived in the villages and on the cooperatives, worked in the fields, and shared food, stories, hopes, and culture with their Nicaraguan counterparts. When Nicaraguans traveled to Mexico, they lived on the ejido and saw first hand the benefits of over ten years of sustainable agriculture. They not only learned techniques but saw the *process* by which the Mexicans had developed their own agriculture.

The Nicaraguans also had a political impact on the Mexicans. Alicia

Alicia Sarmientos of Mexico (in cowboy hat) teaches gardening in Nicaragua

Sarmientos, one of the two young women who went to Nicaragua in the first visit spoke of her first trip away from home:

> I was eighteen years old and went along to teach organic gardening. The people were interested, but lived in fear of being attacked by the contras [counterrevolutionaries]; there was a lot of pressure. I shared many things with the family where I stayed—knowledge about medicinal plants—and I learned some new dishes. I was very taken with what was happening in Nicaragua, how the children were dying of hunger. It made me think a lot about what was happening in my own country, in my region. It marked a change for me, it matured me, and it especially made me value all of the things I have learned through the Grupo and everything I have had in my life. Sharing my work with the people from this country made me more determined to learn.[18]

Rogelio Sánchez, one of the leaders of Grupo Vicente Guerrero remembers,

> At night we slept wondering if in any moment the contras would come. We had the sensation of being insecure. Of course, we came from a country where there was no war. Some of the compañeros had to adapt to sleeping in hammocks or beds made from boards. But as campesinos willing to put up with limitations, this was not so difficult. We had made a promise to [the Nicaraguans], we saw that this was their reality and we adapted ourselves, this was not an obstacle, this was a lesson they gave to

us. I don't know if the technicians trained in universities could adapt to the conditions we did.[19]

Deep and long-lasting friendships between campesinos from different villages, regions, and countries become the basis for the Campesino a Campesino movement. Roberto Vega, the Mexican *metodólogo*[20] who helped implement the SEDEPAC project within UNAG, attributes the identification among Mexican and Nicaraguan campesinos to a common culture of centuries-old maize cultivation: "I think that the principal basis is the shared culture of maize, the history and the legacy of the ancestors, these are the principal bases for developing the Campesino a Campesino movement in Latin America and the Caribbean; it is a solid point of departure for the search of real alternatives, to find solutions" (Ramos Sánchez 1998, 68). The politically grounded, horizontal learning between campesinos reflected the type of cultural depth that Paulo Freire claimed was the basis for a liberating education (Freire 1973b). Campesinos were not simply transferring technologies, they were "making culture" (*haciendo cultura*). On the strength of this cultural base, knowledge, information, and wisdom were shared. The oft-mentioned peasant resistance to change looked quite different from an insider's perspective. The importance of agroecological experience and good-sense farming was essential to effective technological diffusion. As Mexican promotor Gabriel Sánchez Ledezma asserts, "Campesinos might listen to a fool (*un tonto*), but they will only follow a wise person (*un sabio*)."[21]

Wisdom could be shared between campesinos, but experience was the best teacher. The job of the promotor was to provide the learner with the information, knowledge, and hands-on experiences that would make him or her a wise farmer.

Campesino a Campesino Becomes a Movement

Day by day, the peasants make the economist sigh, the politicians sweat, and the strategists swear, defeating their plans and prophecies all over the world.
—Teodor Shanin, 1972

UNAG held huge rallies and campesino conventions in an effort to unify campesinos around the Revolution. Leaders portrayed UNAG, the peasantry, and the Revolution as one and the same "movement." (The active presence of the peasantry among the contras was, of course, strong evidence against this claim.) To outsiders, campesinos often say one thing but think or do another. This axiom was dramatically illustrated in the First National Convention of Sandinista Cooperatives held late in 1988 in the modern

Olaf Palme Convention Center in Managua. Over 2,000 campesino cooperative leaders gathered in the main conference hall to listen to the Sandinista leadership explain the political importance of the cooperative movement. It was an impressive scene: the Sandinista-UNAG leadership sat in the front facing the "masses" of campesino delegates. The wall behind the podium was emblazoned with revolutionary flags and slogans. The national anthem and the Sandinista hymn were sung by all. One by one, the UNAG leadership took the podium and hammered out the party line. Most of the campesinos ignored the speeches and chatted among themselves. When Comandante Jaime Wheelock, minister of agriculture, took the podium there was a polite hush as he began to extol the virtues of the Agrarian Reform. Then, suddenly from somewhere in the middle of the audience, Don Ernesto Herrera, a campesino promotor from Santa Lucía, Boaco, stood up and, hoisting an enormous bean plant over his head, enthusiastically interrupted the proceedings.

"I just want to show all of you what the Campesino School for Soil and Water Conservation is producing in Santa Lucía, Boaco," he shouted. "This bean plant has over sixty pods and we've produced them with eighty and as high as one hundred and twenty," he continued to a truly impressed audience. "I invite all of you to come to Santa Lucía to see and learn soil conservation! As a token of our esteem, I want to present our minister of agriculture with this bean plant, to show him what we patriotic campesinos can do!"

Counting the pods on a 120-pod bean plant in an MCAC workshop in Nicaragua

Don Ernesto made his way to the podium amid the cheers of the campesino delegates to the open-mouthed minister of agriculture, and did just that.[22]

The moment was the turning point that transformed the UNAG Soil Conservation project into the Campesino a Campesino *movement*. After the convention, campesinos from all over Nicaragua traveled to visit the Santa Lucías. At first they came on their own, in twos and threes from remote villages. Later, as word spread, NGOs sent groups for cross visits. By 1989, two years after SEDEPAC had introduced farmer-led development methods to the country, development consultants documented the extensive adoption of sustainable agriculture techniques spreading from campesino to campesino across Nicaragua (Holt-Giménez 1989; Annis 1992; Baumeister 1995; Merlet 1995).

There are several reasons the Campesino a Campesino movement took off in Nicaragua. First, the peasantry as a class was a key political actor in the Revolution. The internal struggle between the different development approaches during the war had accelerated land distribution, "creating" 120,000 landed peasants, many of them armed. While revolutionary promises of prosperity were overblown and the means for attaining progress were contradictory, there was an unmistakable climate of change and effervescence in the Nicaraguan countryside. Traditional peonage was broken. In the renowned Literacy Crusade, campesinos learned to read and write. They received different types of training and education and organized in cooperatives. Working as volunteers alongside campesinos, thousands of foreign "*internationalistas*" from around the world brought in new ideas and perspectives. National and international cultural groups traveled throughout the countryside putting on plays, concerts, and other cultural events. Outside the war zones, campesinos moved about the country freely and even traveled abroad. Farm organizations from Europe, Canada, and the United States sent farmer delegations to Nicaragua to learn about the Revolution and share their expertise. This was all possible through the Sandinista "mass organizations"[23] and the ministries of health, education, and culture, with the help of the many international NGOs and solidarity groups that supported the Revolution.[24]

Institutionally, the fact that the Soil Conservation Project was part of a national farmers' union rather than an NGO gave it access to campesino communities throughout the countryside rather than within a circumscribed project area. The small technical team in the national office was able to extend the approach and respond to demands in the municipalities by coordinating with regional UNAG offices. Interested campesinos and dedicated promotores used the UNAG network to access and mobilize human and material resources across large distances over extended periods. Over time, strong relationships grew between promotores and communities. The low overhead involved with this mobile and flexible approach had a tremendous advantage over project-centered NGO strategies for development that needed to build entire programs in each community then hope for spontaneous diffusion of successful techniques (Bunch 1985). In comparison, promotores in Campesino a Campesino could mobilize instantly and continuously. There was no need to maintain bureaucratic structures and expensive professional personnel during the down times between farmer-led training. Campesino a Campesino was able to take advantage of UNAG's continual presence in the countryside, thus investing their human capital only during the windows of opportunity in the crop production cycles.[25]

Two other factors influenced the explosion of the Campesino a Campesino movement in Nicaragua: Hurricane Joan (1988) and the collapse of the Sandinista economy (1989), both of which led to the beginning of the end for the desarrollistas' capital-intensive agricultural development strategies.

"La Juana" destroyed the Atlantic town of Puerto Cabezas, leveled a massive swath of tropical forest, and swept away millions of tons of topsoil from the hillside farms in the central highlands. Along with the soil went the seed and fertilizer of that year's corn crop. But Santa Lucía, directly in the western path of the hurricane, fared differently. The soil conservation ditches and terraces held against the deluge. That year was a bumper crop for promotores. The comparisons between their fields and their neighbors' were stark and dramatic.

"La Juana" was followed by the complete collapse of the severely eroded Nicaraguan economy and the end of cheap credit, hybrid seed, and agrochemicals for campesinos. In one year, the Nicaraguan countryside went from state-subsidized, state-controlled, capital-intensive, high-external-input agriculture to "free market" agriculture. This also meant the end of technical assistance. Campesinos returned to subsistence farming using primitive slash and burn techniques. Most peasant farming systems had lost their natural fertility and responded poorly. By contrast, the application of green manures, conservation ditches, selection of local seeds, and crop diversity had dramatic positive impacts on productivity. The farms using Campesino a Campesino's techniques stood out as fertile patches against the degraded agricultural landscape.

In 1987, the Ford Foundation funded the Proyecto Campesino a Campesino (PCAC). PCAC's promotores traveled across the country at the invitation of NGOs, extended families and acquaintances, staging workshop after workshop. The first national and regional Campesino a Campesino *encuentros* (gatherings) were held where farmers exchanged knowledge and information, seeds, and "recipes" for natural pest control.

The surprise electoral victory over the Sandinistas by the U.S.-backed candidate, Violeta Chamorro, in 1990 and the dramatic dissolution of the Sandinista state will provide political analysts with food for thought for some years to come. The Sandinista party was caught completely unprepared. Formerly dependent on the party-state for their existence, the mass organizations were forced to reorganize or dissolve.

During the Sandinista years, the mass organizations, linked to the state through the Sandinista party and funded by international NGOs, had dominated civil society. There was little professional or financial support and little political space left over for local NGOs. But the loss of control over state resources provoked a financial crisis for the Sandinista party. Hundreds of professional cadres were laid off.

In a parallel development, many of the international NGOs financing the Sandinista Revolution through the party, the government, or the mass organizations were left without counterparts.[26] They quickly helped ex-cadres and rural development workers to form their own, local NGOs to take the place of the Sandinista organizations. Practically overnight, NGOs sprang up across Nicaragua (Sollis 1995). As development and social workers looked around the country's programmatic wasteland for new project themes, they saw a few trees still standing. One was PCAC. The project had never depended directly on the Sandinista party or the state. Independent "Campesino a Campesino" projects quickly emerged throughout Nicaragua. Many of these were legitimate efforts on the part of NGOs to support local promotores who were interested, or already participating, in the Campesino a Campesino movement. In an interinstitutional sense, Campesino a Campesino achieved a dramatic "scaling up." It is important to note that this expansion was preceded by several years of extensive work by promotores working from within UNAG. Their work established the technical, methodological, and social basis for the growth of Campesino a Campesino–style projects among Nicaraguan NGOs.

By 1989, just two years after the project's introduction, the eight promotores of Santa Lucía had extended soil and water conservation techniques to 15 percent of the town's farmers, who constructed eighteen kilometers of ditches, over 100 compost heaps, six kilometers of terraces, and nearly a mile of windbreaks (Blokland 1992). Within five years, the techniques had swept through the country's central dry zone and were spreading to the semihumid mountain regions and the humid tropics of the agricultural frontier. By 1991, the dozen or so promotores from PCAC had given over 500 workshops to some 3,000 campesinos. Twelve NGOs had loosely organized into a Movimiento Campesino a Campesino coordinating body led by PCAC (Holt-Giménez 1992). In 1995 there were an estimated 300 promotores and 3,000 members in PCAC alone.[27] By 2000 PCAC boasted 1,487 promotores and claimed to serve 28 percent of rural Nicaraguan families (PCAC 2000).[28]

The Technologies

Technologically, the expansion of Campesino a Campesino as a movement (MCAC) owes much of its success to velvet bean, *Mucuna pruriens*. Originally used in the southern United States as a green manure, velvet bean was first detected by researchers in southern Mexico in the 1970s and later in eastern Honduras, where it was used as a cover crop or *abonera,* replacing traditional fallow (Buckles 1994b). Working in Honduras, professionals from COSECHA and CIDICCO (Centro Internacional de Información Sobre Cultivos de Cobertura / International Center for Information on Cover Crops) saw the bean's potential for the production of organic matter, nitrogen fixation, and weed control, and introduced it into the farmer-to-farmer projects. Once they had the bean, campesinos used small-scale experimentation to develop different intercropping and fallow practices (Bunch 1990; Flores and Estrada 1992). Velvet bean produced up to 30 tons per hectare per year of organic matter, fixed up to 150 kilos per hectare per year of nitrogen, and effectively smothered weeds.

The bean spread quickly because it efficiently overcame the limiting fac-

Velvet bean and maize growing together

Juan Aguirre of Ometepe,
Nicaragua, with velvet bean

tors to production that were widespread in campesino agriculture: as a green
manure, it was a rapid and continuous source of organic matter; as a mulch,
it protected the soil from the erosion, conserved water, and suppressed
weeds. Importantly, it overcame nutrient immobilization problems of acid
soils (Bunch 1990). While it was aggressive when intercropped with corn
or plantains, different management practices evolved, shortening the labor
time required for pruning and resulting in an overall reduction in weeding
effort. Best of all, velvet bean was free. It required no credit, incurred no
debt, and did not need expensive extension programs to promote its adoption. A handful of seeds, a desire to experiment, and a bit of advice given by
one farmer to another was all that was needed for widespread diffusion.
Above all, velvet bean was successful because it worked.

Unlike the chemical-based *paquete tecnológico* (technological package),
velvet bean raised yields by improving ecological functions in the agroecosystem rather than by substituting them with external inputs. While the
paquete degraded the agroecosystem over time, velvet bean improved it.
Farmers using velvet bean often perceived other system benefits, such as
reduced crop damage from pests, drought resistance, and higher-quality
grain.[29] Velvet bean and several other green manures from Honduras were
introduced to Nicaragua through MCAC in 1990, driving the expansion of
the movement throughout the Pacific plain and the central highlands.
PCAC and UNAG took the bean to the Atlantic coast where it spread

Countless observations and hands-on experience in discovering local solutions to local problems across the diverse agroecosystems brought COSECHA to the conclusion that common limiting factors and critical ecological points in tropical, campesino agroecosystems had common solutions. They developed a simple set of principles for sustainable agriculture in the humid tropics:

1. The vast majority of soils in the tropics, though often quite poor, can be made highly fertile by maximizing the production of organic matter.
2. Migratory agriculture is frequently motivated by decreasing fertility, increased weed problems, or both. Mulches of crop residues and fast-growing green manure/cover crops drastically reduce the weed problem by keeping the soil covered. (Erosion and solation are also controlled.)
3. Shallow soils and/or steep slopes, which contribute to erosion in the tropics, can also be significantly controlled by zero tillage. The secret to zero tillage in the tropics is the application of massive amounts of organic matter to the soil—in this case through cover crop/green manures.
4. The prevalence of plant diseases and insect pests in tropical agroecosystems is managed by maintaining biological diversity . . . there are over sixty green manure/cover crop species in use by campesinos developing sustainable agriculture today.
5. Plant growth can overcome the "hostile" (acidic, low-fertility) soils of the tropics when plants are fed through mulch.

Consonant with the claims of the world's leading agroecologists (Altieri, Gliessman, Hecht, et al.) Roland Bunch (1995) surmised, "In order for tropical agriculture to be both highly productive and sustainable, it must imitate the highly productive, millions-of-years-old, humid tropical forest."

It is noteworthy that campesinos, when given the support, were able not only to adopt and develop appropriate techniques, they were able to extract the underlying principles for sustainable agriculture in the tropics from their own empirical experience. Of course, campesinos have done this type of empirical agricultural development, albeit very slowly, since the beginning of agriculture. What is highly significant about this experience is the time frame: less than twenty years.

(left to right) In-line terracing; Conservation ditches; Polyculture contributes to conservation and biodiversity

rapidly, consolidating the influence of both PCAC and UNAG in the humid tropics (PCAC 2000).

Like the aparato-A that allowed farmers to lay out their own contour lines, as velvet bean spread throughout Mesoamerica, it carried several methodological and ideological messages. First of all, farmers asked why agronomists and agricultural extensionists knew nothing about this useful plant and at best appeared disinterested in its potential. Second, the ease with which farmers could obtain small amounts of seed, and the rapid and recognizable results (within one season) that velvet bean often produced, lent the technology to farmer experimentation. The overall effect among campesinos in the movement was a strong affirmation of the effectiveness and autonomy of farmer-led agricultural development and a profound disillusionment with agricultural researchers, agronomists, and technicians.

The initial field research on velvet bean by Mexico's CIMMYT (the International Center for the Improvement of Maize and Wheat) split along agronomic, anthropological, and economic disciplines. Ignoring the fact that in campesino farming systems velvet bean was characteristically grown with local landraces, agronomists at CIMMYT tested it with hybrid corn and concluded that velvet bean reduced grain yield when intercropped (Barreto 1994). Anthropologists suggested that velvet bean was spread widely farmer to farmer because it served various agroecological functions in campesino farming systems (Buckles 1994b). Finally, CIMMYT economists pointed out that maize intercropped with velvet bean provided higher profits and returns to labor than monocropped maize cultivation (Sain et al. 1994).

The fact was that farmers had already seen the benefits of velvet bean and were adapting and adopting it widely, without any help from formal agricultural research and extension. NGOs, viewed by farmers as allies in the development of what was essentially a farmer's technology, gained considerable institutional status among farmers because of their role as facilitators for the bean's diffusion.

Campesino a Campesino: Project or Movement?

I am proud to be a campesino that can speak, teach, choose, and give my opinion any time and place I want here among the people of Nicaragua. This fills me with courage, that we are an example in Nicaragua, thanks to a Revolution. We can say what we feel, what we think and what we desire as campesinos. We are the majority in this world. When I hear of the problems from other campesinos in Honduras and Guatemala, I see you are just like us . . . in your way of feeling, in your way of thinking, in your way of teaching. We campesinos are realists. We may be timid, but that timidity should not silence us! It should give us courage; to

José Jesús Mendoza (Don Chepe Chu) of Santa Lucía, Nicaragua

think, to speak, to choose. But the minority has been very astute. They have suc-
ceeded in keeping us, the majority, divided. This is what plagues us as campesinos:
our divisions! That is why Campesino a Campesino is an alternative that makes
me very happy. Every time I hear a story from one of you, that you have found
a positive solution to a problem and that it is bearing fruit so quickly, it makes me
feel as if you, were me. It makes me happy because it is the alternative of being
independent! We are not birds to live in the sky . . . neither are we fish to
live from the sea. We are men to live from the land!
—José Jesús Mendoza, International Campesino a Campesino
workshop, Boaco, Nicaragua, 1989

During the 1990s, Oxfam-England capitalized on the Campesino a Campesino experience through its "South-South" program, which brought Central
American farmers from NGO projects together in a series of *encuentros* to
popularize the movement. The recognition by Oxfam that Campesino a
Campesino was a *movement* (MCAC) rather than simply a project had political implications for the UNAG Campesino a Campesino *project* (PCAC).
Like Solomon, Oxfam placed PCAC at the head of the Central American
movement. PCAC coordinators were instrumental in planning the first
regional gathering held in Nicaragua. This made sense, since even though
Nicaragua was not always the origin of the movement's technical and
methodological innovations, PCAC was by far the largest Campesino a
Campesino program in Central America. International forums were a spe-
cialty for the Sandinistas, and UNAG was accustomed to attending and
hosting international events. By supporting Oxfam's Sur-Sur (South-South)

project, PCAC (and by association UNAG) reinforced their progressive international profile. But while UNAG agreed to place PCAC at the head of the regional Campesino a Campesino movement, it insisted that PCAC was "just a project" within Nicaragua. UNAG reserved the role of leadership of Nicaragua's campesinado for itself. Byron Corrales, the head of the training section of UNAG, insisted emphatically, "The campesino movement in Nicaragua is UNAG! There is no other movement!"[30]

PCAC offered UNAG a way of providing a high-profile service to their peasant sector, which, while comprising the vast majority of union membership, held little political power in the union. It also provided a socially important, progressive, and green public image for the European NGOs that funded UNAG.[31]

But PCAC's presence within UNAG did not translate into substantive changes in UNAG's approach to agricultural development. This remained tied to larger, conventional farming interests. In his introduction to PCAC's thirteenth anniversary report, UNAG president Daniel Núñez did not even mention sustainability or farmer-led development. Rather he referred to PCAC as part of a UNAG "integrated rural development program" (PCAC 2000). But the majority of the campesinos and promotores in PCAC are not even members of UNAG. At the second international Encuentro Campesino a Campesino in 1995, Núñez insisted that UNAG membership be obligatory for promotores: those present refused to carry out the directive. Dolores Lanzas (Don Lolo), one of the founders of Campesino a Campesino in Nicaragua, peasant revolutionary, and longtime UNAG member, stated simply, "UNAG has not earned the privilege of the promotores' membership." Don Lolo was referring to the fact that while UNAG provided important institutional space for PCAC, it did not share any political power with its promotores. There were no promotores on UNAG's national board of directors, and control over the national PCAC budget rested exclusively with the UNAG board of directors, not the promotores. (See Appendix A.)

The Regionalization of MCAC

Though UNAG insisted on relegating MCAC to the status of a simple project, this did not stop the promotores from identifying with MCAC as a movement. By referring to themselves as a movement, promotores were able to travel and work with other projects and campesinos not associated with UNAG. This was especially important in those areas where UNAG was seen as being controlled by large landowners or intermediaries or where anti-Sandinista sentiment was strong. For those promotores working with NGOs outside UNAG, identification with MCAC provided increased mobility and access to new knowledge, tools, seeds, and other opportunities. MCAC allowed campesinos to access resources and to move as independent agents within the development interface of NGOs, research institutions, and farmers' organizations.[32]

The movement of promotores, as well as the methodologists and professionals associated with MCAC, was active beyond the borders of Nicaragua as well. During the Sandinista Revolution (1979 to 1990), Nicaragua became a magnet for revolutionaries and progressives from all over Latin America. European social democratic governments and liberal-left NGOs supported the Revolution in defiance of the U.S. proxy war and helped the Sandinistas maintain a high international profile by financing international and regional conferences in Nicaragua. Rural workers from across Latin America traveled to Nicaragua, anxious to learn about the agrarian reform, the mass organizations, and the literacy and health crusades. Representatives from Nicaraguan mass organizations and the Sandinista party were in high demand at international conferences and rallies all over the world. The International Relations Section of UNAG took great pains to establish international solidarity linkages, both to obtain desperately needed funds for UNAG and to reaffirm political support for the Revolution. Working through PCAC, the promotores from the MCAC took advantage of these opportunities to travel, receive visitors, and exchange information. After the fall of the Sandinistas, international NGOs continued to fund national and regional campesino workshops and gatherings throughout Central America and Mexico. Some of these, like Sur-Sur, promoted MCAC directly. Others addressed agricultural themes such as organic agriculture, fair trade coffee production, integrated pest management, and farmer experimentation. Promoters from MCAC, frequent participants at these events, shared ideas, swapped stories, and exchanged seeds with other farmers. Professional rural workers and a new generation of agricultural technicians in sustainable agriculture helped to organize, document, and follow up on these activities. The farmer-to-farmer methodology spread rapidly, as did the idea of a farmer-led movement for sustainable agriculture.

Campesino a Campesino in Cuba: Agrarian Transformation for Food Sovereignty

For a long time the priorities for agricultural development [in Cuba] were directed toward large-scale production in which mechanization and technical intensification were considered the most important factors for increasing production and yields. As a consequence there was a progressive dependence of the farmer on external inputs, a loss of biodiversity, and a reduction in food security. In addition, the country was faced with serious economic limitations

*starting in the early nineties that affected Cuban agriculture with the reduction
of inputs, fuel, and other factors of production that kept it from reaching
the potential and necessary agricultural yields for the volume of food
needed by the Cuban population.*
—ANAP, The National Association of Small Farmers (Perera 2002)

Another country in which the Campesino a Campesino movement is expe-
riencing dramatic expansion is Cuba. During the Sandinista Revolution,
professionals in MCAC attempted to spread news of the movement to Cuba
via UNAG. The UNAG president Daniel Núñez, the vice-president Ariel
Bucardo, and even Training Section Director Sinforiano Cáceres all had
extensive ties with Cuban officials and the leadership of the progovernment
ANAP—the Cuban small farmers' organization. For a time, Cáceres even
had a personal secretary on loan from ANAP. However, since these relationships primarily functioned in support of political objectives between the
Sandinista party and the Cuban state, they did not result in any exchanges
between MCAC promoters in Nicaragua and smallholders in Cuba. It took
a national food crisis in Cuba and the support of an international NGO to
open the campesino a campesino link between Mesoamerica and the island.

Ironically perhaps, given the extensive political ties between Nicaragua
and Cuba the MCAC response to Cuba's food crisis came not from Nicaragua but from Mexico. The link between Cuban farmers and MCAC promoters was established not through party or government channels, but
through international civil society.

The Special Period

Before the collapse of the Soviet Union in the late 1980s, the bulk of Cuba's
food came from Eastern Europe's socialist trade bloc.[33] The government
relied on comparative advantage, producing sugar cane for export in
exchange for subsidized crude oil, which Cuba refined and resold for foreign exchange. Cuba's agricultural sector enjoyed cheap, virtually unlimited
access to petroleum-based fertilizers, pesticides, and herbicides. This created a culture of dependence on external inputs and foreign food sources.
As Miguel Dominguez of Cuba's National Association of Small Farmers
(ANAP) described it, "Traditionally, Cuban campesinos, since the Revolution . . . have had an abundance of fertilizers, pesticides, and machinery . . .
that created a culture of producing with all the [external] resources. Logi-
cally, agriculture deteriorated because it degraded the soil. There were
unnecessary fertilizer applications, problems with machinery . . . but a culture developed that didn't lack for any external input."[34]

But this "culture" of input abundance received a severe shock when the

Soviet Union, Cuba's main trading partner, dissolved in 1991. According to food security analysts Peter Rosset and Medea Benjamin, "The favorable terms of trade which Cuba obtained for its sugar and other exports made it cheaper for Cuba to export sugar and import foodstuffs than to produce sufficient food domestically." Over half of the total calories consumed in Cuba came from overseas. The loss of its major trading partner plunged Cuba into a profound agrifood crisis, forcing it to "double food production while halving [agricultural] inputs" (1994). The government declared a "Special Period in Time of Peace" in 1990 and took desperate measures to regain its food security. Food crops were cultivated and brigades of students and urban workers went to the countryside to help with planting, weeding, and harvests. Many professionals and urban dwellers turned to gardening and farming to meet their nutritional needs. Said Miguel Dominguez,

> The situation in the nineties drove us to substantive changes in our way of acting, thinking, and living. Before, we didn't think about having vegetables, meat, or grains at the table because our supermarkets were full. With the fall of the socialist bloc and the tightening of the embargo we had to try alternatives. Many of us professionals left on weekends with our fathers, friends, and families to go and plant rice and beans on farms . . . we had to ensure that each family produced enough food for five to six months, or even a year.

Cuba's numerous agricultural research stations and agricultural universities worked to develop bio-fertilizers, integrated pest management, and other techniques for low external-input agriculture. It soon became clear that the scale and industrial organization of Cuba's large, mechanized state farms were inappropriate for developing low external-input agriculture. Reforms were enacted to scale down collectives and cooperatives, placing greater control over farming and marketing directly into the hands of the producers. In an attempt to meet immediate demand with traditional methods, ANAP sought out older campesinos who remembered how to plow with oxen and fertilize with animal manure. This, however, was only the first step in what is perhaps the most remarkable agroecological transformation of conventional agriculture in the Americas—one in which both ANAP and the Campesino a Campesino movement play a pivotal role.

The Campesino a Campesino Agroecological Movement

Interestingly, and somewhat by accident, Cuba's Campesino a Campesino movement first began with the urban agriculture groups operating in the multiple greenbelts around the capital city of Havana. Luis Sánchez, an agricultural extensionist with the Council of Churches recalls

From the beginning there were situations in Cuba that led to Campesino a Campesino appearing first in the periphery of Havana. Havana has fifteen municipalities and twelve of these are really rural, so, with more agricultural than urban space, it produces a good part of the food consumed in the city. . . . In 1995, several organizations, including ANAP, received an invitation to visit the Vicente Guerrero Group [in Mexico] so we formed a delegation. As a result of that visit, we invited three compañeros to Cuba to put on a workshop on soil and water conservation. We invited El Padrino [Teodóro Juárez], Emiliano [Juárez], and Manolo [Manuel Moran Madrid]. They came in June to give the course but apparently we did not coordinate well and ANAP didn't realize they were coming until they were on their flight [expecting] to give a course to twenty people. I was an agricultural extensionist then, working with the community of Santa Fe in Havana's periphery. So [ANAP] came to me and said, "three promoters are coming and we have no people for the course or anywhere to put them. Can you help?" Yes, of course! "And can you bring in twenty people by Monday?"

> (Personal communication, 2004)

Sánchez managed to organize the five-day soil and water conservation workshop with twelve of Havana's urban farmers. Afterwards, two farmers and a technician who took the course put the new knowledge into practice. In August of 1996 in the midst of Cuba's agricultural and food crisis, the farmers put on the first Cuban Campesino a Campesino workshop for their neighbors. Sánchez describes it:

People worked out of pure solidarity and altruism. At that moment Cuba was going through a very critical period that we call the "Special Period" and the situation was complicated. The year before, our urban economy had hit bottom. So this was even more valuable because these folks received nothing except the spirit of helping others. We started giving workshops in November. We gave people three months to put what they learned into practice. We started giving [Campesino a Campesino] workshops in all of the municipalities with producers and facilitators [many of these were technicians that worked in the government's citizen agricultural committees].   (Personal communication, 2004)

A year later, the group had trained over six hundred urban farmers. Bread for the World, a German nongovernmental, Christian aid organization, supported the work and helped Sánchez and other extensionists from the Council of Churches to teach the methodology to other extensionists and researchers in the Ministry of Agriculture. Sánchez acknowledges it was a rocky beginning:

We started to develop a process for "formation." At first they resisted. They didn't understand. The technicians didn't want to take on something they had not been trained for. They said, that might work in Nicaragua or Guatemala, but not in Cuba! Well, later they publicly admitted they had been mistaken. The professionals realized that it was much more productive to work with the promoters. The coverage grew. The campesino-promoter was not just the arm of the extensionists, no! The extensionists supported the campesino's own process. They helped him in that. The extensionists were changing their own vision of things.
(Personal communication, 2004)

Because of the need for an agroecological alternative, and because of the extensive and highly active presence of a national small farmers union (ANAP), the Campesino a Campesino movement grew very quickly in Cuba. In February 1997, Sánchez put on a workshop series organized by ANAP with farmers from agricultural cooperatives in Matanzas and Colón provinces. Later that year, ANAP hosted the Seventh Regional Gathering of the Campesino a Campesino movement (the region being Mesoamerica and the Caribbean). ANAP formally joined MCAC and was promptly elected regional program coordinator (Perera 2002). With the help of Sánchez, Bread for the World, and technicians from the Campesino a Campesino program in Nicaragua (PCAC), ANAP began working in the Villa Clara province in November of that same year. Heinz (Enrique) Kolmans, agricultural consultant for Bread for the World, emphasizes the complementary convergence between Campesino a Campesino and ANAP:

I started talking to ANAP to see about the possibility of Campesino a Campesino. I realized that they liked the idea and that they saw the importance that it had for their work during the Special Period. . . . The incredible thing is that ANAP has the capacity to reach campesinos. . . . The country had no food. . . . It was terrible! There was a great debate about the importance of agriculture and of recovering and improving the traditional campesino, something more agroecological and sustainable. There was a lot of tradition around less input-dependent, diversified agriculture.   (Author's interview)

ANAP quickly expanded the Campesino a Campesino project in Villa Clara to a national program for agroecological development. The organization promoted Campesino a Campesino through its fifty rural radio programs and distributed literature regarding the movement to its national, regional, provincial, and municipal offices. The newly dubbed "Campesino a Campesino Agroecology Movement" was integrated into ANAP's national organizational structure through a system that linked producers on production and on service cooperatives through campesino-promoters, technical "facilitators," and program coordinators. The program focused on recovering traditional agroecological practices, the validation and adaptation of new technologies, and farmer-to-farmer exchanges (Perera 2002):

> Through new experiences with projects ANAP created the Agroecology Movement using the Campesino a Campesino methodology. At first we were helped by a few NGOs—Bread for the World, another French organization. ANAP used the structure of its own organization. This gives us the possibility of linking up all campesinos to spread knowledge to its very core. We have a network of national, provincial, and municipal coordinators that work with facilitators in each cooperative, that work directly with the campesino-promoters that have best implemented sustainable practices. We work more and more with these promoters, and with the help of the personnel that we have put at the service of agroecology, more campesinos follow the example of the promoters, who are really their neighbors.[35]

In 2000 ANAP held the first national gathering of Campesino a Campesino promoters in the town of Villa Clara in Santa Clara province. The social base for ANAP's promoters came from its cooperative and individual producer members:

> How did we form promoters? Well, first we started with those campesinos that still used traditional practices, the ones who had held on to tradition and had not degraded [their ecosystem] so much. We had found many of these during the Special Period when there was no fertilizer, pesticides, or petrol. At that moment the campesinos of Cuba controlled around 20 percent of farmland. And produced 51 percent of the food, meat, vegetables, grains. I am not talking about tobacco or sugar cane. These campesinos were those least affected by the Special Period. They did not have all [the] resources that the large state farms had. After that we went to the Agricultural Production Cooperatives, and then those smallholders that had not suffered [in] the Period too badly.[36]

For their part, these co-op farmers saw the agroecological practices of Campesino a Campesino as a culturally and socially appropriate solution to their livelihood and food security problems:

> We joined the Agroecology Movement out of economic need. Due to mismanagement, our cooperative fell into a financial crisis during the Special Period, with many difficulties because of the blockade that limited our access to external inputs. We then saw the need to look for alternatives to solve these problems. And we had to find them among the co-op members while we covered the needs of the same cooperative members. We needed to raise production and lower costs. Our motto was "do

A Cuban promoter's prize garden

more with less." This is difficult because campesinos don't always understand what you mean. The campesino understands what he or she sees.
They believe what they see. To teach, you have to demonstrate. In order
to reach the point that one can do more with less, use less and have higher
production, one must enter into the world of agroecology.[37]

Nearly all of Campesino a Campesino's production is organic, or nearly
organic, in Cuba. The presence of organic vegetables has had a profoundly
positive impact on rural and urban diets. A promoter explains:

What motivated me to change was my own health . . . that, and the policy of intensification that the government had to increase the cultivation
of vegetables . . . both those things; marketing, too. When I switched to
growing organically, I opened a fruit and vegetable stand. They came all
the way from town to buy my vegetables. Now they don't come any more
because there are vegetable stands all over the place! But this farm is a reference for all and we have different crops planted all year round. We
always try to keep things looking good in case visitors come, because this
has to spread. Our municipality is a candidate for a national reference.
This is the result of all our work. Everyone receives good quality, fresh
produce that is not bad for their health. One's body has to eat good,
clean vegetables not contaminated by pesticides to offset all the other
bad things.   (Author's interview)

The capacity for experimentation and innovation basic to Campesino a
Campesino was easily accessed by Cuba's agricultural scientists for field tri-

Silvia Hernández Martínez, Cuban Agricultural Co-op president, explains the results from one of dozens of crop experiments the co-op has on its farm

als, demonstration, and diffusion—not only of new varieties and cultivars, but of the notion of enhanced biodiversity itself. Silvia Hernández Martínez farmer, experimenter, and president of the Pedro Orlantín Vanguard Cooperative in La Palma, Pinar del Río asserts:

> Before we entered [the movement] we were campesinos with two varieties of beans, one or two of corn, one or two of each crop. We didn't have any more and we never even measured our yields. We lived, as they say, planting as the seasons dictated. We never worried about planting another kind of seed because we didn't have any. But . . . I lost my peace and quiet with experimentation! Now we have hundreds of varieties of things! If one variety is better, if another somewhere else is even better, I need to go and see. . . . I've lost my peace and quiet, but I now I have economic security, for me, for other campesinos, and for society also. Because right now we are in a great experimental phase. But this will pass and another, happier time will come when everyone will have more. Well, we understand now that where there is greater diversity, the pests and disease attack less. The crops live better in groups of plants, they develop better. This farm has gone through big changes. My mind has gone through even bigger changes than the farm! For example, before all my fences were lined with *piña de ratón*. Now, on our farm the boundaries are all fruit trees, plantains, coconut, and even royal palms. So where I used to produce nothing, now I have hundreds of plants that start pro-

ducing in three years because we learned to graft them to speed up the flowering cycle.   (Author's interview, June 2004, Villa Clara, Cuba)

From Food Security to Food Sovereignty: The Agroecological Transformation of Cuba

In eight years, the Campesino a Campesino movement of Cuba grew to over 100,000 smallholders. It took the movement nearly twenty years in Mexico and Central America to grow to that size. What made the difference? Clearly, the extraordinary conditions of the Special Period in Cuba brought sustainable agriculture to the forefront. The organizing capacity of ANAP played a key role in the movement's rapid spread. Another important factor is the relatively high levels of education and excellent health care enjoyed by Cuban smallholders compared with those of most of the developing world. Further, Cuba's technical capacity in agriculture is not only very high, it is fairly decentralized. Agricultural scientists and technicians are widespread, and work directly and extensively with the many cooperatives throughout the countryside, often living on the co-op itself. When the time came to concentrate their efforts on bio-fertilizers, integrated pest management, and other agroecological approaches to farming, they did so quickly. Most importantly, the decentralized nature of Cuba's technical capacity in agriculture allows it to direct research and adapt practices to ecosystem-specific agroecological problems. The agroecosystem approach to sustainable agriculture is a key principle in agroecology. In Cuba, it has had big payoffs. Finally, the importance of secure land tenure and a guaranteed market for campesino agriculture cannot be underestimated. The government of Cuba had provided many incentives for people to work the land, but the most important are the agrarian reform and the mixed (private and state) market system. Smallholders have easy access to land, credit, and markets. Producers may either sell at their own local fruit and vegetable stands, through their cooperatives, or directly to the state. Because no producer need sell below the price the state will pay for their product, this price serves as a floor on agricultural prices.

These factors reflect a favorable policy context, not only for sustainable agriculture, but for campesinos as dynamic social actors. But what drives this policy context? What is its normative principle? A speech given by Lugo Martínez, president of ANAP, to a Campesino a Campesino gathering provides the answer:

> I would say that for Cuba and the Cuban revolution agricultural sustainability and food security, and the sum of these two, is the same as national sovereignty and national security. Cuba is the only country in the world

with an embargo. No other country in the world has resisted a blockade like Cuba. Each day there are new measures. And we try to overcome this cruelty and maintain our dignity. . . . And we Cubans resist. Each day we consolidate our food security. We are being threatened. Everyone knows this. Threatened with invasion. . . . We have always struggled. We have always worked. We have always sacrificed to avoid war. No intelligent thinking person can be in favor of war. These wars of terror to finish off everything we have built in this world. We realize that the only way we can win this war, without going to war, is to let the enemy know that we are prepared to defend ourselves to the ultimate consequences. The countryside is fundamental to the security of the people. What gives us security is working with our campesinos and our producers toward sustainable agriculture; using organic fertilizers, biological pesticides, as we have already done by working with animal traction and the sweat of the men and women of the countryside. This must be the future of Cuban agriculture! In times of war and in times of peace, the best road is the road of agroecology. I want to say that in good conscience, we have not walked very far yet on this road. We have worked since 1994 with our partner organization Bread for the World in the project that we started in Villa Clara . . . with the methodology of Campesino a Campesino. And we will continue this way because it is a methodology that allows us to advance firmly in the work of sustainable agriculture.

We found it necessary to develop this movement, not because we were so ecologically aware. . . . If a boat came with fertilizers most Cubans would not tell it to turn around, they would say, "unload it!" That's the way it is, sincerely speaking. So we realize what we are up against, what we have to do, because we have to transform people's awareness. And transforming awareness is the most difficult task of all. Cuban campesinos have an important job. They were used to having a lot of chemical fertilizer. Then the just trade relations we had with the socialist bloc—especially with Eastern Europe—disappeared. Chemical fertilizers, insecticides and fuel disappeared. We couldn't just sit there with our arms crossed . . . but for two years we were unable to provide our people with meat because the bulls we used for beef were needed to work in the fields. Today we have increased the oxen teams by several hundredfold. Most of our agricultural machinery was from the Socialist bloc and had a twenty-five-year use-value and a total lack of replacement parts. We had no choice. To give you an idea, the Pinar de Rio province cultivates 1,600 *caballerías* [16,000 hectares] of tobacco every year. Ninety-two percent of this land is prepared with oxen teams. Not one single tractor is used. I just want you to understand the effort we had to make here. This is agricultural sustainability!

It has also been necessary, because of the biological war imposed on us, and because of the lack of chemical pesticides, to produce biological pesticides. I'll give you an example: thrips. In the Havana-Matanzas corridor during the potato harvest, we saw the plane from the United States dump this insect from the sky. It was very difficult the first year. When thrips were discovered they were already established. But today, because of the products which we produce, one doesn't hear about thrips in Cuba. Now it is a friendly insect. This is agricultural sustainability!

We have been working with silos. We are making them, but not like the ones made in other countries where unfortunately farmers have to store their grains because they can't find a market, or when the price is too low. In Cuba, the campesinos have guaranteed market for 100 percent of their production. They also have a just, secure price that provides them with economic viability. Cuban campesinos do not need to save anything to sell later. The silos are to save *seed*. That is agricultural sustainability! The campesinos can save their seed and what they need for food. And this is agricultural sustainability and national security. Because if someday I have to tell someone from the city to go to the countryside in defense of the nation, that campesino will have food for their own family and food for whomever has come to help. That is national security and food security.

Reflections

Campesino a Campesino is a far-flung and multifaceted movement. It is shaped by smallholders' cultural responses to development and change in Mesoamerica and the Caribbean. The failures of conventional agriculture have led farmers in MCAC to develop their own tools, technologies, and agroecosystem management strategies to reclaim ecologically degraded land and give them greater control over production factors. Rather than substitute ecosystem functions with chemical inputs, these methods aim to enhance the ecological functions of the farm system as a means of stabilizing productivity. In doing so, campesinos create space to develop farming styles tailored to their specific agroecosystems and socioeconomic capabilities. This leads to greater levels of autonomy in relation to the state and the market. MCAC's focus on the agroecological basis of production situates it firmly on the cutting edge of global trends for sustainable agricultural development.

The dramatic rise of MCAC in Cuba provides a *structural lesson* in sustainable agricultural development. Good methodologies and techniques are important—after all, if farmer-driven sustainable agricultural development does not raise and stabilize yields, conserve natural resources, and improve livelihoods, what good is it? These are necessary conditions, but they are not sufficient. For sustainable agriculture to become the norm rather than the exception, they must be accompanied by radical changes in agricultural policy that favor smallholders and agroecological approaches to farming.

As I will show in Chapter Three, methodologically, MCAC drew from simple, people-centered development principles, and from the revolutionary, pedagogical practices of popular education to fashion nonhierarchical learning techniques that stressed experimentation and mutual aid for the farmer-led development of sustainable agriculture. The resulting "campesino pedagogy" was normatively anchored in values drawn from deep cultural frameworks shared widely by campesinos in the region. Over time, agroecological knowledge became encoded in MCAC in forms that were easily adopted by programs in sustainable agriculture development. Small-scale experimentation provided opportunities for researchers to engage with the movement, and farmer-to-farmer training methods attracted NGOs interested in increasing levels of farmer participation in development.

Paradoxically, MCAC grows fastest in times of crisis, like the Cuban Special Period or the "lost decade" of the 1980s, when war and debt ravaged Central America. The failure of conventional development strategies on one hand and the proliferation of NGOs on the other, combined with the transinstitutional naure of MCAC, allow for the spread of its philosophy, methods, and technologies. This institutional mobility allows MCAC to adjust to changing institutional and political circumstances and to take advantage of opportunities on local and regional scales. Not only does the capillary nature of the movement's growth allow it to permeate research centers, farmers unions, and NGO projects, these institutions in turn draw from MCAC's technical and methodological experiences, resulting in paradigm shifts and trends for participatory, sustainable agricultural development.[38]

Formal efforts at sustainable agricultural development in Central America frequently call for a dual partnership between research centers and NGOs because it is believed that researchers can provide the science if NGOs provide the farmers—a way of thinking familiar to the Green Revolution. But the existence of sustainable agriculture on the ground through MCAC demonstrates that researchers are not the only source of knowledge in sustainable agriculture. Neither are they the most prominent or the most effective. Sustainable agricultural development as it actually exists is largely the result of decentralized, horizontal processes of innovation and diffusion, rather than centralized, vertical processes of technology generation and transfer.

As a movement, MCAC is less the result of programmed actions leading to change, but rather the result of changes and actions that lead to programs. While it is true that NGOs are institutional vehicles for the development and spread of MCAC, they did not plan it, and did not determine its emergence. Farmers' culture, actions, and informal networks were accessed (even captured), but not invented, by NGOs. The emergence of MCAC has not followed any linear course, but has evolved unevenly and unexpectedly in response to unforeseen events. MCAC's development suggests a widespread mosaic of human potentials that interact as opportunities and avenues for communication appear.

Some development institutions claim MCAC's success as their own and interpret the movements' growth as a result of the participatory paradigms for sustainable agriculture currently in vogue. This view fails to consider that from a campesino perspective, it is development institutions that participate in *campesinos'* projects for livelihoods, not the other way around.[39] This position also relieves development institutions of any accountability from below in the sense that *their* participation as institutions is rarely seriously evaluated by farmers. Behind the hubris of programmed development, it is campesinos who give the social and cultural meaning to MCAC, and it is the promotores who, after the professionals leave, stay on to do the work.

While MCAC offers many lessons in agroecology and horizontal training methodologies for sustainable agriculture, these are not singularly unique and are shared with hundreds of development programs. Perhaps the most valuable lessons to be learned from the MCAC lie not in the participatory methodologies employed by development professionals but rather in how "marginalized" campesinos, through MCAC, have affected and continue to shape the way professionals think about and carry out sustainable agricultural development.

TWO

Tales from Campesino a Campesino

We have worked and gained experience, but it is hidden. There are many organizations here and many experiences, but no one knows about it. Not even the government. What are our successes in San Martín? What do we need to move forward? I think it is good for us to put out this book because it will show that everything started here in San Martín. It hurts me to say it, but it has to be said: There are many people who document experiences and put them in their books, they sign their name and are the authors of the book. Where did the experience come from? Who knows? They pirate the experience. We don't want pirates. We are the ones with the experience and we want to bring it to light.

—*Felipe Tomás, San Martín Jilotepeque, Guatemala*

THE CAMPESINO A CAMPESINO MOVEMENT has its roots in the deep indigenous cultures of Mesoamerica—in the languages, communities, and extended families that coevolved with the rain-fed landscapes of maize, beans, and squash. It is part of the campesinado's constantly changing forms of cultural resistance to outside domination, from the Spanish Conquest to corporate globalization.

The following testimonies will present the reader with a rich body of related experiences that disregard Western notions of progress. The origins of Campesino a Campesino are less geographic than cultural, its levels are nonhierarchical, and its stages are not evolutionary. To ascribe a linear process to histories is always arbitrary, and often tells us more about our own cultural assumptions than about the people we study. Sometimes, less is to be learned by analyzing than by simply listening to the voices that unfold and interact—appearing, disappearing, and reappearing in new forms, places, and spaces.

The voices in this chapter belong to the actors who ultimately shape life on the ground in the Mesoamerican countryside. I have chosen a loosely ordered chronology that follows the people and experiences in Campesino a Campesino that I was able to follow personally. Testimonies jump back and forth with events, ideas, and people in the Movement. It is my hope that sharing the voices from the Movement in this way will help dispel romantic notions of the traditional peasant Other and expose the violence behind the "disappearance" of the peasantry. Most of all, I hope that I can help the reader get to know these extraordinary men and women struggling for survival and self-determination. Perhaps this will help clear the way to see ourselves in their experiences.

Tales from Guatemala

San Martín Jilotepeque in Chimaltenango, Guatemala, is the *mera mata*—the rootstock—of the Campesino a Campesino movement. This is no accident. The Movement's most compelling resistance stories come from the Kaqchikel experience of economic and cultural repression. In response to blinding poverty, exploitation, natural disaster, war, and ethnocide, the Kaqchikel Mayans reached deep into their culture for the keys to their survival. Their efforts gave birth to the philosophy and the methodologies that eventually spread throughout Mesoamerica from campesino to campesino. Though the Movement was brutally repressed in Guatemala, virtually disappearing during the 1980s and much of 1990s, it returned after the signing of the Peace Accords in 1996. With the return of the promoters to San Martín Jilotepeque, Chimaltenango, Campesino a Campesino has been healing and reconstructing indigenous communities devastated by war and disaster.

THE FERTILE GROUND OF EXTREME POVERTY

EVERYTHING HAS A REASON. Every uprising has a cause. The elders will agree with me . . . in the 1970s we had a lot of emigration here. This was not voluntary but obligatory. We campesinos had to emigrate to the coast to cut cane, harvest cotton. This was not voluntary but obligatory. Extreme poverty obliged us to emigrate to the coast. Because of emigration, poverty in Guatemala was great. Here in San Martín we could say that now everyone has a piece of land, but back then we didn't. We lived in extreme poverty. Because of this everyone had to emigrate to the coast because in the seventies everyone had a card that had to be validated by the *patrón* on the coast. That is the history up to the seventies. That is how our cause began and that is when the institutions started arriving and cooperativism began. . . . World Neighbors arrived. Oxfam started working in San Martín. They found fertile ground. What was the fertile ground? Extreme

poverty. They said, cultivate your land! You have a plot, you should cultivate the land, and if you do, you will have food and you won't have to go
to the coast. That is how the story began. We started village by village,
community by community, with the themes of agricultural development,
soil conservation, and water conservation. It meant building terraces and
constructing contour ditches. We can say that the martyrs were Roberto
Chicoac and Vicente Hernández of Santa Rita Las Canoas. These were
compañeros of ours who never spoke about the guerrilla or armed struggle.
We were talking about improving our crops so as not to emigrate to the
coast. So in this way, our history is based on a reason, and the reason is
that back then we lived in extreme poverty.

And I want to tell you, unfortunately, what always happens is that when
a storm blows; the poor suffer the most; when the earth shakes, the poor
suffer the most; if there is violence, the poor suffer the most. That is what
happens. These programs started to raise awareness. We had barely started
to raise awareness and agricultural yields when the earthquake destroyed
86 percent of our homes. . . . Unfortunately, the poor are the hardest hit
by these things. Thanks to this, that the earth shook, they started helping
us, and that motivated people to organize and build houses. The earthquake left organization. The agencies that arrived found fertile ground
because we lived in extreme poverty. We had this need. Nearly 90 percent
of us have at least a patch of land. The earthquake left organization and
gave us space to organize.

But then in 1979 and 1980, just as these organizations found fertile
ground because of the exploitation, the guerrilla organizations found fertile ground for the guerrilla. That is why of San Martín's 169 communities,
approximately 100 were organized by the guerrilla. This meant that the
army high command classified the zone as a guerrilla zone, and they confused those who believed in revolutionary concepts with those who were in
the guerrilla. These people were organized, but they weren't guerrillas. Only
those who belonged to an armed front fought. Nonetheless, because they
were organized, the army high command classified it as a dangerous zone
for the Guatemalan state and implemented a scorched earth policy. . . .
That was the beginning of another tribulation. In San Martín there were
3,879 victims. It cost San Martín its organization . . . it destroyed our feeling and our unity. This was destroyed by violence. It destroyed our homes
and the ability to say, "We are compañeros, let's struggle together." That
is how, out of fear, since then, everyone is now asleep. You know we are
still afraid! If I go to a community and ask if they were organized in the
guerilla, they tell me no, and I respect it. . . . Our fear is greater than we
are. Our spiritual situation is bad. To be well we have to be well economically and spiritually. If I ask, "How are you?" and you say "Good.". . . No.

Spiritually you are not well and economically you are not well. We are not well! We need to support our organization so that it grows again. Why? Because they tell us that electricity is development. Potable water is development. Roads are development—fine. But we need an economic base. Electricity is no use to me if I can't pay for it. The road is useless if I have no money for bus fare. We have to be organized! We have electricity, we have water, we have telephones. What do we need to become stronger? Agriculture. Why talk of industry? We are not industrialists. We have to talk of agriculture if we want to move forward.

In 1996 the Peace Accords were signed and the organizations we have today were formed. There are several NGOs working (again) in San Martín, but it has been hard for all of us to begin the work. San Martín is again a fertile ground to do what we need to do, but it will depend on each one of us to spread the work in our communities. I want to tell you about everything we have experienced and everything that has yet to happen to us. I give thanks to God that we live each day, and I prepare myself for tomorrow. When morning breaks tomorrow, we can give thanks to God we are alive and live that day. Our point of departure has to be our work because this is what provides us with everything, our food, our clothes, whatever we need. Today we have the opportunity to be at the forefront of organizations that have the desire, the harmony, the hope in our *pueblo* (people) who have suffered so much and have always needed help. We are not poor because we are indigenous, we are poor because we never had the opportunity to develop ourselves. Let's lend a hand, but let's lend a hand to ourselves and this way we will develop ourselves one to one. I want to tell you that we also are in a great stage in regards to our Mayan cosmovision. We are in the era of reflection. After the reflection we can see that development will come because we will understand each other. The Popol Vuh [the Mayan "Bible"] . . . teaches us that everything has a moment and a space and a reason. For each thing you must look for the reason. And the reason here is that many organizations are looking for justice. And when we find justice peace will reign. We will live in peace and our economic situation will change.   —*Celso, San Martín Jilotepeque*

SOIL CONSERVATION AND THE KUCHUBAL:
THE SEEDS OF INNOVATION AND SOLIDARITY

FROM THE 1970S TO THE 1980S there was a great movement of farmers through the catechist groups. There was a gringo there named Roland Bunch who talked to us about soil conservation and green manures, about a lot of things. But we campesinos did not understand him. What is this "soil conservation?" What are "green manures?" We knew only about chemical fertilizer then. Not what the numbers meant, just the brands. Work started in the seventies and eighties. There was a big movement. From 1972 through 1974 there was training, gatherings of campesinos from different villages. . . . We also had a group of promotores that took us to Tecpán with Don Sorino Salazár, who had an excellent farm. They also took us with Anastacio Muj who had a plot in Paticilla. We knew nothing about green manures, about *choreque* bean, or how to plant it. What is important is that the work we saw, we started to do ourselves. We started to visit other campesinos. That is how Campesino a Campesino began here in San Martín. The experiences of a campesino in Chatalju went to Las Lomas, the experience from Las Lomas went to Xetu, to Xitafor . . . then the movement started working with contour ditches, with live barriers. A great man was with us named Marcos Orozco. He was a person with thirty-five years experience in the Ministry of Agriculture. He taught us all he knew. We learned and put it into practice.

In 1976 the earthquake hit us all. We set agriculture aside a bit and started to work building houses because all our homes had been destroyed. There were promoters in construction, a program for masons and one for carpenters. The group of agricultural promoters worked in this. There was also a group of women who learned about health, nutrition, and hygiene. It was a great movement of carpenters and health workers in the 1970s and 1980s. . . . We solved these "minor problems" after the earthquake, and returned to agriculture.

In 1979 came the bad smell of violence. They started killing our leaders, one here, one there. In the eighties it was even worse. But we had the great experience of Campesino a Campesino because it did not come from anywhere else, it was born here, in San Martín, through the kuchubal. The earthquake taught us to work in kuchubal because one, by himself, could not lift the wooden beams, the tin roof . . . we needed help from others. We didn't have any money to pay for helpers so we had to help each other. We had to organize. Between six neighbors and friends we built a house. That was the work of kuchubal. The kuchubal taught us many things . . . how to organize and to work together.

This is the story of Campesino a Campesino. We learned so much from each other. Sure, there were technicians. The technicians know a lot of things, but they fail when it comes to practice in the countryside. By the same token, if you say to us, "go work technically," we can't. We know how to use the hoe, the machete, but not technical things. Well, back then, the techniques filtered in little by little, and we gained experience. Actually, we didn't know anything like the agronomists. We were campesinos, we worked the land, we used hoes, we used machetes, we used soil, we used everything! But we didn't know about content, process, and development. Thank the Lord, a group of catechists were in the convent listening to the gospel and a gringo [Roland Bunch] came from World Neighbors. World Neighbors started training us. But we didn't know what to do. We learned what the agronomist knows. Learn, learn! We started working. Someone decided to go and visit someone else to see their work. What were the mistakes? What were the successes? One makes a lot of mistakes on a farm. Many received training and put what they learned into practice. We went to see all this work. They took us to Piticilla, San Jose Churucuyu, Tecpan. . . . We were receiving classes but look, there was a problem: we couldn't do it alone. That is where we got the idea of Campesino a Campesino, because these farmers were not agronomists, but campesinos. We began to believe in our experiences. Many of us started working. Some are still alive, others are with our Lord. They left us a lot of work and that is what we are doing today. We began to go to other countries. I remember that a number of promotores came from here: José Cupertino, Angel Mario Moreno, Don Timoreo Turíz. They went to Mexico to give courses. But sadly, when the violence came, when the repression came, we all had to flee. I left, too.   —*Felipe Tomás, Quetzaltenango*

THE EARTHQUAKE AND "THE VIOLENCE"

The Guatemalan earthquake of 1972 destroyed hundreds of villages in the country's highlands, home to many indigenous people. Over 10,000 people, mostly poor peasants, were killed and tens of thousands left homeless. In the aftermath, international aid agencies converged on the countryside with materials, supplies, and organizational support for reconstruction. This aid was frequently conditioned on religious or political affinity. Earthquake survivors found themselves negotiating a minefield of political alliances made all the more dangerous due to the opportunistic maneuvering of the rural elite who, with the help of the military, saw the earthquake as an opportunity to further dispossess peasants of their land and their labor. The Guatemalan revolutionary movement emerged from the jungles of the Petén, and its ranks filled steadily with poor, indigenous peasants. To confront the crisis, indigenous communities reached deep into their culture, reviving traditions of trust, mutual aid, and solidarity. Paradoxically, the very qualities that allowed them to rebuild their lives after the earthquake targeted them as "subversives" in the scorched-earth counterinsurgency war subsequently unleashed by the Guatemalan military.

Ever since the U.S. Central Intelligence Agency backed a military coup in 1954, Guatemala has been governed by a string of dictatorial presidents, ruthless in their protection of the political and economic privileges of the army, the landed elite, and powerful industrial interests. Resistance is brutally crushed, particularly in the countryside. The peasantry suffered forced conscription, massacres, disappearances, and military occupation throughout the 1980s and into the 1990s. The campesinos refer to this period simply as *La Violencia*: The Violence.

While the people centered agricultural development approach promoted

MARÍA: IN DEFIANCE OF SORROW

The survivors of San Martín's Campesino a Campesino movement were telling their stories. They spoke hesitantly at first, cautiously avoiding references to the decades of violence that had shattered their lives. María, a young, widowed Kaqchikel mother listened silently as others spoke in general terms of the terrible history of the region, making oblique, polite references to those no longer present.

After Celso's testimony about the "fertile ground of extreme poverty," María's hand went up. She moved to the front of the room and grabbed the digital recorder from my hand. With her child on her hip she began her story. She told of the day the soldiers came when she was taking breakfast to her father in the field. She ran to the house to warn her family. Her mother ordered her to hide in the forest. Afraid, she refused, but her mother shoved her baby brother into her arms and pushed her out the door. She hid in the bushes and watched as the Guatemalan military dragged her father to the house and beat him to death, then shot her grandfather. María cried openly as she spoke of the years of fear, hunger, and sorrow that followed. She spoke of finding happiness and hope with her new husband only to lose him in an automobile accident. She finished her story by urging everyone to speak clearly and to come together despite *la pena insoportable*—the overwhelming grief—that they all carried inside. The grief that kept them frozen in their fear. There was an uncomfortable silence. Then hands shot up. Everyone wanted to tell their story.

María handed me the recorder. It had accidentally been turned off the entire time. I turned it on and passed it to the next speaker. I marveled that people with such a tragic history of repression could meet again in spite of the permanent threat of violence. In their hearts, they rebel against La Violencia and its terrible loneliness. Willing themselves to speak, they reach past their fear and come together in defiance of their sorrow. For the Kaqchikeles, overcoming grief is an act of resistance.

María Paula Matu and son

by World Neighbors was seen as an alternative to armed resistance in the 1970s, by the 1980s its promoters and participants were targeted as subversives, guerrillas or guerrilla sympathizers. Men, women, and children suffered assassination, torture, and exile. It was the beginning of a long, dark, and pain-filled night. The embryonic Campesino a Campesino movement was "disappeared." The bereaved survivors became refugees in their own land. The story is told of farmers who filled in their conservation ditches with cornstalks and covered them with dirt so as not to be openly identified with the movement. The conservation ditches were to remain hidden for nearly two decades.

WE ALL SUFFERED DURING the armed conflict of 1980 to 1984. What the seventies taught us is still good. As a woman, I learned with my compañero. I saw him work in a group, in kuchubal. We are not going to blame the earthquake for anything. God brought it. All of the agricultural work, terraces, minimum tillage, I learned with my compañero. When the Violence started we could not work . . . we couldn't get together in groups because they would call us guerrillas. We stopped, we abandoned it, we left it behind. The Violence came. With the Violence *we* were abandoned . . . we lost people. I lost my compañero and I was left with three children. What did I do then? I worked. I suffered with my children to earn our daily bread. If I didn't work I couldn't feed my kids. Not only did we lose these histories, it was another story of armed conflict. The armed conflict left us destitute, with no clothing, no food. It left us without family. This is all pain to us now . . . to everyone who has victims. The young today don't remember because they were little. But of everything the armed conflict left us, it left sadness. For me, sadness is to be left without a father, without a mother, without brothers, without children. That is sadness. On top of that, we lost all the work we had done on our fields.   —*Mariana Cadena Casqui de Xatalun, San José*

I THANK ALL OF THE FAMILIES that have helped us so that we don't die of hunger. Thanks to all of the compañeros for what they have shared because it helps us a lot. I have been a widow since 1985 and I belong to the group of war widows. I am thankful for this because I am alone with only God to help me, and my family who also helps a little. Thank you for the path you have given. I am very sad, but find myself very passionate about this path that lights up my happiness a little because when I get out in the open air I open up, I am happier . . . thank you.
          —*Juana Hernández Balám, San Martín*

F OR A TIME I WAS DIRECTOR of the agricultural program at the Kato-Ki cooperative. During the war years all the compañeros who worked in soil conservation came from the village of Las Escobas. If you go there you will see the grass barriers, rock barriers, contour ditches, and pasture. They couldn't travel from Las Escobas to San Martín because transit was prohibited. They had to go by way of the capital or Chimaltenango because the institution that supported us needed reports. We wrote reports and took pictures. That is how we got together. I remember that no one could travel here from the villages. One of the compañeros that was a promoter and worked in La Virgen was persecuted and captured in this very cooperative.   —*Lorenzo Hap, Kuchamul Cooperative*

I AM NOT A KID, NEITHER AM I SO OLD. The only thing I can say is that I have suffered . . . as a child and as an adult. My father, who is dying now, showed us to make contour ditches. I was able to see the work World Neighbors left. There was a problem, they taught good things but sadly, the Violence sent all the promoters into exile. Their lessons—the ditches, the terraces, all that . . . our fathers could not continue. Now, thanks to the organizations that support us, we can continue the work. When the Violence came, we all suffered. We talk about migration. Everyone is leaving. We all do it for the same reason, because life is so difficult here. But one thing, some go to accomplish something, others do nothing. When the Peace Accords were signed, it was important because we were able to organize openly. We organized into different groups.

—*Campesino from San Martín*

W E WERE SPOILED WITH AGROCHEMICALS. But it was foreigners who took us down this path. Big countries that didn't do us any favors because we abandoned the manure of the chickens, the pigs, the rabbits, the goats. In the past, I remember as a child my father had twenty goats. He would have us collect manure from the fields. Why couldn't I do more? Because we were poor. There was no money to maintain enough animals to produce enough so that we can produce . . . ourselves, our children, our grandchildren. Unfortunately we lost our animals because we went to the coast. Then the earthquake hit us hard. The Violence came and hit us even harder. We went to the coast and we were left penniless, no clothing, no food. . . . We walked barefoot, with no hat. But we shared . . . we shared out stories. We ate wild fruit, raw corn without cooking it because we couldn't make a fire. Thank God, we all ate . . . uncooked, but we shared. This is a great tale to tell all our children and grandchildren because they will not even believe it. But it will live on in this book. We

RETURN TO LA MERA MATA

After many years in exile, Don Lázaro Aguín is back in San Martín Jilotepeque, farming, experimenting, teaching, and reorganizing the Campesino a Campesino movement. "This is *la mera mata*," he says, referring to the movement in San Martín as the rootstock. "This is where it all began."

Lázaro has gone from farm to farm in San Martín, searching for the seeds and the survivors who make up la mera mata. Many are gone. Others remain, but they are impoverished, and painfully silent. Some are the sons and daughters of promotores fallen in La Violencia.

Today, dozens of villagers have gathered on Lázaro's farm to share their stories from the Movement everyone thought had been disappeared. Amid the terraces, compost heaps, and cover crops, the campesinos and campesinas of la mera mata come together to share the task of rebuilding their lives. It is a kuchubal of the heart. They walk Lázaro's brilliantly renovated farm, talking and meditating on the work, the production, and the possibilities. One farmer jokes, "If Lázaro has risen, why can't we?"

After the field visit, the group retires to Lázaro's spacious patio for a meal and cool drink. In the shade of a large jacaranda tree, Lázaro recounts a visit to a hillside farm in the far reaches of the municipality. The old terraces on the farm were built during the heyday of the Campesino a Campesino movement. The original promotor was murdered in La Violencia, but his son, recently returned to San Martín, is preparing the land again for planting. The vegetation is sparse and the ground is hard from years of overgrazing by neighboring sheep. Despite the terraces, much of the topsoil has washed away. It will be difficult to raise a first crop. But the son is not discouraged. He takes Lázaro to the field and plunges his machete into the earth along the inner edge of a terrace, turning up a handful of dark, rich, loamy soil. It is an old conservation ditch. Every terrace has one. During La Violencia, the army accused the promotores of digging ditches for military purposes. Before his death, the young man's father filled in the ditches with cornstalks and dirt. Today, the young farmer is digging them out again, and will use the rich composted soil to fertilize his new crops.

Everyone agrees the young farmer is a lucky man. It will be much easier to restore his farm with all that compost. All he has to do is dig it up. Lázaro smiles broadly at the men and women he has found from la mera mata. Gathered together openly after so many years of hiding, he thinks, "Campesino a Campesino was not 'disappeared' in La Violencia, it hid. All one has to do is dig it up." San Martín is very lucky, indeed.

will share our story with other countries this way. And they will share with us. Why? For the good of all of us, our children, our grandchildren, the things that happened, how we shared and survived.

—*Andres Osorio, San Martín*

EXILE

DURING THE VIOLENCE I HAD TO GO INTO EXILE. Look, there are a lot of things about exile I just can't explain. The experience of exile is very sad because one leaves one's family and finds oneself alone in other countries without friends, with no one to talk to. The saddest thing about exile is to stop speaking our native tongue, Kaqchikel, because I could not communicate with my compañeros. I had to learn Mexican Spanish to survive. It is not the same as Guatemalan Spanish. This is very sad and it hits me in the heart. I think that all of us who have been in exile have lived this sorrow. Of course, we were among other human beings, talking, conversing. I kept my ideology of working with other campesinos. I started to work with campesinos and I learned from them. I had to adapt to their culture and learn a lot of swear words, because you know, Mexicans are Mexicans! I had to learn their culture. I had to live with them and share with them. I learned much from these campesinos. I learned about their agriculture. This was a great experience for me. While in exile I had to bring my family from Guatemala to Mexico. With the family, I was a bit happier, calmer, and able to concentrate more on work. Anyone who is in exile alone just goes around in circles. With the family one is happier and works better and produces more.

After a long time helping the Mexican campesinos (who are in the same situation as we are here in Guatemala), one day I asked myself, "What am I doing here?" Of course I was helping campesinos, giving advice, supporting farming . . . but what of my Guatemalan brothers and sisters? What are they up to? They need help. If I have all this experience, I should return to Guatemala now that the situation has calmed down. My heart was moved when I realized I had to return and help my brother Guatemalans that also needed me because they were in the same situation as the Mexicans.

On the one hand it is good in exile because one learns about other cultures. But it is a sad thing to leave one's land. That is one of the things. I had to return to my birthplace. Thanks to God, I am here, in Guatemala, helping, supporting with this experience. In exile there is great experience. There is sorrow. There is happiness and sharing, but one always thinks of one's own land.   —*Felipe Tomás*

Felipe Tomás was in exile in Mexico for seventeen years. He was among the Kaqchikel promoters to flee to Mexico with the help of World Neighbors.

The farmers of the Campesino a Campesino movement in San Martín Jilotepeque would like to dedicate their section of this book to their families and loved ones who were murdered by the Guatemalan government during the violence:

Huenceslado Armina Estrada · Francisco Estrada Loreoj · José Cupertino Suue · Rodrigo Jacobo · Mateo Xajil Elias · Aguistizo Estrada Culajay · Hilario Xajil · Sebastian Taj Cusauero · Maria Victoria Estrada Lozaj · Eulogio Xajil · Cipriano Estrada · Tomás Culajay Tay · Hilario Camey · Antonio Culajay L. · Cristóbal García Cajón · Encarnación Garcia Cajón · Encarnación Culajay López · Serbando Osorio Yool · Catalino Osorio Yool · Luciano Canas Camey · Herminia Canas Lorenzo · Santiago Coy Lopez · Ignacio Tacen Aimira · Miguel Angel Ambrocio Estrada · José Agustín Marejón · Agusto Morales · Ernesto Curajay · José Curajay Taren · M. Edmundo Fay Balan · Perfecto Fay Balan · José Gabriel Fay Balan · M. Monica Fay Atz · M. Virginia Morales · Clemente Mic · M. Angélica Saban · Encarnación Jacobo · Buanaventura Balan · Celso Jacobo · Celso Baxac Lopez · Eulogio Jacobo · Felipe Germinal · Antonio Lopez · M. Franquilina Gusanera · Victor Zay · Felipe Saban · Julio Osorio Jacobo · Esmerejildo Balan · Patricio Culayay Tacen · Pedro Culayay Tacen · Clemento Jacobo · Bernardo Bajxat · Juan Ramira Culajay · Silverio Tejax · Mario Agusto Tay · Filomena López Chajchaguín · Miguel Ispach · Grineo Ambrocio · Reyes Cajtí · Jerónimo Cajtí · Susana Cajtí · Delfina López Osorio · Seferino Yool Xajel · Paulo Yool Xajel · Tomás Yool Xajul · Joselino Yool Xajel · Eduardo Barar · Martina Bajar Culajay · Bonifacio Caj · Alejandro Cay · M. Jesús Borror · Juan Xajil · Marcos Pineda · Dominga Pazán · Antonio Penanada · Doroteo Fejáx · Santos Fejáx · Martina Fay Atz · Juan Fay Marcelo Fay · Adolfo Fay · Pedro Lopez · Victoria Canel · Marta Pineda · Agusto Pineda · Bernardo Avila Ajbal · Lucrecio Casecio Camey · Edmundo Martin Yool · Darío Martin · Catalina Martin Yool · Rosaria Marin Yool · Francisco Martínez Martín · Ricardo Hernández Sutuy · Isac Varitue extensionista de la cooperativa Estancia de la Virgen · Catequista Chi Gonzalez · Felipe Chamule · Crisanto Fay · Francisco Estrada · Marcos Estrada · Victor Estanislao Aguín · Dominga Aguín Garcia · Antonio Ambrosio · Benita Telán Mejía · Cristóbal López Vargas · Alicia Aguín García · Matilde Lem Fun · Luis Lem Mica · Rosendo Martin Garcia · Rosalio Martin Garcia · José Brígido Martín Guerra · Nasario Pino Yool · Daniel Pinol Ambrocio · Eladio Muteute · Asisclo Coroyo · Policarpio Estrada · José Felipe Catu · Marcial Catu · Angel Guicoy · Miguel Estrada.

Don Felipe Tomás, promotor in San
Martín, Jilotepeque, Guatemala

He was taken in by the same Mexican promoters that he himself had trained
several years before. Upon his arrival in Mexico, he found the Mexicans had
formed a local, farmer-led group and were actively teaching sustainable
agriculture in Vicente Guerrero, Tlaxcala.

Tales from Mexico

The story of Campesino a Campesino in Mexico begins with a rural devel-
opment project in the state of Tlaxcala, Mexico, started by the Mexican
Friends Service Committee (MFSC) under the direction of Rogelio Cova
Juarez, in 1977. "Roge," a native to the area, was dedicated to environmental conservation and social justice. Under his leadership the MFSC
embarked on a variety of development projects, including the project for
"Alternative Technology" in the village of Vicente Guerrero (1976 to 1979).
With help from villagers, North American volunteers for the project established a "model farm" to demonstrate the viability of French intensive-
biodynamic gardens, rabbits, milk goats, and solar heating. But villagers
were facing other issues, none the least of which were potable water, deforestation, soil erosion, drought, lack of income, poor health, and the grind-
ing corruption of government officials.

In 1978 a small group of farmers received training in soil and water conservation from Guatemalan promoters. The course inspired villagers to send
a group to Guatemala to learn more about soil and water conservation from
the Kaqchikeles of San Martín Jilotepeque. Upon their return, the group
took over the school gardens program from the volunteers and began practicing and promoting soil and water conservation.

Political differences between Rogelio Cova and the board of directors of

---

FINDING INSPIRATION

My first achievement was the opportunity to go to Guatemala and learn from that great experience that I dreamed about as a campesino—to see abundant production on a campesino farm while I just couldn't get my own plot to produce. So, the knowledge I gained in Guatemala, of seeing different plots from what I was used to, left me with a sense of wonder. From the moment I went to Guatemala my head started to imagine all kinds of things. Man! I wanted to have a small, high-producing plot like those compañeros!

—*Gabriel Sánchez Ledezma, Vicente Guerrero, Mexico*

---

the MFSC eventually led him to leave the that group. The staff walked out with him and together they formed SEDEPAC (el Servicio de Desarrollo y Paz, Asociación Civil, or the Peace and Development Service). For a time, the campesinos from Vicente Guerrero continued their work in farmer-led sustainable agricultural development through SEDEPAC.

I N 1981, WHEN THE GROUP WAS CONSOLIDATING, compañeros escaping difficult circumstances in Guatemala arrived. Repression of the Movement was strong and two Guatemalan compañeros came supported by World Neighbors. They came and were incorporated in the work. What is important is that the work was already defined: conserve soil and water, improve soil fertility . . . farmer experimentation, trying new seeds. The Guatemalan compañeros reinforced this work with their experiences from Guatemala.

The first thing that happened was our break with the Mexican Friends Service Committee. That was the first problem we had. . . . We were already committed to community work here in the region when we had to think, "Well, the financing is over with the Friends Service Committee, now what do we do?" We met with Rogelio Cova and he said, "Look, from now on there is no money, nothing. Who will stay and work? Who wants to go on to see what we can do?" Some said they couldn't, others of us said, "Yes, let's keep going as long as we can." We worked as volunteers. Why? Because, personally, I was convinced that our work was an opportunity and that I was learning more new things each day and that sharing this with other campesinos was a tremendous experience. I was enchanted with life! Before, I was paid for three days' work a week. As a volunteer I gave four! I just thought, "Let's see how far we get!" Our commitment was strong, and Rogelio Cova started writing proposals and that is how SEDEPAC was formed.   —*Gabriel Sánchez Ledezma*

THE BREAK WITH SEDEPAC

After having founded and directed SEDEPAC for several years, Rogelio Cova left the organization in the late 1980s. Rafael Reygadas from the PDP (Partido Democratico Popular) succeeded him as executive director. The organization brought in party members to occupy many staff positions. Tension developed between SEDEPAC and the Grupo Vicente Guerrero when nationally determined political priorities of the PDP clashed with the locally based initiatives of the Campesino a Campesino Movement. This tension led to a break between the Grupo Vicente Guerrero and SEDEPAC. While difficult, it gave the Grupo the opportunity to become Mexico's first independent campesino group dedicated to sustainable agricultural development. One of their first accomplishments was to win the presidency of their own municipality based on a platform of anticorruption and Campesino a Campesino development (see Chapter One).

WE WORKED WITH SEDEPAC, which ran six programs: Rural Area, Urban Communities, Summer Projects, Refugees, Women, Sweatshops. . . . It grew so fast that at first we thought it was very good, but we didn't realize it was going to turn into another political issue. So we left SEDEPAC and we started this movement to eradicate all the *caciquismo*[1] in the municipality. This was an empire and the caciques said "Okay, you will be president now, then, you will be president. . . ." Right? In this struggle we managed to break the empire and up to today the caciques have not been able to gain control of the municipality again. The Grupo Campesino has been a good experience. It's a good thing there have been so many ruptures because one learns and has to grow.

—*Gabriel Sánchez Ledezma*

IT WASN'T PLANNED . . . but I think it was for the best. It was tough, but it made us stronger. SEDEPAC went off to work in other areas and we took on the challenge as a campesino group. We survived from 1988 to 1993 as a group. We carried out limited activities, we promoted our work, we kept up our profile, but in 1993 we were lucky enough to get a visit from Bread for the World, and we were made stronger, but this time as a local group. . . . In 1993 we formulated our own strategy and started working hard. New generations came in, new leaders to reinforce the process, and since that time we have kept up the work and kept on moving forward. As a group we have gone through evaluation and planning processes. We have had to reflect on what to do.

—*Rogelio Sánchez, Vicente Guerrero, Tlaxcala*

In 1986, the promotores from Vicente Guerrero began a series of learning exchanges with campesinos in the Nicaraguan farmers and ranchers union,

One of my personal triumphs has been to have joined the Campesino a Campesino movement. In the first place, we were a very numerous family of eleven brothers and sisters in very difficult economic circumstances. A number of the older siblings went to bed hungry. So ever since

I was young I had to go work in a factory. All of the human capacity to learn, to dialogue, to share, to be listened to was lost because when one becomes a slave like that one is limited in all aspects. This is why I say it was a personal triumph to join the Movement in those years. This changed my life. In [the Movement] I learned about freedom, of opportunities to learn, opportunities to share,

Rogelio Sánchez, promoter from Vicente Guerrero, Tlaxcala, Mexico

and for personal growth. . . . Gabriel, Roque, and Teodoro had already begun [conservation] work. There was a school farm with a lot of soil and water conservation work. They planted a school orchard and it looked very pretty. I was really interested in this kind of work and put in some of the practices on a small plot of land I inherited from my mother. Little by little I got into the process of farmer experiments and I hooked up with the process that the compañeros had been into for some time. I became convinced of the need to contribute to Campesino a Campesino, so I just kept getting involved.

—*Rogelio Sánchez Ledezma*

UNAG. The visits had a profound impact on both the Mexicans and the Nicaraguans, though for different reasons. Nicaraguan campesinos had recently received land as part of the sweeping Sandinista Agrarian Reform. They often received a land title and a rifle—to defend the land from attack by the contras, the counterrevolutionaries trained and financed by the United States.

DURING THE PERIOD WE WERE WITH SEDEPAC, we had the opportunity . . . to start a program of farmer exchanges (visits). Before that no one used the term "campesino a campesino." We went to Nicaragua in 1986, 1987, 1988, and some of us went in 1989 and even 1990. We had some very interesting exchanges with all that accumulated knowledge of farmer experimentation between SEDEPAC and UNAG, but there were also specific people. Among them, Rogelio Cova, Roberto Vega, and Eric Holt-Giménez set up the exchanges. The team from Tlaxcala and some from Michoacán went in the first exchanges. This was very fruitful because we worked directly in the fields. We were not used to working with a rifle on our shoulder. All of the Nicaraguan compañeros carried rifles as they worked and it felt strange, right? There was a revolution in process. The land had been controlled by the rich so the poor people in the countryside had not learned how to manage the soil. They had recently received land [under the Land Reform Act] but there was war and hunger in the countryside and a need to learn how to care for and manage the soil. This helped out the process a lot. Many interesting things happened.

When we arrived and gave the first farmer workshops we showed them how to dig contour ditches and make terraces. People just stared at us but didn't say why. What we didn't realize that in a war, a ditch can be a trench for combat because the contras could attack the cooperative and attack the promoters. But people didn't say anything to us. We saw that they were worried! But we had not yet gained their trust. They were unsure of our work. It was difficult. Things did not just start magically. It was not until the third or fourth workshop people started to respond. Then they said, "Japanese technicians have come. North American technicians have come. Technicians have come from all over the world and none have been able to contribute significantly to our agriculture. These poor little Mexicans! What will they do?" We were just silent because the exchange was a process. At night we heard the gunfire from the AK-47s. We were sleeping and we would wake up afraid. . . . But one worked with courage and the Movement was made stronger with these shared moments and experiences. The team took on the challenge and we said, we are going to make this work because we think that these compañeros are going to do something good.

Something of great transcendence in my personal life and for the group was the experience we had in Nicaragua. When one travels and sees the local context of other communities, of other producers, of other campesinos, one starts to reflect and appreciate the things that surround us. That's when you say *"Hijole!"* How have these people, living in these conditions, accomplished so much? And I, who am in another context and in another situation, have not taken advantage of what I have. So I think this has been transformative because it has permitted us to reevaluate and acquire a greater commitment and have ideas of what to do.

—Rogelio Sánchez Ledezma

Gabriel Sánchez Ledezma at a field visit
with armed campesinos in Nicaragua
in 1986

Tales from Nicaragua

The appearance and rapid spread of Campesino a Campesino in Nicaragua
during the Sandinista Revolution was no coincidence. The Revolution was
a beacon to Latin American social movements. Intellectuals and activists
from around the world were drawn to the Sandinistas' bold political project
for social change. These "internacionalistas" actively supported the government's populist development programs in literacy, health, and agrarian
reform. Many expatriates were middle-class professionals who contributed
valuable skills. Others were young, idealistic volunteers irreverently called
"sandalistas" because they came in jeans and sandals, carrying backpacks.
Other visitors to Nicaragua were the campesinos who, with the help of progressive NGOs, came to share their agricultural knowledge and to learn
from the revolutionary experiment. It was a time of great political effervescence and, because of the U.S.-backed counterrevolution, also a time of
danger, sacrifice, and desperate hope. It was transformative. In revolutionary Nicaragua, the farmer-led approaches to agricultural development pioneered in Guatemala and Mexico were the tools of farmers' political
solidarity. The Mexican campesino's agroecological knowledge and farmer-
to-farmer methodologies were reciprocated with the Nicaraguan's revolutionary experiences. This cultural exchange of information, knowledge,
wisdom, and politics became known as Campesino a Campesino.

In the winter of 1987 I drove a nervous group of Mexican promoters to
Santa Lucía, Boaco, for what was to be the first farmer-led soil conservation
workshop in Nicaragua. It was wartime and we had difficulty buying gaso-

line and finding food for the event. The mountainous territory around Santa Lucía had been infiltrated by counterrevolutionaries, and ambushes were common. The war had divided the countryside. As an outsider, it was impossible to know if one was speaking with an informant, a spy, a combatant, or simply a farmer trying to keep her family alive. This thought crossed my mind when I stopped to pick up an elderly campesino sitting on a sack of grain at the turn-off. The man thanked us for stopping and offered to show us the way to Santa Lucía. The Mexican campesinos chatted with him about the crops and the weather. As we entered town he discreetly inquired as to our business. The promotores explained, somewhat less discreetly, that

---

ALICIA SARMIENTOS

From the moment I was invited to participate in the Grupo de Promotores, my life changed. Before that, I was just in the house. I had the opportunity to finish grammar school and after that I kept to the home. I had no vision of what happened around me because a lot was going on, but I saw only what hap-

pened at home. When I had the opportunity to go to Nicaragua, I met other women who fought for land and work and that motivated me a lot and opened a wider vision that we should not just do everyday housework, but there were many things we could do as women.

When I returned from Nicaragua and rejoined the Grupo, I discovered many communities close to mine. I didn't even know my own municipio because I had been

Alicia Sarmientos, promotora from Vicente Guerrero, Tlaxcala, Mexico

stuck in the house! I discovered that there were other lives, other women who struggled against what they were not allowed to do. They weren't allowed because of repression. Above all, machismo was very strong and it did not allow us women to develop ourselves. At that time I didn't understand it as machismo . . . more like "limitations," as if we women were good for one thing and that only. I started to discover that we could do different kinds of work as groups of women and that we could talk about what was happening to us. We could plan activities and work together. . . . I learned that we actually had a lot of capabilities and for that we had to learn to improve every day.

they had come from Mexico at the invitation of the Nicaraguan Farmers Union. They were to give a workshop for other farmers on soil conservation. The man looked from one to the other incredulously. "Turn this way," he said, directing us to a small farmhouse where a dozen campesinos stood waiting. Grateful to have arrived safely, I offered to drive him home. "You already have," he said, smiling, "Welcome to Santa Lucía! My house is your house." We had just met José Jesús Mendoza, better known as "Chepe Chu," the farmer who would become one of the founders of Campesino a Campesino in Nicaragua.

IF THERE IS ANYTHING THAT TRULY SATISFIES A PERSON, it is helping others; to collaborate so others improve; collaborate so others overcome obstacles; collaborate so that others can live differently all those things one suffers from in the countryside. I have felt such beautiful things through these experiences even though I never had any schooling. When someone wanted to teach me something, I was ashamed because I thought I wouldn't be able to understand them. But with Campesino a Campesino, the Mexicans came to give us a workshop here in Santa Lucía, and everything changed. Before, when technicians came to give workshops, I never understood what they were talking about. But when the Mexicans came, I understood everything because I understood their experience. This filled me with enthusiasm to keep learning about organic agriculture, the alternative for those that love the land and love nature. For me it was like opening a book, a book without letters, a book that says very deep things; immense, great, glorious, marvelous dreams come true! This is the book of life. It has taught me many things and given me things I never thought I would have.

Campesinos came and gave us workshops and I liked what they taught because they taught what they practiced. That was the main thing: *do* to be able to teach. This has been my mission, to do things in order to teach them to others, which is the best way to improve life in the countryside.

That was in 1987. It has been seventeen years and I can see the fruit of the dreams I had when I went to my first workshop. I never imagined the setbacks I would have, but I have been able to assimilate their lessons. Each day the school of life teaches us new things, beautiful things, precious things. Above all, when a dreamer has positive, concrete things that lift him up, criticism is not important. Campesino a Campesino is one of the most glorious experiences of my life. Some might ask, "What have you done?" They don't want to see these marvelous things, or see that one can live better with everything that nature gives us. But I feel fulfilled because I have been able to help many people healthily, purely, without prejudice.

—*José Jesús Mendoza, Santa Lucía, Boaco*

The early workshops put on by the Nicaraguan promotores were filled with hope and a sense of purpose. Many Nicaraguans felt they were at the center of a historical social change. The campesinado—both the backbone of the Revolution and the bane of the Sandinistas—had a mission: to defend the land, produce food for the revolution, and provide hope for the campesinos of the world. One of these campesino visionaries was Don Ernesto Herrera. A master teacher and a tireless organizer, Don Ernesto saw MCAC as an opportunity to lift the countryside from poverty.

THIS PROGRAM IS VERY IMPORTANT for all of us and important for all of humanity. This program is concerned with conserving and improving what little land we have left, because otherwise we will die of hunger. Because, these young people here are going to get married and they go off on their own and have kids and that means we will need more food. So I invite all of you to make a pact with us to be *multiplicadores* (multipliers). We can't be egocentric if we want to change the world. We can't just contemplate the world, the world is lovely, but we change it day by day with the cooperation of all of us. If we want to improve Santa Lucía, we can't wait for the government to come in here with a magic wand and transform Santa Lucía. It is all of us, our collective force that will transform Santa Lucía and feed Nicaragua.   —*Ernesto Herrera (Zurita 1991)*

The power of a good example, the desire to share, and the strong sense of purpose of the campesinos from Santa Lucía turned out to be a powerful

Don Ernesto Herrera, promotor of Santa Lucía, Nicaragua, planting a seedbed

Mamerto Mendoza, promotor of Santa Lucía, Nicaragua (on right)

combination. Peasants from across the country traveled to the village to see the benefits of agroecological farming for themselves. Soon, Don Ernesto's "multiplicadores" began to appear throughout Nicaragua.

I SAW HOW THE CAMPESINOS of Santa Lucía harvest. From a small plot of ground they harvest a lot! Meanwhile, I plant a large plot of ground and harvest just a little. Why? Because I don't improve the land, I don't use contour ditches, I don't use minimum tillage. But from now on, of course I am going to work to plant a little and harvest a lot. Because I saw how they did it in Santa Lucía. . . . That is why I like this program and I won't forget it. And what I learn, of course, I will teach to someone else.
—*Campesino at a workshop (Zurita 1991)*

FOR DECADES, technicians from banks and companies have provided agricultural training, but this never really reached campesinos. This gave rise to a need that started to be felt in Guatemala. That was the beginning of Campesino a Campesino. Then the Mexicans started doing it. They brought it here, and now we understand that training wherever it is, has to be 100 percent from campesino to campesino.
—*Mamerto Mendoza, Santa Lucía (Zurita 1991)*

DURING THE FIRST EXCHANGES with Don Chepe Chu and Don Catalino Conrado, we didn't really understand what the objective of PCAC was. But when the self-education process began, we started training one another. The first training was about soil and water conservation. I was especially interested because my land is on a hillside. I also like the idea of planting legumes.

One time I had to go fertilize a field with compost, but I didn't really know what it was. The first participants from the cooperative did not really understand PCAC. At that time we had abundant chemical fertilizer, tractors, we were not interested in something that was more work, even though it helped the soil.

Without any technical assistance, PCAC became an alternative; we saw the harm we had done to the soil. Then we had a change of government, and we realized that PCAC was an alternative for change, also. We started to experiment with organic fertilizer, comparing it to chemicals.

To farm [this way] takes more labor. After several years of initial sacrifice I see it giving fruit . . . it takes time to receive what one has invested, but you come to love the piece of land that you have. The importance of the forest and knowing about the life of the soil helped me to buy more land, not to become rich, but to live better, in other conditions. Love of nature is not learned in school, but by being in contact with her. We are in our fields all day, every day. The traditional farmer thinks that he needs to work the same way always, but we are constantly thinking about improving what we have. Maybe not great things, but at least we will eat better.
—*Santos Nicoya, Rivas, Nicaragua (PCAC 2001)*

One of the young campesinos who answered Don Ernesto's call was Ramón Sequeira. Like many peasant youth during the Sandinista revolution, Ramón had recently been trained as an agricultural technician and had dreams of working on a large state-owned farm. Campesino a Campesino changed his mind forever. Today Ramón is the program leader for one of UNAG's regional Campesino a Campesino programs.

FROM THE FIRST DAY that I received the Campesino a Campesino training from Rogelio Sánchez, I realized I would never go to work for a big company. With the tools he gave me I said, "this is my alternative." It changed me and I was able to change my father's thinking too. He didn't want to stop burning his fields. I told him to make contour ditches. "No," he said, "I will do it my way." He laid them out straight with a rope. Of course, when it rained they broke and made a big gully. I said, "You see, Papá, you had to use the A-frame." "You're right," he admitted. The old folks are difficult!

Stories and personal testimonies help a lot. For example, there is a story about buried treasure on a farm. The guy goes and digs up the whole field. He never found anything, but turning the soil results in a good harvest. The treasure was his production. These stories help to interpret good and bad. Small-scale experimentation also convinces people. A promoter who is convinced of something is unstoppable! All these things have convinced

Ramón Sequeria, UNAG technician, and his wife

me to change my attitude. I used to kill birds with my slingshot. No more. I have monkeys on my farm. If anyone kills one of them, I'll have them thrown in jail! We need to protect the land, our resources, and all of the animals. One reflects on these things, and changes. For these changes we need stories and testimonies. These are the treasures that transform us as people.

I have never felt any competition with the promoters. Actually, I have asked them for help. I have never said, "I am the king, the wise one." One never stops learning.   —*Ramón Sequeria, Santa Lucía*

Campesino a Campesino has helped agronomists and technicians stand the development notion of "participation" on its head. Development institutions originally designed participatory extension techniques to enroll farmers in externally driven development projects. In MCAC, "participation" refers to the ways technicians and agronomists join in farmers' livelihood struggles; it is less about project targets and "smart" objectives and more about establishing enduring human relationships.

OUR TECHNICAL KNOWLEDGE is important, and a great step forward because now the technicians learn from us. The Movement in the countryside does not depend just on technicians, but on all of us. The Campesino a Campesino program is like a school for today's technicians. Many young technicians come to our farms to do their theses based on our work. We have gatherings with technicians here, we have debates and they are left thinking.   —*Carlos Vidal, Rivas (PCAC 2001)*

Something that will stick with me all my life is the fact that there can be a good idea, a brilliant idea, a great idea, but if the people don't see it as part of them, if they don't feel involved and identified with this brilliant idea, that might even be able to solve some problem for them, if they don't take it as their own, forget it. That great idea will stay an idea.

Participation is not just asking, "Ok, what do you want? Speak!" Sometimes, being participatory means being sufficiently humble to just stand aside. Just be quiet and let people make their own mistakes and learn. Often, in good faith, we want to run and help. In order to be a proactive movement, people have to feel things as their own and get involved and think and reflect. It is a process.

—Jorge Irán Vasquez, UNAG technician

This has been somewhat difficult for me—to adapt to campesino life, to be out in the sun all day long. I don't think any of us as agricultural technicians are used to that. But when you are close to the farmer like that, you see and value their work. You don't just value whether or not they come to your meetings and trainings, you value them as a human being.

—Nubia Vargas, technician,
Proyecto Agricultural Sostenible, Isla de Ometepe

Proving Sustainability: Measuring Campesino a Campesino's Agroecological Resistance to Hurricane Mitch[2]

Around eight at night we knew it was bad. I lit a candle and waited.
If Mitch wanted to take me only God knew . . . and one does not
play with God.   —Promotora campesina

Despite impressive results in soil and water conservation, productivity, agrobiodiversity, and organic production, MCAC, its promoters, and its technicians are continually challenged by proponents of conventional agriculture to prove their claims of sustainability. An opportunity to prove the value of their practices came in the wake of one of the worst natural disasters in Central America's written history: Hurricane Mitch. In October of 1998, Mitch slammed into Central America, causing US$ 6.7 billion in damage—an amount equal to 13 percent of the region's GNP. Widespread flooding and landslides destroyed bridges, roads, homes, crops, and animals. Over 10,000 people died, and 3 million people were displaced or left homeless. Vulnerably perched on Central America's deforested hillsides, poverty-stricken campesinos were the hardest hit, leading Central Americans to call Mitch "the Hurricane of the Poor."

Hurrican Mitch's destruction on a hillside in Nicaragua

WE ARE NORMALLY HAPPY PEOPLE, but everyone felt awful because the aftermath of the hurricane was not a happy sight. We are poor people but Mitch made it worse because it destroyed our food sources. . . . The hurricane ruined us—*nos fregó*. We lost everything: our green harvest and our people. We dried up—became ill with grief—and the sadness just won't go away. A moment came when I thought I would never see my parents again. The river took everything as if it were a game. My heart filled with panic and pain. Here, strong men have cried like babies.

—*Campesino, Estelí, Nicaragua*

Soon after the storm, as Central Americans engaged in relief and began to talk of reconstruction, reports filtered in that MCAC's sustainable farms had suffered less than their conventional neighbors. MCAC's terraces, contour ditches, cover crops, and reforestation had resisted the impact of the hurricane and saved crops, animals, and topsoil.

Agronomists, technicians, promoters, researchers, and over 2,000 campesinos carried out a massive study in Guatemala, Honduras, and Nicaragua that compared hurricane damage on MCAC's sustainable farms to damage on the conventionally farmed neighboring plots (Holt-Giménez 2001). (See Appendix B.)

The research gave MCAC's farmers a chance to test their own practices for sustainable agriculture against the conventional model. It was also an

"MITCH NOS FREGÓ PORQUE ERAMOS VULNERABLES"

Anasonia Recinos Montes is a psychologist and rural methodologist who has spent years working within Campesino a Campesino. She has been instrumental in the Movement, helping men and women share experiences with each other and with the rest of the world. Her account of Hurricane Mitch amplifies the voices of the campesinos who survived the hurricane, and, through MCAC, began to reconstruct their farms and their lives:

> Mitch was not the most powerful hurricane in our history. So why did it cause so much destruction? Because the countryside was unprotected, especially the hillsides. The deforestation, the extensive cattle ranching, and conventional agriculture left it without any protection. This increased the erosion, the landslides, and the gullies. Monoculture left the countryside vulnerable. It will take decades to recover. Of course, for fifty years campesino families have been pushed up onto the hillsides and onto fragile soils. This weakened the countryside and it weakened us. Mitch ruined us because we were vulnerable. Mitch came on top of the crisis in the countryside. Over the last ten years the services for farmers have disappeared. The price of inputs goes up and the value of our harvest goes down. There is no credit, no marketing services, no technical assistance. The campesinos, the ones who produce the food in Central America, have been abandoned.   —*Anasonia Recinos Montes, Nicaragua*

Anasonia Recinos Montes, methodologist, with promotores from Santa Lucía, Nicaragua

opportunity to begin the task of reconstruction by reaching out and assessing each other's damage. In the face of widespread ruin, campesinos, promotores, and technicians formed teams to gather measurements. They found they also needed to work to pull stunned communities out of shock.

THE CAMPESINO A CAMPESINO MOVEMENT saw the need for campesinos to reconstruct the countryside, sustainably. So they called for "participatory, sustainable reconstruction." But, we had to prove the sustainability of our agriculture. We said that the agriculture that resisted the hurricane the best had to be the one that was most sustainable. This was the kind of agriculture we had to reconstruct.

We did a study of the *parcelas gemelas*—twin farms—where we compared the agroecological resistance of neighboring farms, one sustainable, the other conventional, because we didn't really know, scientifically, if the sustainable farms really were sustainable. We did paired observations to make sure everything was fair: the sustainable twin and the conventional twin had to be on the same hillside and had to have received the hurricane's impact under the same conditions of slope and orientation.

As technicians and promoters in the Movement, many of us already had experience solving problems by using small-scale experiments and were used to measuring, comparing, and analyzing the effectiveness of our innovations. We already knew how to diagnose our land, take slope measurements, do soil profiles, and assess soil texture. We were used to working in teams and we knew how to teach things to one another. This helped us to form farmer-technician research teams and carry out the study. After over twenty years of developing it, the Campesino a Campesino movement was ready to compare our own agriculture to conventional farming.

—Anasonia Recinos Montes

The "parcelas gamelas" (twin fields for paired observations) of the Hurricane Mitch study

IT TOOK US DAYS before we could walk into the community, but what is important was that we found them. When I finally got to my village and I saw the people I attend to, how it hurt! They were like abandoned children! As a technician, I suffered like a parent. I felt pain for the village.

—MCAC technician, Estelí, Nicaragua

I THINK THERE HAVE BEEN other hurricanes, but times have changed because before we had vegetation covering the land and our resistance was greater. Our soil lost the capacity to retain water. It used to rain for ten days and the water didn't erode so much soil . . . the environment, the country and nature are weaker now and are affected more by this. I am here because I need to know more about my farm. I need to learn for my community. The hurricane hit us so hard in so many places. We women should know and be prepared. We have to learn in order to teach our children about hurricanes.

—Conventional campesina farmer, Matagalpa, Nicaragua

VULNERABILITY IS the other side of the tortilla of sustainability. Vulnerability is being unprotected from the forces one can't control. Vulnerability depends on human practices. Ten winters of rain fell in four days. One has to ask, which kind of agriculture lost less? Can we call ours sustainable if it doesn't resist? If my agriculture is "reinforced" then it will resist more. The capacity for resistance is one aspect of sustainability . . . there are different levels of resistance in the face of natural phenomena. What is sustainable is what is maintained and keeps on producing.

—MCAC promoter, Estelí, Nicaragua

WE ALL REVIEWED the history of the Campesino a Campesino movement and of sustainable agriculture in Central America together and we saw that it was important to conduct a study to scientifically test what we had been saying for years: that sustainable agriculture is the best alternative for campesinos.

In campesino experiments the farmer often uses a furrow or small control plot to validate or compare the new seed or practice they are trying out. With the parcelas gemelas (the twin farms) we did the same thing, only instead of validating a single practice, we evaluated the whole farm. Also, instead of only being interested in measuring yield, we compared ecological factors like soil, moisture, and vegetation. So the comparisons would be fair we did them between parcelas gemelas under the same conditions. The only difference was that one was managed agroecologically, the other conventionally.

We had to measure agroecological resistance to the hurricane in the

---

IT IS TIME FOR SUSTAINABLE AGRICULTURE TO SPEAK!

Campesino a Campesino has cost us, no one gave it to us. We are not going to invent anything here. All promotores from Campesino a Campesino know this. You don't get this experience in the university; it is found in the countryside. If we are the ones with the experience, then we should do the study. To succeed in this study we have to have a common understanding of things. This is the first time campesinos are going to carry out research like this and we will be criticized. Fine, let everyone see that the "yokels" of Central America did this study. The only way to convince people is to work with rigor. Thanks to the study we will be able to show that the problems brought on by the hurricane can be avoided with good practices. It is fabulous! When this study is over, each farmer will know the condition of hundreds of farms. It is like being among family again.

At first we were criticized, but times have changed and conventional agriculture is falling apart because it is part of the problem. Now we won't have to wait for ten years to validate sustainable agriculture. The old way of doing things can be compared to sustainable agriculture. There are studies that show that conventional farming is more economical because it uses less labor. But these don't take into account that with conventional agriculture we lose our principal resource: soil. We can no longer be ignored because now we have a test—it is Mitch, and we have to see who resisted most. It is time for sustainable agriculture to speak!   —*Campesinos discussing the Mitch study in village meetings*[3]

---

same way on both farms without interference from other factors in order to fairly evaluate the effects of the agricultural practices. It was so important to be rigorous and precise with the procedures and measurements.

Even with all our precautions, we made mistakes. Sometimes we confused the measurements. Sometimes, out of fatigue, or because the field sheet was long and complicated, we lost our concentration and we wrote things down wrong. For this reason, the coordinator and the technicians checked everything. There were times we had to go back to the field and redo the work. We could not afford to make mistakes because one's mistakes would affect everybody.   —*Anasonia Recinos Montes*

THIS IS LIKE A *pelea de gallos* [cockfight] where one puts up their best rooster, only here we are going to put up our soil and water conservation practices and agroecological methods! This business of the parcelas gemelas is like a marriage: if we select well, the study will give a good result. It is like when one raises kids . . . you have to be fair with all of them. A machete is no good if it is dull. With this study, the blade is the data. It has to be sharp!   —*Campesino promotor, Nicaragua*

The study was a social event. Families and neighbors gathered around the campesino-técnico research teams to watch as they inventoried practices and calculated damages. They dug soil profiles, measured field moisture and erosion, and calculated percentage vegetation and slope. Long before the results were quantified and the statistics run, campesino research proved to be a valuable learning activity.

WE FARMERS GO for months without seeing any money. The best thing that happened to us was to learn to value the soil that we do have. There were farms with conservation practices where our picks just sunk into the topsoil [it was so deep]. It was beautiful! By doing the study we saw the benefits of conservation—the conserved farms resisted more. We also saw that the sustainable practices protected neighboring farms from damage. The study helped me because we were able to calculate costs and clearly prove the need for sustainable agriculture. These rural experiences are the best because we are able to link theory and practice.
                                    —*Sustainable farmer, Nicaragua*

IF ONE IS CLOSER to the farmer, you can appreciate him more, understand his problems, and get to know the family. It was really nice, we invited the farmers and their spouses. We sat down with the whole family and talked about what we were going to do. The families were interested in the work and went out into the field with us. It was a great thing to see the children out there, doing the same research as the adults. The little ones would repeat all of the procedures and measurements!
                                    —*MCAC technician, Nicaragua*

IT WAS SO PRETTY! We saw all the colors of the soil! A sustainable farm is not the same as a conventional one . . . it has little animals, like worms, and a diversity of trees and plants. The beautiful thing was, we saw that the little animals that live in the soil are also farmers—they work day and night! We had the opportunity to take slope measurements of our fields and to measure differences in the soil's organic material. With the promotores we learned that we can fix and conserve the soil. We saw that with more conservation there is more life. We are going to keep going back to Mother Earth. She needs us and we need her.
                                    —*Campesino children discussing the Mitch Study fieldwork*

WHERE DO THINGS START? With the parent. I am just a campesino and I don't have a lot of abilities. My parents taught me to slash and burn the land and I ended up ruining it. Now I have learned that I have to change. I asked my children, "How many children do you have? Great. How many centimeters of soil do you have? Good. Now how much soil are you going to leave to each child?" It was so good that the grandchildren were in the field with us. This strengthens our bonds—that is where one teaches, learns, and is educated.   —*Campesino elder, Nicaragua*

By an overwhelming margin, and with irrefutable statistical certainty, MCAC farms were found to suffer less damage, conserve more soil and biodiversity, and experience less economic losses than their conventional neighbors (see Appendix B, Hurricane Mitch: A Case Study). The study had a profound impact on the participants and the villages where the research was conducted.

I WILL NEVER FORGET how much we came to love *los técnicos*! Now we know what kind of técnicos we really have. They worked all day in the sun with us, they ate tortillas with us. We became aware of their true capacity because it was not office work, it was in the field. I never felt alone, my técnico was always with me. We walked together, there was a lot of support, and that is a great thing. It was a time of intense training, but also of a lot of caring.   —*Nicaraguan campesino*

IT WAS A GREAT EXPERIENCE. The way the people came together was wonderful. The organization was very good because there are networks of promotores between communities. As técnicos, we didn't have a clear picture of the damage. I became sensitized when I saw so much damage and how it impacted the people. The farmers were so interested in understanding their farms. They wanted to know everything and they invited their neighbors to come too. You should have seen how excited they got with the study!   —*Nicaraguan técnico*

The study also uncovered serious problems in the countryside, both for the development of sustainable agriculture and for campesinos.

IT WAS SO SAD. We found widows and single mothers who could not benefit from development projects because they didn't have enough labor on the farm. There are campesinas who are all alone and can't do soil conservation . . . we have to pay attention to this. What is not good is that many institutions just have projects for men because they have more time.

BEFORE, PEOPLE NEVER EVEN SAID HELLO . . .

Betania Blandón was a young agricultural technician whose first post was a remote municipality in the mountains of Estelí, Nicaragua. Female, unmarried, and inexperienced, except for some unbidden flirtation, she was largely ignored by local farmers. The hurricane and the study changed that:

In the communities where I work, the conventional farmers who worked on this study are now agroecological farmers. They organized work groups and they joined Campesino a Campesino. It was difficult because they are all on steep hillsides. One producer told me he was ashamed of how his farm made out in the study. Now he invites people to his farm to see his [reclamation] work. When the conventional farmers compared the two farms [sustainable and conventional] they thought, "Wow! Look at my farm! My neighbor is winning." Now there are many communities with sustainable practices. People learned from the study and started to work. I look at the map from last year and compare it with this year. There are about 40 percent more sustainable farms now, and we have not received any financing for reconstruction.

Before, people never even said hello to me in the village. I just arrived and gave orientations. But now all of the children know my name and come looking to greet me. I feel like this has been a great experience in my life and am thankful that it taught me so much. I grew as a woman and as a professional.

—*Betania Blandón, PCAC technician, Matagalpa*

Conventional farmers often have reasons for not adopting agroecological practices—for example even though their neighbors may be sustainable farmers, they might not have their own land.

If the people have to search high and low, borrowing and renting land, they will never conserve. If they ever legalize our land, we will see that people will stop moving around and they will start conserving soil. This business of land tenure is critical. There are communities that are aware of conservation but they don't have their own land, they always live on someone else's. We have to take into consideration that the people who don't have land are forced to engage in migratory agriculture, they always live on someone else's land. Emigration tears families apart and these separations affect the entire community. The unjust distribution of land is the cruel reality in our country . . . it is a structural problem.

Time and lack of labor power is also a problem. People don't conserve because the cost is too high. The campesino has to leave his land and look for work in the city. Sometimes the land is left to single women who can't lift all the rocks. One has to invest to conserve, and we campesinos plant just to eat. Of course, one needs patience to see the fruits of sustainable agriculture.

There are no incentives for this kind of agriculture. There is no culture for buying our organic products. A lot of farmers don't want to take the first step because it is difficult and there is no credit.

—*Campesinos at a village discussion after the Mitch Study*

H OW IS IT POSSIBLE that for one neighbor, labor is an obstacle and for the other it is not? How is it possible that one has information and the other doesn't? We see that the adoption of sustainable agricultural practices has a lot to do with the particular situation of each campesina family. Some have more labor power than others. The single women have a difficult time with soil conservation, for example. Others are prisoners of a vicious cycle of debt and seasonal migration and don't have time to take advantage of their neighbors' knowledge. More than land tenure, the problem of insecurity over land use is a disincentive to constructing conservation structures and organic agriculture because the campesino can't be sure that they are going to benefit from their investment.

—*Anasonia Recinos Montes*

Reflections

The people sharing these stories from Guatemala, Mexico, and Nicaragua do not pretend to speak for the hundreds of thousands of farmers who are a part of the MCAC experience in Mesoamerica. It is important to realize that while some of these stories often describe a difficult and sometimes distant past, because the underlying causes leading to conflict in the countryside have still not been addressed, the problems are as relevant today as they were then. Campesinos rarely speak in the name of others—they tell their own stories, no more, no less. However, in speaking, they offer a strikingly consistent view of agroecology, resistance, and survival. This perspective, from the protagonists, is a guide for those of us trying to understand the Movement, its people, and the processes that ultimately link us to them.

THREE

Campesino Pedagogy

Los hombres crecen, crecen físicamente, de una manera visible
crecen, cuando aprenden algo, cuando entran a poseer algo,
y cuando han hecho algo bien.
—José Martí[1]

Una de las principales cosas es poder hacer para enseñar. Hacer
las cosas para enseñar a otros, que es el mejor método que
existe para avanzar en el campo.
—José Jesús Mendoza, Santa Lucía, Nicaragua[2]

Introduction

THE DIVISION CHIEF of the farmers' union was clearly annoyed.
"Decide once and for all! Is Campesino a Campesino a method, a
project, a movement, or what?"

The two technicians from the Campesino a Campesino program fid-
geted uncomfortably. I looked to the posters of Che and Sandino on the
sparse office walls for inspiration. At the end of a rickety wooden table, the
young cadre stared us down, waiting for the right answer. Before we could
stammer a response, he rose, sliced the air with an upraised index finger and
summarily pronounced, "Then it is a *methodology*!" Having ruled on the
issue, he ushered us from his office.

Though the distinction between method, project, or movement may
seem esoteric, the coordinator had shrewdly selected the term "methodology" both to distinguish and control MCAC. Seen as a simple project,
Campesino a Campesino was notable, but nothing extraordinary: there
were dozens of sustainable agriculture projects in the country, and many
used farmers as extensionists. Seen as a movement, Campesino a Campesino
would have challenged the leadership of the farmers' union among the peasantry. The term "methodology" used in this context conveyed an apolitical
professionalism that both raised the promoters of MCAC above other farm-

ers and placed them firmly below the political leadership of the farmers' union. In other words, rather than describing a broad-based *movement* of cultural resistance, in this instance "methodology" described a technocratic *program*, institutionally embedded within a political hierarchy.

I would suggest that that is precisely what Campesino a Campesino is *not*.

The development literature has often described "farmer to farmer" as an innovative and cost-effective method of transferring sustainable agricultural technologies. To the extent that it is recognized in formal development circles, Campesino a Campesino is valued because of its ability to broadly disseminate these technologies. What is not always appreciated is that this technology "transfer" is really the reflection of a deeper, culturally embedded exchange in which *knowledge is generated and shared.*

Knowledge, we are often reminded, is power. While inspirational, the "knowledge-is-power" adage falls short in describing the power struggles that take place over knowledge itself. The ability to absorb doled bits of information is not the same as free access to knowledge. This, in turn, is not the same as the ability to generate information. Moreover, the *possession* of knowledge in and of itself is no guarantee that it will not be co-opted, appropriated, subsumed, replaced, or erased by knowledge systems wielded by those more politically and economically powerful.

The agroecological knowledge generated in MCAC not only forms the basis for its methodology and the dissemination of its sustainable agricultural techniques, it also challenges the structures and content of much of the agronomic knowledge thrust upon the peasantry since the Green Revolution. Further, the way campesinos generate their own knowledge challenges not only the centralized, hierarchical structures of formal agricultural research and extension and the unaccountable actions of professional experts, it questions hierarchical power per se, including the power of professional advisers, political cadres, NGO coordinators, village caciques, and, sometimes, male promoters.

For the campesinos in MCAC, the ability to access, adapt, create, use, and defend agroecological knowledge on their own terms is an exercise in autonomy. Combining theory and practice, Campesino a Campesino draws widely from campesino sources, as well as from technicians and scientists. In this sense, Campesino a Campesino is an epistemic community that accesses, generates, and shares knowledge for its own ends. Methodology in MCAC is more than a collection of farmer-to-farmer extension methods; Campesino a Campesino has its own logic and conventions regarding what constitutes knowledge, as well as its own normative principles regarding farming and the environment. Further, because the methods for sharing knowledge are dialogical and based on campesino led inquiry and action, the Campesino a Campesino methodology is probably best described as a praxis-based, campesino pedagogy.[3]

Because the techniques employed by Campesino a Campesino are open access resources and very easily appropriated, the campesino pedagogy itself is an area of negotiation and struggle. Here, the goals, objectives, and tools that define MCAC are in constant dispute. Further, this pedagogy continually evolves in response to changing conditions. Thirty years of farmer-to-farmer exchanges have not standardized or homogenized MCAC's pedagogical practices. Rather, experience has deepened and diversified the movement's body of knowledge. Continual innovation and sharing among farmers has led to a dynamic process of social learning, rooted firmly in campesino culture. Nonetheless, certain basic principles and procedures have emerged for generating farmers' agroecological knowledge and for defending the crucial *relationship* between farmers and their knowledge. This chapter describes the logic of MCAC's campesino pedagogy.

Background

As described in Chapter One, Campesino a Campesino has its cultural and methodological roots in the Kaqchikel communities of Chimaltenango, Guatemala.[4] World Neighbors and Oxfam-England must be credited as the first development organizations to recognize the development potential of the Chimaltenango experience. By employing technicians to support local farmers *in the development of their own agriculture* rather than through simple technology transfer, they inverted the conventional top-down, expert-driven intervention approach to agricultural extension and initiated a new farmer-technician relationship that produced agroecosystem-specific knowledge for agricultural development in situ. Following Korten and Klaus (1984), Roland Bunch (1985) described the basic principles for "People Centered Development" as follows:

- Motivate and teach farmers to experiment
- Attain and utilize rapid, recognizable success
- Use appropriate technologies
- Start with just a few, well-chosen technologies
- Train villagers as extensionists

Bunch saw the development of local capabilities as an inverted pyramid in which farmer-extensionists experimented with one or two new technologies every year. If these were successful, they encouraged other farmers to experiment with the same technologies, and to teach others. In this way, human capacities and the technology base grew at compatible rates and were mutually reinforcing. The focus was on campesino innovation and the sharing of technology as a strategy for what Bunch later referred to as *agricultural development* (Bunch 1996).

This approach ran counter to the Green Revolution's Transfer of Technology (TOT) strategies based on "diffusion theory" (Rogers 1962, 1969), which emphasized centralized, expert-driven development of technology and diffusion through professional extension to "early adopters." It also ran counter to the conventional, integrated rural development programs advanced by the official development agencies that attempted to address all of the village's problems at once.

These strategies required high levels of expert intervention and management of the development process; the former because of its focus on command and control of science, and the latter because managing the institutional complexity of integrated rural development programs was beyond the capabilities of most villagers. The low level of success of these strategies was blamed on bad extension and farmer "apathy." Extension approaches attempted training and visit (T&V) methods, while integrated development programs embraced "stakeholder" strategies and material incentives to get farmers involved with development. In contrast, in an attempt at farmer-led (rather than expert-led) development, the people-centered, agricultural approach put basic tools for innovation and extension directly in the hands of farmers.[5]

Bunch's people centered, agri-cultural approach found fertile ground among Popular Education practitioners. The Popular Education movement, led by revolutionary-minded social workers and intellectuals, drew heavily from Paulo Freire's work. Freire advocated education for liberation through a peer-driven, "horizontal" process of *concientización*, or political consciousness raising, based on praxis.[6] Popular Education overlapped with the Christian "base" communities that had sprung from the liberation theology movement. Liberation theology was a spiritual and sociopolitical response to the severe political and economic oppression that characterized the Latin American countryside during the 1970s. The base communities reflected on liberation aspects of the New Testament and organized for social and economic justice. Popular Education's praxis-based, dialogical approach to learning merged with liberation theology's "preferential option for the poor."[7] The net result was the formation of thousands of motivated, village-level advocates of social change.

In a parallel development, progressive humanitarian foundations and some social-democratic European governments were concerned that the United States' bilateral aid to oppressive governments was intensifying rather than resolving the politico-military conflicts in the region. Given the unworkable political systems of the repressive regimes, they attempted to strengthen the culture of democracy indirectly by strengthening civil society. This was accomplished primarily by funding thousands of NGOs to work with the poor.

The explosion of NGOs in the 1970s and 1980s in Latin America coincided with a growing interest in sustainable agricultural development. Though sustainable agricultural development was pioneered in Mesoamerica by NGOs, it was later taken up by the International Agricultural Research Centers (IARCs). Both adopted some form of the "participatory" development approaches in vogue at the time.

The emergence of agroecology as the science of sustainable agriculture (Altieri 1987; Norgaard and Sikor 1995; Gliessman 1998a) followed these initiatives in Mesoamerica. As more and more scientists and technicians were trained in agroecology, many made their way to the NGOs and formal research programs that worked in sustainable agriculture. This convergence of factors led to a small boom in sustainable agricultural development projects. All of these actors engaged with sustainable agriculture at the development interface, where they disputed and negotiated the meaning, direction, methods, means, and resources for sustainable agricultural development (Holt-Giménez 2002).

The promoters of Campesino a Campesino were eagerly sought after by professionals and NGOs seeking to implement or expand their research and extension activities. The Movement's methods were easily appropriable, and farmer-to-farmer networks fit nicely with the trend toward participatory development. This brought the promoters into direct engagement with scientists, technicians, and NGOs at the development interface. The approach and methods of Campesino a Campesino have been forged as much at this interface as in the smallholder communities where they are implemented. Indeed, sometimes it is not always clear where Campesino a Campesino as a "movement" leaves off and where Campesino a Campesino as some research or development institution's "participatory methodology" begins.

Methodology or Pedagogy?

The men stood in a circle, sweating, scratching, and glancing around sheepishly. Our instructor, Felipe Tomás, waited, poker-faced, pen poised over his notebook.

"Well?"

Gabriel sighed, and then spoke for the group,

"The thing is we don't know how to do math. I mean, we can all add and subtract okay, and multiply some. But we don't know how to divide. We never went past the second grade. . . ."

Everyone looked in my direction, but Felipe Tomás shook his head.

"No, the gringo won't always be around to help. In fact, he doesn't exist," he said, dismissing me with a wave of his machete and moving to stand between me and the group. He had effectively eliminated the only person within kilometers who knew how to divide.

"*Ai cabrón!*" The men laughed.

It was the second day of the workshop in Guatemala and we were learning how to take the slope of a hillside. Armed with a tape measure, a carpenter's level, and two meters of string, we scrambled up and down the steep, eroded cornfield taking measurements. One man held the end of the string on the ground. The second grabbed the far end and pulled it taut in the direction of the slope. A third man stood in the middle, attached the carpenter's level to the string and instructed the second to raise or lower his end until the bubble was in the middle of the level, indicating the string was perfectly level. Then, the fourth man measured the distance from the downhill end of the string to the ground. I wrote the measurements down in a small notebook: Fifty-five, eighty-three, one hundred and ten. . . . When halved, the measurement gave us the percent slope.

Hacked out of the lush forest, the *milpa* had given several years of good harvest until the intense tropical rains washed the precious topsoil away. Rills had appeared on the upper slopes and, following the natural depressions in the field had converged, forming a deep gully that channeled torrents of water and soil onto the road below, "paving it with topsoil." Before any soil amendments could be added, the slope had to be protected and reclaimed, a task, we were assured, that would take several diligent years of hard work. The field was steep, and the terrain broken. Under the noonday sun, heat rose in waves above the bare subsoil, baking us as we worked. Nonetheless, we had just spent several days in a cramped truck traveling overland from Mexico to Guatemala and were happy to be outside getting our hands dirty and learning new techniques. After a few practice runs we organized ourselves as a team, dividing up the tasks to work more quickly.

We needed to determine the distance between the conservation ditches to be built. The steeper the slope, the closer the ditches needed to be in order to counter the tremendous, erosive force of water and soil moving down the hillside. When we had five slope measurements, taken from five different sites, we stopped to take the average—a simple operation of adding up the measurements and dividing the total by the number of observations. Simple, that is, if one knows how to divide. Now, the men were perplexed, embarrassed and no doubt annoyed with their instructor for creating a situation that revealed their ignorance. Felipe Tomás broke the painful silence with his own admission: "I never went to school and can't divide either," he shrugged. "But, this problem requires intelligence, not schooling. Compañeros, please take off your hats."

Given the blazing sun, this was less than appealing. Felipe pointed to the road a hundred yards down the steep slope. Cows, sheep, and goats had ambled past all morning on their way to pasture.

"Now please do me the favor of going down and collecting a handful of sheep droppings, each of you. I'll wait here," he said, moving to the shade of a tree on the side of the field. He ignored further questions by burying his nose in his notebook and scratching away with a pencil. I waited silently in my invisible exile.

"Gringo, you exist again," he pronounced without looking up. "Go get some caca."

Grumbling, we stumbled down to collect sheep shit. When we got back, hot and bewildered, Felipe Tomás had us count out droppings for each measurement (Fifty-five, eighty-three, one hundred and ten . . .). Then we placed it all in one big pile.

"How many in total? Two hundred thirty-two. How many times did you stop to take slope measurements? Five times? So, put down five hats in a circle," he ordered. "Now, put a dropping from the big pile into each hat." We did. "Again." We did it again. "Now keep doing that until they are all gone."

When we had finished, he instructed us to count the number of droppings in each hat. Three of us had forty-six droppings in our hat. Two of us had forty-seven.

Felipe Tomás tossed the extra two droppings away, "The average slope is forty-six percent," he announced.

There was a brief silence as the lesson sank in. Then Gabriel fairly exploded.

"Division! *That* is division! All these years, I never understood . . . it was a mystery . . . division!" Elated, he shook his hatless head in amazement and looking in admiration at Felipe Tomás said simply, *"Ai cabrón!"*

The Canasta Metodológica

The strong oral traditions within the campesinado open up innovative ways of communicating abstract concepts. Promoters often use simple demonstrations to illustrate basic agroecological processes such as the erosiveness of raindrop splash, organic matter's high capacity for water retention, or soil texture. This understanding of agroecology—often ignored by approaches relying on the simple transfer of "sustainable" technology—is essential to the practice of sustainable agriculture.

A two-year Mesoamerican study of MCAC's campesino pedagogy found that the movement had developed an unwritten but sophisticated methodology that allowed campesinos to learn and apply agroecological concepts to sustainable agricultural development (Holt-Giménez 1997). The methodology used demonstrations, games, and group activities (cross visits, sociodrama, songs, poems, folktales, etc.) to teach a series of agroecological themes (small-scale experimentation, diversity-stability, fertility, integrated pest management, etc.). This collection of learning aids was a loosely grouped methodological basket, or *canasta metodológica*, that could be drawn from selectively for workshops, field days, or impromptu teaching. Farmers could tailor their teaching to correspond with the agricultural seasons and farmers' livelihood strategies, and with individual, family, and vil-

TABLE 3.1 · LA CANASTA METODOLOGICA			
	PROBLEMATIZING	EXPERIMENTING	PROMOTION
Demonstration	"Equilibrium & Sustainability"	"The Limiting Factor"	"The Scales"
Objective	Reflect on concepts of "environmental equilibrium" and "agroecological sustainability"; formulate local terms and related concepts	Review the importance of "limiting factors of production" for determining an experimental agenda based on the most important production problems	Understand water retention properties of organic matter
Game	"The Ecological Ball of String"	"The Three Blind Men"	"The Barrier"
Objective	Define ecosystems	Reflect on the importance of experimenting in groups	Reflect on the barriers to communication between technicians and campesinos
Activity	"Field Survey"	"Field Visits"	"What Is Organic?"
Objective	Relate changes in productivity over time with agroecological history	Compare practices and problems between farmers' fields	Identify organic materials for making compost
Creative Representation	"The Eroded Heart" (drama)	"The Sick Person" (drama)	"Ecological Agriculture" (poem)
Objective	Emphasize the importance of doing a field study to identify problems before prescribing solutions	Reflect on the importance of controlling variables in field trials	Inspire motivation, self-expression

Orlando Cruz Mora, technician from Ometepe, Nicaragua, shows "la balanza" (the scales), a campesino demonstration of the water-retention capacity of compost compared with that of poor soil.

lage capabilities. There appeared to be three, overlapping, and cyclical phases in this pedagogy:

- Problematizing: Farmers learn basic agroecological concepts through group inquiry into the limiting factors of production and the ecological risks on farms and in watersheds. Farmers analyze the causes of principal common problems and pose possible solutions.
- Experimentation: Farmers design experiments to test possible alternatives while learning to formulate working hypotheses, make consistent, unbiased observations, and take precise measurements. They concentrate on making valid and fair comparisons, on controlling experimental variables, and on conducting group experiments and sharing results.
- Promotion: Farmers learn to put on workshops and field days; they also learn different techniques for peer training and agroecological knowledge sharing and group communication skills. The objective is to share the knowledge behind basic soil and water conservation techniques, fertility, integrated pest management, etc.

Promotores designed paced learning experiences that repeated key agroecological concepts in several different ways (spoken, demonstrated, and experienced), allowing farmers time to codify new information within their own cognitive frameworks (see Table 3.1).

A series of modules were also discernable, splitting the original two-week farmer-led soil conservation classes into weekend workshops timed to coincide with farming seasons and geared to the particular situation of the participants (see Tables 3.2, 3.3, and 3.4). In this way, participants did not have to spend time away from their farms or families, and new knowledge and innovations were tested and gradually adapted and adopted to local farming systems.

TABLE 3.2 · FIRST MODULE: FIELD DIAGNOSIS

(to be held after the last harvest at the beginning of the dry season)

THEMES	ACTIVITIES	OBJECTIVES
Day 1		
Agroecology	Equilibrium and sustainability The Eco-Ball Critical factors	Compare concepts and establish terms for agroecology and sustainable agriculture
The field diagnostic	Soil profiles Slopes Vegetation and crops	Make a first approximation of problems, critical ecological factors, and limiting factors; relate fertility and production with environmental equilibrium, diversity, and organic material
Problematizing	Problems Causes Possible solutions	Establish an agenda for farmers' experiments
Day 2		
Soils and organic matter	Texture and structure The balance scale What is organic?	Understand the basic properties of soil tilth and fertility Identify forms of organic matter
Manures	Making compost	Prepare compost and apply manures
Day 3		
Farmer to farmer	Field visits to promoter farms	Share understanding of problems and observe experiments and innovations in the field

TABLE 3.3 · SECOND MODULE: SOIL AND WATER CONSERVATION

(to be held in the middle of the dry season)

THEMES	ACTIVITIES	OBJECTIVES
Day 1		
Field visits	The promoters share their experiences as a team	Establish the team's credibility Show innovations and organization
Day 2		
Erosion and conservation	The ramp Raindrop splash and filtration The level coconut The mini A-frame Building an A-frame	Show the basic steps in the process of erosion Show how contour lines are laid out Learn to build and use an A-frame, rustic clinometer
Day 3		
Contours, ditches, terraces	The average Teams	Learn to take average slope and lay out contour lines Establish an experimental plot with conservation measures Organize teams for future work

TABLE 3.4 · THIRD MODULE: SMALL-SCALE EXPERIMENTATION

(to be held just before the new agricultural cycle)

THEMES	ACTIVITIES	OBJECTIVES
Day 1		
Experimenting	Visit to experimental plots of promoters	Demonstrate advantages of small-scale experiments
Day 2		
Problematizing/alternatives	The Limiting Factor Review list of problems, causes, and possible solutions	Review of experiment agenda Introduce basic concepts for designing the group's small-scale experiments
Experiment design	The Backache The Three Blind Men Farmers' Memory	Organize group of farmer-experimenters Decide on experiments
Day 3		
Implementation	Design experiments and forms for recording data and observations	Establish experimental plots in the field and capacity for follow-up

"Erosivity," a campesino demonstration showing how a raindrop splash starts the process of erosion on bare soils

Los Talleres: The Campesino Workshops

We really feel the gatherings are important and the workshops teach us so much. The exchanges of ideas are important because you can't buy ideas. For example, if these organizations were to put money in our hands, they will finish us off. But if we learn a practice, an idea, we will never stop. We should consider this seriously if we want to move forward.
—Gabriel Corea Almira, Guatemala

Campesino a Campesino workshops, or *talleres,* are highly active, hands-on learning experiences in which most activities take place in the field. An 80 percent practice, 20 percent theory rule usually prevails. Talleres are generally playful, festive affairs. Perhaps because their childhoods are fleetingly brief, campesino men and women characteristically retain a refreshing attitude of playfulness in adulthood. Because few had the opportunity to go to school, a chance to learn new things is happily celebrated. Classroom sessions are punctuated by songs, stories, jokes, poems, sayings, and games. Sometimes a local band is invited to play music during the break periods. Food is simple but *must* be abundant. Alcohol is usually prohibited during the taller, but often the last evening ends in a big party, sometimes lubricated with the local brew. Frequently, farmers putting on or traveling to the workshop come from far away, sometimes from other countries. Strong friendships are established that over time weave dense networks of reciprocity and solidarity.

Fairs, Encuentros, and Intercambios

A brightly painted, hand-lettered sign caught my eye: "Campesina School of Soil and Water Conservation." It was propped next to a steaming, neatly trimmed compost heap in front of a spacious canvas tent. It was fiesta day in San Martín; the streets were bustling and filled with the smells and noise of dozens of food and gaming booths. Fireworks blasting overhead and music from several record players competed for the destruction of my inner ear. In front of the soil conservation tent, a half-dozen men and women watched attentively as an indigenous promotor (looking somewhat like a carnival barker) plunged his machete into the center of the large compost heap and said, "If after a minute the machete comes out hot and moist, this means the bacteria in the *abonera* (compost pile) are happy and working well. We can turn the pile in two weeks. If the machete comes out hot and dry, they are thirsty, and we must add water. If it comes out cold and wet, we have drowned these marvelous *animalitos* who work for us. . . . You must tear down the compost heap and start over."

The promotor then drew the machete from the compost heap and passed it around carefully for all to inspect. An approving murmur moved through the crowd as they touched the machete and nodded their heads in turn. "They are working!" someone pronounced.

Inside the booth, another promotor was standing next to a scale model of a cultivated hillside. The model was split in two sections; one side showed different aspects of soil erosion, the other side different conservation measures. Whoever built the model had a tremendous eye for detail. Trees, grass, and shrubs were represented with sticks, moss, and leaves. Minute clay figures of cows, sheep, goats, and people with toothpick hoes dotted the "hillside." A house, a road, and a miniature toy truck completed the conservation model. String led from different parts of the hillside to hand-lettered posters on the wall that explained erosion and conservation. As he spoke over the din of the fiesta, the promotor pointed with his machete to each spot on the hillside. He spoke slowly in Spanish and Kaqchikel, repeating himself often and pointing carefully back and forth from the signs, along the strings to the processes and practices on either side of the eroded and conserved "hillside." One onlooker instructed his young son to take notes in a worn school notebook. I realized that the promoter was working carefully because most of the audience could not read or write and were

Campesino workshop, Ometepe, Nicaragua

painstakingly committing the new concepts to memory. What I did not find out until I had a chance to get to see the countryside around San Martín was that the man had made an exact model of an existing hillside. He was explaining the agroecological history of the land he and a neighbor actually farmed.

In another corner, several men were bent over three long thin planks, busily constructing an aparato-A, the rustic clinometer used for laying out contour lines. A table held several bottles of sedimented soil at which people peered closely as another man explained the properties of soil texture. Women in long, handwoven skirts and richly embroidered *huipiles* (blouses) spoke animatedly in Kaqchikel over a table with different food products and prepared dishes. The walls were covered with drawings done in colored pencils depicting different agroecological aspects of farming and conservation. The overall effect was mesmerizing.

The Kaqchikeles were the first to make use of traditional town fiesta days to put up booths about soil and water conservation. Virtually every town in Latin America has a patron saint whose day is religiously celebrated. National independence days are also important festive holidays. Saint days and independence days are often accompanied by processions, parades, speeches, mass, music, and rows and rows of booths where food and drink is sold. It is usually not difficult to obtain permission for a booth, and the promoters of Campesino a Campesino often spend days setting up their exposition. They take turns tending the booth as other farmers drop in to learn about sustainable agriculture. It is a relaxed and culturally dynamic way to spread the news, make contacts, exchange seeds and information, and try out new products. True, the occasional drunk can wander in and disrupt activities (I once saw an inebriated farmer fall face first on the hillside model), but this is not a tragedy in campesino culture and is summarily taken care of.

As Campesino a Campesino grew in strength and legitimacy, the agroecological fair was followed by the farmers' *encuentro* (gathering) in which smallholders present their experiences in sustainable agriculture and listen to new ideas from technicians and scientists, much in the image of a formal scientific conference. The encuentros tend to draw government and NGO professionals as well and often provoke debate about the direction of sustainable agriculture.

The *intercambio* (exchange) is perhaps the least structured of MCAC's socialization methods. It is simply a visit by one group of farmers to another. While intercambios are commonly used by NGOs to stimulate interest in a project, they are also used extensively and informally by campesinos to get to know one another and to see sustainable practices at work. The intercambios can be afternoon or weekend affairs, or they can extend to a week or more if hands-on experience in a technique is desired.

Typically, a group of farmers visits another group to see their sustainable agricultural approach first-hand. If the visit sparks interest, those with sustainable practices hold a workshop in the village of the interested group. Farmers learn some basic concepts in agroecology and some conservation methods and small-scale experiments are designed. Later in the season, there may be another intercambio to share results of the experiments, this time with local as well as visiting farmers.

For all their seeming informality, the intercambios are actually concentrated moments of interaction in which culture is shaped and reshaped

An MCAC "encuentro" or campesino gathering

between actors. Tools, seeds, information, and knowledge pass from hand to hand, not in the sense of a one-way technology transfer, but as part of a shared cultural praxis. Safely bundled in shared culture, sustainable agriculture technologies are adopted and adapted, spread and modified, not through extension of exogenous information and techniques, but as part of a process of endogenous agricultural expression.

Solidarity and Innovation

I want to talk about the kuchubal. For six or seven years after the earthquake we worked in groups working the soil. When we finished with one, we went to the other's land. It was good because on your own, you couldn't do the work. I liked the kuchubal a lot. To do soil conservation, it's very important. The government should support this work. As a state it should help in conservation. I remember that ten of us worked like this. That's how we did it. The same with building houses, between five or ten we built each other's house.
—Farmer, San Martín Jilotepeque, Guatemala

KUCHUBAL: THE BENEFITS OF MUTUAL AID

The Mayan kuchubal is at the social and organizational root of Campesino a Campesino. Originally, the kuchubal was a social form of labor used by extended families and neighbors to share work during peak agricultural periods. Most peasant societies used some form of the kuchubal at one time or another, and though its practice may have disappeared with the advent of less labor-intensive forms of agriculture, it is still strong in the cultural memory of many rural communities.

On the precarious hillsides and brittle dry-land mesas of Mesoamerica—where most of peasant agriculture takes place—soil and water are frequently the most limiting factors to production. Conservation practices such as ditches and terraces are often the first measures to be implemented in the transition from conventional to sustainable agriculture. Because conservation typically requires a lot of initial effort, the kuchubal emerged as a logical response to a high labor demand. Farmers work in small groups of three to ten people. Typically, they meet weekly to work on the farm of one of the members of the group. They may spend a day laying out contour lines, moving stones, and digging—there is always lots of digging! The following week everyone works on the land of another member of the group. The advantage of this form of mutual aid is that not only labor, but information and knowledge, are shared. The reciprocity built in to the kuchubal encourages trust and good will. This can lead to long-term farmer-to-farmer solidarity.

In an "intercambio" or farmer-to-farmer exchange in Nicaragua, promotor Sebastián Durán shares agroecological knowledge with other campesinos.

Variations on the kuchubal have followed Campesino a Campesino across Mesoamerica, giving rise to the promoter teams that share knowledge and experiences. Teams work together to teach others in workshops, field days, and one-on-one exchanges. Campesino a Campesino teams share knowledge and skills among the group. Some members are good at experimenting, others excel at teaching groups, others simply share their experiences on-farm; some may have more experience in insect management, others in fertility; others know more about conservation or seed selection—Campesino a Campesino teams are fluid. Entering farmers become promoters by innovating, sharing, and learning the methodological "ropes" from those with more experience. Basically, farmers teach each other new things much in the same way they learned to farm—by doing, observing, and reflecting together—much as an extended farm family does. Those with more time in the group often retire from traveling or giving workshops to devote more time to their own fields. Or, leaving the care of their field to a family member, they may become Campesino a Campesino consultants for an NGO or a sustainable agricultural development project. The point is that the group is ideally a dynamic, fluid entity that adapts to changing conditions and capabilities. This provides a resilient locus of constant innovation.

This is contrasted with the more individualistic approach associated with the lone farmer-extensionist at the service of a research or extension programs. This farmer is usually selected by the technician or scientist to par-

"NADIE ES PROPHETA EN SU TIERRA. . . . PORQUE SOMOS COMO SANTO TOMÁS"

"Sometimes it is hard. . . . One is out here working, sweating away, then people walk by and whistle at you [ridiculing] . . . "

"People made fun of me. They laughed, and that hurt me."

"They said I was crazy."

"One failure is that it is difficult to be a prophet in one's own land. Criticism starts within one's own family Or with the community, when they find that a compañero has had the possibility of starting a new way of working that people recognize. This has been a stone in the shoe of the Movement, and we haven't been able to shake it out easily. . . ."

The promoters in Campesino a Campesino do not earn social recognition from their neighbors as easily as one might think. Frequently their new ideas are rejected by other family and community members. Until they show "recognizable results," their efforts may be seen as folly. Ridicule is a powerful force for maintaining normative behavior in village societies. Farmers are often unwilling to try new things that might not work, not just because of the risks involved, but because failing in front of others is embarrassing . . . public mistakes are usually not forgotten.

It is not unusual for early innovators to be recognized by farmers from other villages, sometimes far away, before they are appreciated at home. "No one is a prophet in their own land," they say. However, this stage is usually overcome when one or two friends or family members set aside their fears and join up with the innovating farmer. Often a group visit to another village with a successful Campesino a Campesino team is all that is needed to get a local group going. Once three or more farmers are organized, they provide each other with moral support in the face of the "doubting Thomases" that surround them.

The story is told of the farmer who experimented by intercropping maize with velvet bean (*Mucuna pruriens*) on a degraded patch of land in his field. Because it was an experiment, he planted only a small amount. If the bean failed, he stood little to lose. The field was visible from the road and other farmers passing by commented, "What is that *pendejo* [fool] doing planting on that lousy little patch of ground?" While hurt, the farmer went on with his experiment. The velvet bean grew luxuriously, providing nitrogen and choking out weeds for a bountiful corn crop. When neighbors saw his successful experiment they exclaimed, "Pendejo, he should have planted more!"

ticipate in field trials of on-farm experiments. In some cases he or she is selected by members of the local community. A lot of time and money is often invested training the farmer-extensionist, who typically must ingest a wide array of exogenous ideas and techniques to become the village "expert." The problem is that "experts" tend to distance themselves from their neighbors. Other farmers are often leery of them because they receive so much support from outside sources and doubt if they themselves can recreate the same practices and obtain the same results on their own farms. Knowledge tends to accumulate with the expert, who gains status and recognition not from his or her fellow farmers, but from the technicians and scientists who are anxious to see their practices implemented. The endogenous process of farmer innovation never gets off the ground.

The best promoters in MCAC are generally self-selecting. They come forward of their own interest, train, and become promoters on the merits of successful farming and social learning. They obtain social recognition by sharing practices with others. Promoters often refer to the biblical passage, "One recognizes a tree by its fruits," to aver that one recognizes "a promoter by his or her fields and the people he or she has trained." As farmers improve their agriculture through collective processes of innovation, their expertise and methods are recognized. The more they share their knowledge, the more they gain prestige in the eyes of others.

EL COMPROMISO MORAL:
TENDING THE "KNOWLEDGE COMMONS"

Helping others in campesino culture is neither instrumentalist nor altruistic in the same sense that most urban, Western cultures might understand it. "Help" is not necessarily seen as a quantifiable (and therefore repayable) favor but as a logical way of reducing overall social vulnerability to hard times. In this sense it is not "selfless" giving either, because it is offered to others who are embedded in the same network of community relationships in which both giver and receiver are a part. In this context, helping others helps oneself—indirectly, but certainly not intangibly.

The primary motivation to share what one has learned is a combination of age-old campesino reciprocity and cultural solidarity. The campesinos who receive knowledge from others in the Movement talk of a *compromiso moral* (moral obligation) to give back to the Movement by teaching others. It is not necessary to give directly back to the person who shared their knowledge. Though this can and does happen often, it is not expected. What is expected is that the person will make good use of the new knowledge and work to enrich the knowledge of the Movement. The experience one gains by trying out something new produces some new form of understanding. This new knowledge is what is asked for in return. The way to return this knowledge, modified by new experience, is to "pay it forward" by sharing it with other campesinos. Of course, reciprocity in this context draws the other party into a *relationship*, based on good will, that ensures the possibility of some form of help in the future, particularly in ways that might reduce risk or ensure aid in times of need.[8] There is also a somewhat spiritual belief operating under the moral construct that recognizes the value of serving others, recognizes mortality, and strives to leave an altruistic mark as a guidepost for future generations. The social character of the Campesino a Campesino knowledge base is very similar to a "knowledge commons" in that it accessed individually but is cultivated and cared for by all.

Another motivation for contributing to the knowledge commons is simply the personal desire on the part of farmers to share their new discoveries. Campesinos are enthusiastic about developing their own agriculture. When yields increase or the ecosystem is improved as a result of new practices, the desire to share is practically irresistible. The knowledge commons is not an "open access" resource in the sense that anyone can take knowledge for her own benefit to the detriment of others' access. Access itself is obtained by sharing. As Teodoro Juarez of Grupo Vicente Guerrero put it,

> As a team, we had the compromiso moral to share what we have learned with more campesinos. As a promotor, I have to share, without receiving anything economically, just give it. We went to various communities; we worked in San Francisco, in San Juan, in Barrio de Torres, in Españita, in three communities of our municipality. We were Vicente, Gabriel, Roque, and me. Before, our parents worked individually, or only with family. They never brought three or four families together. . . . Sometimes people treated us like we were crazy because we wasted our time. They said, "Look, you don't have enough to maintain your own family but you run around teaching." But for me it was a compromiso moral to share my knowledge with other campesinos because what I learned would serve them as well. (Personal communication with the author)

Clearly, as the Movement grows, those involved receive the effort they put into it many times over, in knowledge, in social status, in security, and, concretely, in improved yields and diminished risk and vulnerability. Those who are especially active gain accesses to resources, new experiences, new ideas, and new ways of making culture. By sharing, campesinos build and cultivate the Movement that in turn both reawakens and quenches their thirst for learning and new experiences and brings them to intellectual, social, and political experiences that were previously inaccessible.

THE SECURITY OF THE "KNOWLEDGE COMMONS"

The knowledge at work in Campesino a Campesino is a reflection of a set of social relations revolving around different forms of the "commons." While the European concept of the commons is understood as a land-centered area of community resource management (forests, pastures, water sources, etc.), many other things can and often are cared for collectively for the benefit of all. For example, in many villages and regions, local maize or bean seeds are planted, harvested, and saved individually but exchanged freely and consciously when needed in order to reduce risk and take advantage of specific agroecological opportunities (soils, climate, season, labor availability, etc.). Farmers often trade or give seed away in carefully calculated amounts with the tacit understanding that they will have access to seeds when they need them too. Knowledge of how to cultivate these seeds is also shared along with the seeds themselves. The end result is a community with a diverse "commons" of genetic diversity, essential to the food security of campesino families.

Labor is an individual or family resource that is also often used for community benefit in public works (school building and maintenance, health and water projects, etc.). In some communities labor is organized collectively through the *faena* or *tequio*. Labor is often shared between families during peak agricultural periods (land preparation, planting, harvest, etc.). Labor sharing can also take different forms, such as one to one reciprocity or rotating, or mutual aid work parties like the Kaqchikel *kuchubal*. Again, knowledge is shared along with labor.

Knowledge, while intangible, is an essential community resource. Farming is a complex, time-consuming art learned over many seasons. Farmers must constantly adapt to risky and changing conditions—markets fluctuate, seeds degenerate, new pests appear, weather patterns change. While farmers are often thought of as being secretive, much of what is learned in farming is necessarily thanks to extensive sharing between farmers. Campesinos knowledge and information about farming, deeply embedded in rural culture and society, relies heavily on sharing information. Sharing takes place through a tight web of social relations based on interdependence. Knowledge, along with seeds, labor, pasture, water, forests, and other community resources, helps smallholders cope individually and collectively with the risks inherent in farming.

THE 100² EXPERIMENTAL PLOT

One standardized small-scale experimental plot popular in Campesino a Campesino is the 100² plot that can be measured in whatever units are familiar to farmers (meters, yards, varas, etc.). The experimental test plot "T" is situated in the farmer's field on a patch of ground that best represents the general conditions in the field. The farmer plants the field using the usual practice. In the experimental plot, he or she changes just one thing: a companion crop, seed spacing, a weed control practice, etc. All other "variables" are held constant, that is, in every other way, the farmer treats or manages the experimental plot in the same way as the rest of the field. Then the farmer measures out another 100² control plot "C" in the field. This is the "control" plot and it receives no special treatment. Throughout the course of the experiment, as the crops grow, the farmer observes and keeps a record of the differences in the two plots, experimental and control. He or she may look at vegetative growth, number of flowers, ears or grain set, or at the incidence of insect damage and drought resistance. Whatever the observations are (and they can be many), the farmer consistently compares the test plot with the control. At harvest time, the products from these plots are harvested separately from the main field and measured in units of weight and/or volume. The farmer can then compare the harvest from plots "T" and "C," and by multiplying the results by 100 (simply adding two zeroes), can extrapolate the results to a hectare or a *manzana* (0.7 hectares).

For example, suppose the farmer marked off the plot in meters and the "T" plot was a new variety of maize. The field (and the "C" plot) would have been planted in the usual variety. Perhaps "T" yielded 30 kilos and "C" 25 kilos (it could go either way—it is an experiment!). Since the plot is 100 meters and a hectare is 10,000 square meters, yields for a hectare will be 100 times those in the test and control plot. By adding two zeroes to 30 and 25 kilos, the farmer then knows that the yields were 3,000 kilos per hectare and 2,500 kilos per hectare, respectively, equivalent to 3 tons per hectare as compared to 2.5 tons per hectare. The experiment showed that the new seed produced a half-ton per hectare more maize than the old seed.

The beauty of a small-scale experiment of this sort is that the farmer can lay out several test plots at the same time without jeopardizing the overall crop (T1, T2, T3, etc.). One control plot will serve as comparison for all of the test plots.

Now imagine a group of ten farmers in an experimental farmers' group, all experimenting with two to five different experiments during a crop cycle and sharing their results. That is twenty to fifty experiments per cycle. In areas where two or three crops can be grown a year, from forty to one hundred fifty experiments can be carried out by the group each year!

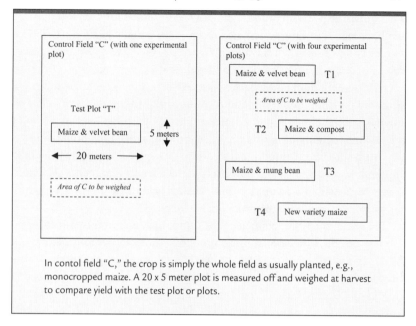

In contol field "C," the crop is simply the whole field as usually planted, e.g., monocropped maize. A 20 x 5 meter plot is measured off and weighed at harvest to compare yield with the test plot or plots.

FROM FARMER EXPERIMENTS
TO CAMPESINO A CAMPESINO RESEARCH

Small-scale experimentation has always been a key component of MCAC's processes of innovation. Unlike the on-farm research of farming systems research (FSR), which was in vogue during the 1980s and 1990s in Latin America, the objective of Campesino a Campesino's small-scale experimentation is not a better technical understanding of the farm system on the part of scientists but a better agroecological understanding of the farm by farmers. Campesino a Campesino's experiments focus on social rather than institutional learning.

Farmer-driven experimentation is itself driven by necessity and by farmers' insatiable curiosity about the agroecological cycles, processes, and phenomena they see at work on their farm. Contrary to what many people think, traditional campesino agriculture is not a static set of ageless practices, but rather a dynamic, socially and ecologically interactive process made up of many small changes and adjustments as farmers respond to the vagaries of climate, variation in land quality, changes in the environment (pests, weeds, etc.), changes in labor availability, and changes in the market. Farmers, cautious yet innovative, have always worked to improve agriculture. Smallholder agriculture in particular is knowledge intensive rather than capital intensive, and relies heavily on cautious but constant tinkering with new seeds, planting densities, crop mixes, planting times, and soil, water, and fertility management (Richards 1985).

Campesino a Campesino's small-scale experimentation techniques are methodological variations designed to speed up farmers' natural tendencies to try out new things in a way that does not put their livelihood strategies at risk. There are many variations on small-scale experimentation because innovation itself does not just take place in the field, but in the patio, in the garden, in the community, in the commons, and in the forest as well. For example, a farmer might come across an interesting plant, seed, or cultivar while working outside his or her village as a laborer. This might first be planted in the patio behind the house, safe from wandering animals, where the family can care for it and watch its progress. Later, after seed is collected, it may be planted in one or more places in the field to see how it does in different soils or crop mixes or on different slopes.

The patio, often the domain of the campesina, is an important locus of innovation. Because women in campesino families are responsible for the health and nutrition of the family as a working unit, they pay special attention to plants and cultivars that will help ensure a good diet. The cultivation and use of medicinal plants are also frequently handled by women. Further, besides doing a large amount of fieldwork during peak labor periods, women usually do all of the cooking, so they are constantly on the lookout for new cultivars that taste good, use minimal amounts of water and cooking fuel, and complement the existing diet. Often the gardeners in the family, they constantly try out new forms of managing fertility, water, and pests—for instance, bio-intensive, double-dug beds. Aspects of these practices are later transferred either directly or partially to field crops (e.g., a farmer won't double-dig an entire field, but he or she might use intensive in-line tillage or begin applying heavy amounts of organic matter). Farmers frequently plant a few plants, change a couple of rows, or try out an application on one or two plants just to see how things work. Yield comparisons may be just one of many factors they observe in order to determine a plant's usefulness. Resistance to pests, drought, and disease, storability, use as fodder or building material, taste, and marketability may all enter in to their final assessment.

GRUPOS DE EXPERIMENTACIÓN CAMPESINA

The social process of innovation in Campesino a Campesino is anchored in individual and collective agroecological discovery. Groups for small-scale experimentation (*grupos de experimentación*) tend to be formed naturally out of the shared analysis and convergence of interests growing from the intercambios and talleres. There are no set regulations for the campesino-experimenter groups.[9] Farmers usually decide on an initial agenda for experimentation, based on an assessment of problems and possible solutions. Frequently, farmers in an experimental group will test one or two possible alternatives (involving seeds, spacings, fertility management, integrated pest management, and so forth) among them. In this way, the new practice is tried out under a diversity of conditions. Rather than trying to hold variables constant between farms, the experimenter groups tend to test the new innovation under different management practices and in different agroecological niches. Results contribute to a better understanding of the new practice's potential over a broad spectrum of possibilities.[10]

The grupos de experimentación tend to organize experiments on the basis of seasonal opportunities and plant phenology. Experiments with soil and water conservation are set up in the dry season (during the *tiempo muerto* or fallow season of the agricultural year) to take advantage of available labor and to be ready when the rains come. Field trials with different crops, seeds, or spacings are initiated at the beginning of the planting season. Integrated pest management, fertilization, and weed management experiments take place during the crop cycle.

The grupos provide a supportive environment for campesino innovation, both because they cushion farmer-experimenters from the frequently harsh comments of the inevitable village skeptics and because they provide a focal point for interaction with technicians and researchers. Further, for their individual efforts, they provide the farmer with multiple returns. As one farmer from a campesino-experimenter group stated, "I came with one experiment to share . . . I left with ten!"

Apart from the immediate returns provided by farmer-experimenter groups, their long-term effect is to increase farmers' overall agroecological capacities and capabilities, in particular on technical and scientific levels. Several decades of farmer-led research were to figure importantly in 1998 when MCAC was called upon to assess the impact of Hurricane Mitch on sustainable and conventional farms in Central America (see Appendix B).

Campesino Pedagogy: Transformative Learning

In campesino pedagogy, smallholders do not make a technical distinction between research, training, and extension. Nor do they separate teaching from learning or learning from practice. All of these activities take place between "teaching-learners" and "learning-teachers" in a nonlinear, overlapping way.

Farmers not only want to learn new technologies, they want to understand how and why these work agroecologically, and they generally want to share their new knowledge with others. Campesino a Campesino allows farmers to share not only information but experience, thus grounding new ideas in local culture.

Experience itself is primary to agroecological learning between campe-

DOÑA CHICA AND THE GRUPO DE EXPERIMENTACIÓN CAMPESINA OF RIO SAN JUAN

"Today it was hot when I went to the field. The velvet bean was not wilted. The longest runner measured 25 cm today and there were sixteen new leaves. No flowers. One worm under the leaves. I pulled the bean runners down from the corn plants. 20 minutes work. Toño [the technican] was supposed to visit but did not. In the afternoon it rained hard. I think the velvet bean is pleased."

My eyes clouded over as I read through the field notebook. In painstaking block letters, Doña Chica's young grandson had recorded each minute observation as dictated by her.

"Keep reading, Ingeniero," she entreated when I paused to reflect on the care she put into her experiment, "I'm sorry, my eyes are no good anymore. Even if I could see the letters," she laughed, "I don't know how to read!"

Doña Chica kept the prized notebook in a plastic bag to protect it from the steamy tropical weather. A widow, she and her three sons worked a forty-hectare rotational plot on the agricultural frontier of Nicaragua's Rio San Juan. Concerned that slash-and-burn practices were no longer effective, and too poor for expensive commercial fertilizers, Doña Chica was determined not to cut down more tropical forest in order to grow crops. Someone told her that *frijol abono* fixed nitrogen and smothered the thick mat of weeds that robbed nutrients from the corn. She heard it provided thirty tons of rich, leafy biomass per hectare. Velvet bean seemed like just the thing to restore fertiity to her farm's thin tropical soils. She joined a Campesino a Campesino experimenter's group, and with the help of Toño, an NGO technician, designed an experiment to test the bean on her land.

This grupo de experimentación campesina [farmers' experiment group] was unlike any other I had come across in Nicaragua. Its farmers were spread for miles along the San Juan River bordering Nicaragua and Costa Rica. Access to town or other farms was by boat or dugout canoe. The two banks of the river were like a before and after photograph of rainforest destruction. On the Costa Rican side, a few lonely clumps of trees stood in a vast expanse of low-grade pasture populated by a few meager-looking beef cattle. The Nicaraguan side was still lush with tropical forest, but was pockmarked with slash-and-burn clearings for basic grain cultivation. After a few years of cultivating, thick weeds ususally took over these plots, leaving "pasture" for the cattle ranchers who then pushed campesino settlers deeper into the forest. Clearing a tropical forest is hard work. Many farmers, like Doña Chica, were looking for an alternative.

Toño, the technician who worked for a local NGO, visited the farmer-experimenters of the group once a week. It took him several days to make his rounds, navigating the slowly moving river. At each farm he reviewed the farmer's observations, checked the test plots, and with a hand-held tape recorder interviewed the farmer regarding the progress of his or her crop. When he returned to his office in San Carlos, the port town where the Rio San Juan flows from Lake Nicaragua, Toño took his tapes to the local radio station. There, with the help on a sound engineer, he made up a weekly radio program that was broadcast the length of the river. Hundreds of farmers followed the progress of the grupo de experimentación campesina as they tested velvet bean in a dozen different locations. By the time the impressive results of the velvet bean experiments were shared over the radio, farmers had a pretty clear idea of the enormous potential of the plant. The experimenters harvested their beans and brought them in to San Carlos. Hundreds of farmers showed up to purchase a half-kilo pack of beans to try on their own fields. Rio San Juan had always been considered a difficult, even impenetrable, region for agricultural extensionists, who usually looked for another posting as soon as possible. The grupo de experimentación campesina, some velvet bean, and a radio transmitter changed that.

Doña Chica shares the record of her field experiments with the author in Rio San Juan, Nicaragua.

sinos. Promoters share information, knowledge, and wisdom based on real experiences in sustainable agriculture. Wisdom (in this case, knowing when, where, and how to implement sustainable practices) comes from experience and can be shared but not taught.[11] (This distinguishes the promoter from the agricultural technician and the agronomist, who rarely farm, and if they

Pedro Sánchez uses a simple picture to talk about innovation, solidarity, production, and protection in an MCAC workshop.

do, rarely farm under the same socioeconomic and environmental conditions as the people they teach.) Sharing learning experiences among farmers has a number of advantages. First of all, while a knowledgeable agronomist is a good source of information, a successful farmer is an inspiration to others. The Campesino a Campesino pedagogy intensifies and socializes farmers' agroecological experience because farmers, confident in their knowledge and supported by their own epistemic community, are eager to share with others. The process can be viewed as three overlapping and interactive foci that move forward in a spiral fashion as the epistemic community increases its capacity for innovation:

The sharing of cultural wisdom produced a set of general normative principles that suggest that MCAC's technologies and methods are deeply rooted in meaning. Codified as a simple stick figure, MCAC is said to "work" with two hands: one for production of food and another for protection of the environment. The Movement "walks" on the two legs of innovation and solidarity. In its "heart" it believes in love of nature, family, and community, and it "sees" with a vision of campesino-led, sustainable agricultural development.[12]

FAMILY-BASED LEARNING

I HAVE CHILDREN who are professionals. I never finished the third grade. But I learned a lot of things along the way, and campesinos have been my teachers, my professors. I learned so much that now I can do the work of an agronomist, and I say this with pride because I have knowledge. I learned it along the way, because it is there, in life's road. Experience gave me everything.

I think many of us dream of giving our children a good education because that is the future. I don't know, but analyzing this, if all the youth want to be professionals, no one will want to pick up a hoe or a machete. I wonder, what are we going to do in the future with our children? Who will cultivate the corn? Who will grow beans? We can see this today. Young people go to work in a factory in Guatemala City. They go to high school and college. Fine. But we see that only older people are working the land. They are the ones who care about the land and our food. They are the ones everyone calls fools because they don't know how to do anything else! We older people who are working the land will disappear some day. We are one step from the grave. And that is where our experience will end up. What are we going to do?

Many young people study for a career, but there are no jobs. What shall we do about the young people who can't get work in the countryside? They join gangs because there is no work. But there is so much to do in the countryside! We have to reforest, we have to conserve the soil, we have to plant . . . there is no end to things to do in the countryside!

—*Felipe Tomás, Guatemala*

Because family farming involves men, women, and children, Campesino a Campesino workshops, field days, encuentros, and farmer-experiments are often highly integrated. Learning agroecology in campesino pedagogy is often a family affair. Because many adults are neoliterate, children and teenagers frequently take notes for their parents. Since the field, the patio, and the household are integrated, interactive parts of the family farm, tended to by different members of the campesino family, innovations, and changes introduced affect the types of tasks, labor time, and relationships between family members. While this chapter deals primarily with the generation of agroecological knowledge, because of the importance of the family unit in agricultural production, promoters in the MCAC often extend their engagement to areas of health and education. Referring to the importance of families and the inclusion of rural youth in MCAC's proves of social learning, one promoter, Rogelio Sánchez, stated:

> We are trying to keep our families integrated because this is part of our culture. With television, our children enter into another environment and aren't interested in learning what their parents know. . . . When they leave [the village], they are ashamed to be sons and daughters of campesinos. The [public] education they receive makes them think like city kids, not country kids. It deforms them to the point they don't feel

ENRIQUE, "EL CALLADO"

One of the most well-known campesino promotores in all of Mesoamerica is Don José Jesús Mendoza. Sage, cantankerous, and a master
innovator, Don Chepe Chu, as he is known, runs his own school for sustainable agriculture on his farm in Santa Lucía, Boaco, in Nicaragua.
He was once a preacher. In his workshops, he holds forth on the virtues
of agroecological farming with all the rich metaphor and conviction of
his past sermons. Lesser known are his two brothers, Andres and
Enrique, who teach with him at the school. During the period that Don
Chepe Chu was becoming known, Enrique shadowed his older brother,
silently participating in the workshops and field visits. He always seemed
a bit skeptical, and was painfully shy. In fact, among the technical advisers who assisted the Campesino a Campesino program, he was known
as Enrique "El Callado" (The Silent One) to distinguish him from the
other Mendoza brothers. It seemed like a clear case of sibling hierarchy.
As the youngest, Enrique always took a back seat. His social status in
the village was defined by his relationship to his more dynamic older
brothers. He seemed an unlikely candidate to be a leader in MCAC.

   One day Enrique pulled me aside. He wanted me to see the soil conservation work he had implemented on his farm. I had visited his five-
acre plot two years earlier and remembered it as a typical, somewhat
underproductive area with corn and beans planted rather noninten-
sively on a fairly steep hillside with a big gully running down one side. I
imagined he had put in some contour ditches, spread some compost,
and perhaps planted a few trees. There was nothing in Enrique's silent
demeanor to prepare me for what I found. As we rounded the bend to
his farm, we walked past an *enormous* compost heap steaming in the
lower corner of his field. The field above us was unrecognizable. He had
terraced the entire field. Several varieties of corn were intercropped with
local beans, soy, squash, peanuts, and tomatoes. The barriers held
Napier grass, lemon grass, papaya, manioc, pigeon pea, and pitaya.
The perimeter was a mix of "live fencing" and several species of multi-
purpose timber for medicine, nitrogen, fodder, and firewood. The gully
had become a controlled channel for releasing excess water from the
field. He had filled the deep gash with terraces, each with a small grove
of bananas. I was speechless. This was just as well, because Enrique was
anything but "callado." He barely let me get a question in edgewise as
he went into detail about the process of converting his farm. His memory for the details of the labor invested, the decrease in erosion, the
increase in productivity, and the complex changes in fertility and insect

problems was phenomenal. He had tested and observed everything, and apparently had forgotten nothing. We stayed in the field until dark as he talked about the agroecology of his farm, his successes and failures, and his plans for the future.

I asked him why he had not brought others to the farm. Smiling, he answered that he wanted it to be a surprise. No one suspected he was just as good a farmer as his older brother. When everything was in place and the time was right, he would share his experience with others. "But when?" I insisted. As soon as the new variety of corn was ripe enough to serve people corn on the cob when they visited, he giggled, beside himself with excitement. Enrique had become a showman!

Many people have visited Enrique over the years. In workshops and in public, he remains "El Callado." When he steps onto his field, however, he is transformed. His desire to share his experience is irrepressible, his enthusiasm contagious, and his eloquence second to none, not even his older brothers.

Don Chepe Chu acknowledged this lesson from his younger brother: "There are people who don't like to talk. We say they don't have what it takes to be successful. This is not so. The desire to speak is something that comes when one wants to teach what one loves. Everything starts with love. If a farmer doesn't love what he does, he can't be a good promotor. He has to love what he teaches and that makes him good. This is the best quality of promotores: they love what they teach. The student becomes infected with this love. It multiplies."

Enrique "El Callado" Mendoza on his farm in Santa Lucía, Nicaragua, with velvet bean

pride in their origins. . . . For us it is very important to recover our cultural values because we have a relationship with the environment. As campesinos, it is a privilege to live in the countryside because we don't have to depend on a lot of things from the city. As farm families we know we are important because if we don't produce the food we eat and that people in the cities eat, our country won't develop.

THE TRANSFORMATIVE EFFECT

They saw other campesinos that taught, and not just other campesinos but
indigenous campesinos. For me, this was the most important because they
have told me so. To follow the example of the compromiso moral and fol-
low the other promoter as they are is not just to reaffirm alternative agri-
culture . . . there is a social figure, the campesino promoter who facilitates
this change. —Roberto Vega, methodologist, MCAC

Projects for sustainable agricultural development that select promoters either directly or through some local "electoral" process miss the fact that promoters are made, not born, and not elected. The capacities for agroecological expertise and local leadership are not limiting in the campesinado. What are lacking are opportunities to develop capabilities. The campesino pedagogy of MCAC provides both opportunities and the cultural, social, and political context for this self-development. Indeed, when campesinos talk about MCAC, they frequently invoke the opportunities the movement has provided.

MCAC's methodologies and ethic have had an impact on a number of professionals working in sustainable agriculture as well, who reached out to the promoters and, incorporating their methods, attempted to influence the development approaches within their own institutions. In particular, farmer-led experimentation provided researchers with opportunities to work with promoters and NGOs to promote innovation.[13]

Method, Movement, or Pedagogy of Resistance?

This chapter is in no way an outline for a Campesino a Campesino "manual" to be applied across cultural-political contexts. The fact that campesino pedagogy is the social learning practice of a *movement* sets it categorically apart, politically and culturally, from project-driven methodologies for agricultural development. This is not to say that there is not tremendous overlap between NGO projects and MCAC. On the contrary, there is a historical relation between the two. Indeed, by enabling the movement with projects, programs, and methods, NGOs have both contributed to campesino pedagogy and have been profoundly influenced by MCAC.

THE PROMOTORES AND THE TÉCNICOS

The relationship with agronomists or technicians is not always easy. Promoters have had a rocky history with the técnicos (government-extensionists), who often lacked farming experience. Extension in general lost status because of the failures of the Green Revolution, and thanks to austerity measures taken on by most Latin American governments, it all but disappeared in much of the countryside. Even in the best of times, extensionists came and went depending on their job placements and rarely developed deep knowledge of the agroecology of the region where they worked or made lasting relationships with the farmers there. This, coupled with the fact that they had no training in ecology, made them an unreliable source of information in sustainable agriculture. Ill prepared, poorly supported, and with little job security, the técnicos often viewed the promotores as a professional threat. In response one Kaqchikel promotor-turned-consultant (Lopez 1996) wrote:

> We do not see village [promoters] as some sort of second-class agronomists—people with the same role as agronomists, but with less education. They are not substitute agronomists—sometimes preferred because they cost less. Nor should the objective of their training be that of teaching them everything about agriculture. The role of the village [promoters], like that of the village health workers before them, is not of having a general, overall knowledge of their particular subject area—of becoming village doctors or agronomists. Their role is, rather, to learn the solutions to the most common problems in the village.

In other words, a promoter was to learn the agroecology of his or her particular area and generate innovative ways of overcoming the limiting factors to production and of minimizing ecological risk. In fact, the threat from the promoters was not that of replacing agronomists or técnicos, but of creating a demand for agroecological information that these professionals were unable to meet.

Nonetheless, the campesino pedagogy embedded in the MCAC transcends the notion of methodology as it is commonly understood by development institutions.

"Farmer-led" and "participatory" methodologies are tools employed by agricultural research and development institutions to bring farmers in to formal programs and projects. But these institutions are, for all practical purposes, unaccountable to farmers. In the best of cases, they provide an avenue for researchers and development workers to participate in farmers' livelihood struggles. In the worst of cases, they ignore conflicts and differences among farmers, temporarily diffuse local resistance to development, and co-opt local initiatives. The point is that smallholders do not need methodologies to "participate" in their own livelihoods. The ways in which farmers in MCAC generate knowledge and share wisdom to develop their own agriculture must be viewed as cultural practice—as a dynamic and pluralistic phenomena. The goal of campesino pedagogy is not "participation," but cultural strengthening of the social and political relations between smallholders engaged in struggles for sustainable, rural livelihoods. In this sense, because the production of agroecological knowledge is a key component to controlling resources in the countryside, it is best described not as a participatory methodology but as a pedagogy of cultural resistance.

I believe that there is wisdom in campesino pedagogy and that this wisdom, rather than methods per se, is what should be shared. I also believe that because of its centrality in the movement and because claims on the methodology reflect claims on the direction of sustainable agricultural development and on MCAC itself, understanding this practice as pedagogy is key to understanding the importance of culture and autonomy, not only in the movement, but in the practice of agroecology.

FOUR

Campesino Politics
of Development

In the countryside we say that a wound festers—*se solapa*. When a
wound festers, it won't stop hurting and it becomes an abscess. This is
what happens when we are ignored. We campesinos are the majority in
this world. And the majority should be listened to. When the majority is
pushed aside, we are dividing instead of adding. But when the majority
is listened to, that is when we have a solid base. If we build on sand, it
will be destroyed. Ah, but if we build on rock! And the base, the rock of
the world, is the campesinado, because when the poor are better off,
then everyone is better off. We ask city people what they would do if a
pound of grain didn't come in? Or a pound of tomatoes, or of beans?
We would die of hunger, they answer. This is what will happen
if we are ignored.   —*José Jesús Mendoza*

We have to insist on the human space in development because neo-
liberalism and the politics of globalization are so violent, not just economically but culturally. When they privatize, they don't just privatize
the service but the links that exist between the people and the environment. There is a strong danger of the loss of cultural identity. Our
campesinos migrate and the drought drives them out. We are living a
process of disappearance. I think that what we are seeing is the resistance of a people who do not want to disappear!
—*Nelda Martínez, development worker, Managua, Nicaragua*

DEVELOPMENT IS A POLITICAL EVENT. Whether through neoliberal structural adjustment or through village-level projects, the main
actors—multinational institutions, governments, and NGOs—all negotiate to establish the terms, implement the mechanisms, and manage the sector's billions of dollars in resources. All this is done, ostensibly, for the poor.
For over five decades, campesinos have been invited to believe in tales of

progress in which poverty, by dint of development, disappears. What is never made explicit in these happy narratives is that campesinos—as the beneficiaries, partners, or stakeholders in development—also disappear.

Development's achievements are uneven, to say the least. While the industrialized world has made out quite well, it is at best unclear whether or not campesinos have actually benefited, and it is even less clear whether development, neoliberal or otherwise, offers them a future.

What do smallholders think of being developed? How do they see their own future? How do they control and manage resources to ensure their survival in the face of a project that essentially programs their disappearance? This chapter attempts to provide a perspective on the politics of development from the point of view of those subjected to it—the campesinos.

Solidarity, one of the "legs" of the Movement, has its roots in the campesinado's culture of mutual aid. The solidarity among campesinos in MCAC takes the form of sharing knowledge, wisdom, and resources. These expressions of solidarity are neither uncomplicated nor gratuitous, however. Imagination, compassion, need, hard work, and a concrete commitment to the campesino "commons" constantly faces individualism, elitism, apathy, mistrust, political manipulation, and hopelessness. Promoters in the Movement face the challenge of cultivating solidarity not only with their neighbors but within their own families and with the professionals working in agricultural development.

Innovation, the other "leg" of the Movement, is a result of constant farmer experimentation with new cultivars and farming methods. This is a permanent part of any dynamic agriculture and is as old as agriculture itself. What distinguishes MCAC's innovators is their strong grounding in agroecology, their tendency to encourage each other in small groups of campesino-experimenters, and the speed with which innovations are generated and shared.

Walking the Legs of Solidarity and Innovation

To UNDERSTAND the soil and water conservation programs [of Campesino a Campesino], one really needs courage. It is like when a young man wants to court a young woman. First she says yes . . . then no . . . then she messes with your head. . . . A campesino is like that! "I'll think about it," he will say.
                              —*Enrique Mendoza, Santa Lucía, Nicaragua (Zurita 1991)*

CAMPESINO A CAMPESINO . . . is a way of bringing down the costs of production. The campesino learns how to innovate, to search out new methods . . . to bring costs down and production up. A campesino usually produces corn and beans, but he has to buy tomatoes, onions, and other things even though he has land? We would have better nutrition growing everything on our own farm; and better health, and we wouldn't have the terrible problem we have now, which is hunger. Here, what has given us life has been these workshops where for the brother who knows less, the one who knows more is teaching him, so that he can help himself. So that he finds solutions on his own and is not dependent on the technicians, on loans, on the banks . . . so he can be self sufficient and know how to improve his own quality of life.

—*Argelio Flores, Santa Lucía (Zurita 1991)*

WHEN I STARTED this work my family were the ones who objected because they said I was wasting my time, I was supposed to take care of them. . . . I had problems with my family because they said, "Look, you take off and you never leave any money!" For example, I would leave to share experiences for three days, and those three days I was supposed to bring in money. . . . But little by little they began to understand. Meanwhile, though, I had problems.

—*Teodoro Juárez, Vicente Guerrero, Mexico*

A LOT OF PEOPLE don't like working with others. To each his own, people say. Sometimes we get together for work and they say, today I'll go . . . tomorrow it's "no." What's missing? Motivation. If I am committed, I learn, even with failures.

The motivation to work in groups. . . . One can do a lot on one's own if one wants to. But working in a group can get us irritated with each other. As if you felt like sleeping and someone comes and wakes you up and says, "Hey, let's go work!" But, between us we help each other. . . . It helps us to stay motivated.

Helping and teaching go hand in hand. This is the only way a campesino can become a complement to another household. It's like a job. It is a way of improving your job in your family work because by training someone else one starts doing things that help to integrate the family. One's successes help to make the family stronger. . . . With training I learned that the soil was actually a live being like you and me. We have to give it food, because if we don't we will have nothing, it will give nothing. I saw how one can plant in different ways, that we can't depend on just one crop, but must diversify our crops. Through the exchange of knowledge from Campesino a Campesino I saw what one can do.

—*Santos Espinoza Garcia, Michoacán, Mexico*

ONE THING THAT has worked is being able to share experiences with other compañeros from other places and countries like Nicaragua, Costa Rica, Cuba, and others. We have had these opportunities through the Campesino a Campesino movement. We feel like we are not alone, like there are people interested around the world who add their "grain of sand" to the process in this movement. There are many, and many have been fortunate. This has allowed us to build and advance as a Campesino a Campesino movement.   —*Rogelio Sánchez, Vicente Guerrero, Mexico*

CUBA TAUGHT ME that in spite of the blockade, they have been able to survive. Maybe they are not 100 percent self-sufficient, but it is an incredible level of self-sufficiency. They produce what they consume. . . . The most important thing about Cuba is the value they place on country people because the city people realize that without the people of the countryside they will die of hunger, that's it! They really value what the countryside produces in Cuba. Because part of production goes to the city, and that is expensive. That has been interesting, they have not become dependent or consumers of other products, for example, the junk that comes from abroad here in Mexico. The difference between Cuba and Mexico is that we Mexicans, unfortunately, are very consumerist. We don't really value what we have and what we produce.

—*Alicia Sarmientos, Vicente Guerrero, Mexico*

SOMETHING THAT MADE a big impression on me was my trip to India to share experiences. I was afraid to get on the airplane. A campesino is used to traveling by burro and on horseback! It was hard. But when I got to India, I got to share experiences with farmers from sixty-nine different countries and it had a great impact on me. So much so that when I returned I got sick because I was so saddened to see how a campesino family there survived on just a handful of rice a day. But this made me more determined because I said, "We Mexican campesinos are screwed, but we are not in *that* bad of a shape." I said, "We have to put effort into this." This motivated me enormously. . . . All the work I put in my field paid off with higher production. . . . This is what I had been looking for. This is what I wanted. . . . I didn't just like what I saw, I liked experimenting and providing examples, right? I liked to experiment with different varieties of corn, varieties of beans, and other cultivars because I wanted to see how well they produced.   —*Gabriel Sánchez*

CAPITALIZING ON FARMER INNOVATION

Jorge Irán Vásquez is a technician who has worked with Campesino a Campesino for over a decade. His work with promoters has led him to focus on farmer-led agroecological and cost-benefit studies as a way to make the most out of farmer innovations:

> With so much sharing of so many experiences, there is a large set of techniques and knowledge. But one has to identify within all of that which will have a positive impact on the farm and in the region. As technicians in MCAC, we don't define this, but we give backup. We don't sit down and say, "Okay, this or that is a priority." We watch what people do and let that guide us.
>
> We have used the farm study to prioritize on the basis of available resources. . . . People are doing these studies all over the country. The objectives and the methodologies differ. Some people do it in order to plan an investment on the farm, depending on the resources and markets in the region. For example, in Matagalpa farmers have always harvested *naranjilla*—wild mandarin oranges—which are very expensive. With his farm plan, one farmer had the idea to plant naranjilla and is now selling it at a good price. It is a fruit that is native, but not common, to the region, and people saw it had a market. On the other hand, the chayote, which is found all over Nicaragua, was not common to the region, and so the farmers started growing it. They are diversifying with passion fruit and lychee as well.
>
> There is a widespread process of diversification going on. I have seen farms that only had a few products diversify with new ones for the local market because the farmer thought about it when they did a farm study, when they analyzed the added value on everything on the farm . . . even the mangoes, which are there just so the children have something sweet to eat, or the coriander for the kitchen have a value. I have seen a lot of analyses that don't include these things, but if you start adding them in, you see how much wealth people are producing that sometimes they don't even realize. We have done comparative analyses on diversified farms and on farms outside the movement. People are not only diversifying their farm and increasing their income, they are generating work because they have a greater capacity to hire farm labor.

Working with the Hands of Production and Protection

ONE DAY I DECIDED to go take a look at my land. I did a careful study and measured the depth of the topsoil. I took five samples. In one it was 25 inches deep, in another it was 19, in another 20, and in another 18. . . . I told my son, we have soil for many years here. I will die, and this soil will be yours. He understood the value of the land. I told my thirteen-year-old grandson to plant a tree. When I got this land it was a bare pasture. Now I have a forest. Plant trees, I said, because that is where life is. If it were not for these trees, the wind would blow all my crops down. This happens in many other fields, but not in mine. Why? Because I have a cover. I have windbreaks. I plant them for multiple reasons: firewood, organic matter for the soil, protection of the environment. . . . I have teak and cashew to market. I work with two hands: protection and production.
                                  —*Orlando Martínez, Ometepe, Nicaragua*

The Movimiento Campesino a Campesino "works with two hands" of production and protection—the production of food and the protection of the environment. The practice of sustainable agriculture is not easy. Campesinos do not control agricultural or environmental policies. Government programs pressure them to accept production credit that can be used only for hybrid seeds and agrochemicals. They have few resources besides their labor, the elements, and a patch of land. Nonetheless, because the limiting factors to campesino production tend to be very basic (e.g., soil and water), and because they rely heavily on ecological processes as production factors (e.g., rain for water, manure and biomass for fertilizer) increases in production often go hand in hand with reclamation and conservation of soil, water, and biodiversity. This agroecological approach is often sought after the farmers have already been "run over" by the Green Revolution—their soil depleted of nutrients, their crops ravaged by induced pests, their families poisoned, and their households broke.

ALL THAT IS COMING—globalization, the free trade agreements—these have never worked for us because they take work away, they take away our opportunities. Remember how we started with fertilizer? They gave ten pounds of fertilizer to my father. Gave it to him! And it costs two quetzales a bag! In those days we only made pennies a day. Do you know what my grandfather said? This won't help because it will burn the soil. Don't use it! But because it was a gift, my father put it on the corn. What happened? The corn came up a rich green and the ears were big! What a miracle fertilizer was! The next year he bought a bag and we had lots of corn. And that's how it went little by little, one neighbor saw it, then another.

Everyone started to use it because fertilizer was God. A bag cost only two quetzales! When people started to buy it, they raised the price. It got to five, then six, eight, ten. It got as high as twenty quetzales a bag! How much is it today! It has skyrocketed and it doesn't produce like it used to. It depends on how we use it. A lot of people just count on urea [nitrogen]. What does urea have, just one component, no more, just nitrogen. The corn needs fourteen elements to grow and give fruit. A triple fifteen is the most complete fertilizer. But we realized that it still does not work for us, because the soil kept deteriorating, it lost its organic material, it lost its body. We made our Mother Earth poor and we want to force her to produce. We don't give her enough food. Organic material is like food for the soil.

Now we say the seed has become "too accustomed" to fertilizer. It's not true. The seed is not "too accustomed" because if you plant a corn seed in a pot with good soil it grows well even though you don't put on fertilizer. So fertilizer is not the solution. I think that the solution we are learning here is organic agriculture. It is sustainable agriculture. We are not sustainable because we are always taking household money to buy fertilizer. We sell a pig, we sell some chickens, we sell a bull calf to buy fertilizer . . . we give our work away. 				—*Felipe Tomás, Guatemala*

ORGANIC, ECOLOGICAL, AND SUSTAINABLE AGRICULTURE

IT IS OFTEN SAID, and one can cite the Bible or prophets, that everything ends, but love is endless. When we construct love for the land, toward the farm, this is the beginning of a victory, because everything begins and ends with love. One needs to take care and love the land and nature and everything in it. Some campesinos think that all insects are bad. This is not true. One needs to love insects. When one enters this reality, one learns many things. Everything changes through love. Love is the basis for ecology. Because of a bad orientation, many people do not have this love. . . . This creates uncertainty and the belief that the land is no good. This is not true. The land is always good, as long as we love it and protect it. 				—*José Jesús Mendoza, Santa Lucía*

WE SAY THE LAND IS NO GOOD. But it has been our management of the land which is no good and that is why it has been destroyed. I think with these [agroecological] methods we will have more life and more production. Here, not one technician has come to help us poor folk. Only now, with our friends who have taken us to Santa Lucía and the campesinos there who taught us, do we have a good life. Because this is life for us. 				—*Promotor, Boaco, Nicaragua (Zurita 1991)*

IT ALL DEPENDS on how we work the land. There is no bad land. All land is good if we know how to work it. If we work well, there is good land that we can give "body" to. We can put spirit back in the land so that it rises up and provides us with food. First we have to plant legumes. Here we have velvet bean [*Mucuna pruriens*]. We have *Canavalia* and we can plant *gandul* [*Cajanus cajan*]. The second year we can put in a lot of organic matter. I am adding 400 to 600 bags of organic material per hectare. Part of it I bring from the outside. Other parts not. There are parts on my land where the legumes are chest high.

Organic agriculture is, first of all, no burning. Secondly, there is no trash. I don't know who invented that word, because it doesn't exist. Even the sweepings from the house are not trash. Because if you collect it, it will rot and it is organic material. I stopped using the word *trash* years ago. What we have is organic material. Why do I say organic agriculture? Because every thing that sprouts, grows, and dies, stays there. I live together with ecological agriculture because I live together with all the animals. Four years ago I made a seedbed for grubs. There are over 30,000 grubs there now, and they are my friends. I live together with the worms. I made a nursery for worms too. I might have a million now. I put forty-five pounds of worms on my field. Why? Because they live in the soil. But first we have to stop burning because if we burn we will kill all those little animals. I haven't burned in thirty years! A man told me, "I don't burn, I just use herbicide." He is burning! Put some herbicide on your own foot and see how it feels!

The truth is that with ecological agriculture there are squirrels, badgers, armadillos, snakes, deer. . . . I call it sustainable agriculture because that is where I get my food. I have not worked for anyone else in two years. I have my food, my breakfast, lunch, and dinner. I buy my shirts, my hat. That is why we call it sustainable agriculture. If we call it sustainable agriculture and we have to go to the coast to work, then it's not sustainable. Sustainable agriculture means you are going to eat. If you get sick tomorrow you will have medicine.

Organic agriculture is a process. The first year you will stop burning. Second year you can loosen the soil, do your contour ditches, the grass barriers, bring organic material, plant legumes for four, five, six, seven, eight, ten years. That is why many of us get discouraged. Are you a mason? Know what a mason does? They want their paycheck every week! Organic agriculture is not like that. You are going to get some profit after three or four years. But we should not get discouraged. The best profession is to be a farmer. Really! I know teachers that at the end of the month have already spent their check they are about to get. There they are in the store paying

their bill and then right away start buying on credit! I am proud to be a
farmer because I always have food. I have a farm that I bought fifteen years
ago and it cost 14,000 quetzales per manzana. Know how much they offer
me now? One hundred fifty thousand quetzales! But I will not sell. Just
here I have my food for ten or fifteen years. All I have to do is maintain it.
Just harvest. Sometimes I disappear for two weeks. I go here and there. . . .
When I get back my farm is still there.

   When I have a lot of work is in summer [dry season]. A lot of people
say there is no work in summer . . . they sit around. No! In the summer
there is a lot of work because in the summer you haul in leaves, you haul
in brush, in the summer you loosen soil and make contour ditches. . . .
In the summer you are going to harvest your grass barriers. Then winter
[rainy season] is easy! All you do is visit the fields. Summer is when the
work is.   —*Lázaro Aguin, San Martín Jilotepeque, Guatemala*

SOMEONE CAME and asked me if I would rent them four manzanas of
land to grow organic sesame. Where? There, in that woodlot, he says.
What! Do you think I'm crazy? No, no, no! Don't you know that that is
life? My life is there, and your life, and all our lives. No, I am not touching
that little forest, I said. We will leave you the firewood, he said. I don't
care. I know why I have that little forest there. You cut down the forest
and then you say the sesame you planted is organic. No, that's not organic,
that is "natural." They say organic because they cultivate land that has
never been fertilized. But organic agriculture requires a whole organic
production process. When I say "organic" it is because my land has been
protected with terraces, has compost, and is cared for.

                              —*Orlando Martínez, Nicaragua*

I THINK WE NEED to put what we see in a field visit into practice because
that is how we get results. Otherwise, we say we've wasted our time. But
I don't think it is a waste of time. I think one has to conserve the soil so
that one can reap the benefits from the time that one "wasted." We call it
time wasted when we don't conserve. But if we conserve the land it is not
a waste of time.

   My husband and I practice organic agriculture. We are doing it little by
little. We belong to a cooperative where they showed us to conserve the
soil, to make barriers, contour ditches, not to burn. My husband is putting
it into practice. It has been six years since he used any agrochemicals. This
is how we learned. When he can't go to workshops, I go and learn and
then share it with him. Whenever he goes to learn, he shares it with me.
Between the two of us we move forward. Maybe as a woman I don't do

everything in the field, but I just tell my husband and he does it. We are practicing organic agriculture, not on a big piece of land, but little by little, we have put about half of it into shape. Little by little, we are moving forward. Those of us women who are married should share what we learn and what we see, and what we hear, with our husbands. . . . We talk to them and then we do it in practice. Even if we go plant by plant, it is not wasted time if we conserve.

—*Sixta Jacobo, San Martín Jilotepeque, Guatemala*

I HAVE COME TO UNDERSTAND the natural resources we have that we had not valued before. For me they are the forest, the water, the soil, and of course, the human beings that live in the area. . . . This had a strong impact on me because I feel that we are part of life with our natural resources. It makes me so sad to see human beings destroying natural resources, because the issue of natural resources is at the bottom of everything. It is the most beautiful thing we have for the lives of the human beings, the animals, and the plants.

This has always been my concern, how can we really move forward in the recovery of traditional agriculture and organic agriculture and how can we reverse conventional agriculture that has taken so much and so badly. It is using up the natural resources. Our government has also contributed to the destruction . . . everywhere their idea is how to get more money opening up farmland by cutting down forests. Then they talk about "conservation."

These things worry me. . . . The butterfly sanctuary is a worthwhile place. But for many people the monarch butterfly is the most valuable. I say all things are valuable, humans, forests, the insects are all valuable. But for many governments, the most important ones are the butterflies, and they want to drive out the people who live in the reserve—send them who knows where just to protect the butterflies.

—*Gabriel Sánchez, Mexico*

Gender

Gender issues have shaped the Movement since its inception. As a matter of course, campesina women put in a *doble jornada*—a double work day— that starts before men wake up and ends long after everyone else has finished working. Women bear and rear the children needed for the survival of the family labor farm and are responsible for everyone's health. Aside from the heavy chores of the home, women's extra work in the field is essential during planting and harvest periods. Women's exploitation is the beginning of the chain of exploitation that is the basis for the campesinado's food and labor subsidy to industry and development. Over the last decade, globalization has increased the exploitation of campesina women, both directly—as underpaid workers in maquiladoras—and indirectly—for the cheap reproduction of the labor force.

No project, program, or vision for sustainable rural livelihoods is possible without recognizing, on one hand, the ways in which women are central to family survival and how, on the other hand, they are exploited in this role. Sustainability must necessarily address gender equity regarding work, as well as women's equitable political participation in the process of change. In the early days, women's participation in MCAC tended to reflect their traditional roles in the campesino household: e.g., gardening and nutrition. War, political upheaval, migration, and NGOs' focus on gender provided opportunities to address broader roles for women in sustainable agricultural development. These changes are reflected in MCAC as women promoters struggle to forge more equitable roles and relationships.

I STARTED DISCOVERING that we could do all kinds of work together as women, and that we could share what was happening to us. We could also organize activities or work together, and I discovered that we were at a higher level of life and knowledge and that we had to learn to be more each day. So I taught myself little by little. We didn't use to address gender. We organized a lot of work with women, but around housework and the home. We didn't see things beyond that until we started looking at gender issues. We discovered that we had rights to land because if we are married and our husbands want to sell the ejido, they can't do it without our consent, if we don't sign. We didn't know that. No one knew it. We thought they were the only owners. It was as if we were on the sidelines. Then we realized that we had this power . . . even if they want to sell, we won't sell. This has been great because many women have not permitted their husbands to sell the ejido. The men have migrated to work, okay, because of economic need. They have wanted to sell the land, but no! We women are defending ourselves now. We can work the land. Many women are a living example of this. I have learned much from them. Their husbands are working abroad and they are working the land. This is a wonderful activity because it involves not just the women but the family—boys *and* girls.

When we started to work on gender issues, I was afraid because it was often misinterpreted. Because when the idea of feminism first came in to the village, it attacked the men hard. This created a lot of mistrust in the communities. If we talked about gender the men didn't want their wives to meet with us because they were afraid of the issue. We found other ways of taking about the issue without calling it gender. Instead we called it "reevaluating our daily work." All of our work is important. We invited our husbands to participate in workshops with the women. One day we used a technique called "a day in the life"—a day in his life and a day in her life. On this day instead of the women doing their housework, we did it the other way around. We made the men do all the work the women do in a day, and the women did all the work of the men. We discovered that in a day women carry out at least forty different activities while men, at the most, do twenty . . . and that is exaggerating! It was good because it allowed the compañeros to see the situation.

We have had some village authorities that truly appreciate women's work and they recognize that thanks to the support that women gave as women and wives, they were able to become community leaders. It has been an interesting process because we have gotten them into gender without them even realizing it. They keep reevaluating and reevaluating.

One achievement has been that in our community, it used to be that women did not participate in community meetings as women, only as widows. But today if you go to the community meetings, 75 percent of the participants are women and 25 percent are men! So when the time came to elect new authorities, the women decided who it was going to be. The older men fought it tooth and nail, but they couldn't change the women's minds. They have their village authority, but the women elected him. They work together. Things are changing little by little.

—Alicia Sarmientos, Mexico

WHEN I WAS FIRST MARRIED, my husband didn't give me permission. I had never been to a meeting. I couldn't go. It was difficult to get out. My husband was always against it; he didn't want it. But I talked to him about discrimination against women. It was common not to give women permission to go out then, one had to stay in the house; and going out was hard because we had double the work because we still had to get all the housework done. When you get back from a meeting you have to start over and see what needs to be done because we have left children at home. One leaves them alone, but it is important to get out because one learns a lot. For example, if I don't know anything about agriculture and don't learn, what about my children who need me to teach them these things which are being lost? So it is important to go to meetings even though for many it is very hard. In the past they didn't value us as women. Many women couldn't participate in Campesino a Campesino because of their husbands. But one has to make an effort to participate and to learn.

—Maria Casquí, Guatemala

BEING IN A GROUP builds enthusiasm among us. If there are problems, we leave them behind and we learn. For example, we go out for a field visit and our minds learn so much. I know that my children are at home and as a mother I think about them. Because my children came home from school . . . they need me to tell them to change out of their school clothes. So we are thinking about our children, but I like to be in the group because of our unity. I can talk with the other women about any kind of problem and they help me find a solution. I also get to meet other people and make friends. It is good to get to know people. When you are a good friend to me, I will keep you in my thoughts because you have taught me many things. So it not all about children.

I don't have a husband anymore for whom to wash clothes, or make food, but I have children. But those that have husbands need to take advantage of opportunity. The man and the woman have the same rights. The main thing is that respect comes first. If we don't have respect, we have nothing. Respect is the most important thing.

—*María Paula Martín Bor, Guatemala*

FOR ME THE MEETINGS are very important. My husband didn't used to let me go to meetings—he didn't even let me go out. But some of us women started meeting anyway and we formed a group and worked together for the well-being of our children. We knew that gardens could help us feed our children well. One year we planted amaranth as a group. We harvested so we could nurture our children with *atol* and *pastel*.[1] It was a success. Now we want to start a small commercial chicken farm as a group so we can be better off economically. As women we don't get a salary to maintain our children so we are thinking about this. We always work in groups as women because we have a great need. We don't have enough with what the men bring home, so we have to bring something in too, because we are very poor. For me it is very important to learn about agriculture because the day our husbands can't work, what will we do if we don't know how to farm? We won't be able to take care of ourselves, and that is important. —*Dominga Morales, Guatemala*

WHEN I WAS SINGLE I NEVER participated in women's groups. When I became a widow I had a need to be in a group. Through the group we started a chicken farm and with this we were able to maintain ourselves. After that we did weaving as a group of widows. All of this gave me strength to go on, and I became secretary of our group. I have continued working up until now. I think it is important to meet, not only for men, but for women too, because first of all, we have our children. I like to work and make more of myself in life. Forward, compañeras, don't flinch! This is our best we can give to them because if we just stay in the house we won't learn anything.   —*Maria Luisa Quilasay, Guatemala*

W E LIVE ON AN ISLAND where we have learned organic agriculture and have learned new customs and have traveled outside our homes with other women even though we used to just work in the house out of touch with everyone. We have learned to move forward with organic agriculture slowly but surely which is of great benefit to our children. We will leave the next generation new soil and new experiences and new techniques and new products. I invite all campesinos of the world to discover new techniques in order to overcome their difficulties. United, we can move forward.

As women we have learned to detach ourselves from our husbands' sexism because it limits us when we can't go to workshops and activities for women. In spite of my age, I have to keep learning, in the field and in the home. We women have to move forward for the good of our sons and daughters and not let ourselves be marginalized by our husbands.

    —*Cándida Espinoza, Nicaragua*

I N MICHOACÁN WE have had a great opportunity to integrate many women because in the eastern part of Michoacán women work the land more than men do. Sometimes the men have to emigrate to the city looking for money. Many men leave and many become alcoholics, which is another big problem there. Others have gone to the United States. So, women have integrated into the movement very well. We have nineteen mixed groups where men and women work together one day a week. There is strength in organization and the work in soil conservation has advanced a lot. Today, without exaggerating I can say we have more than 60,000 meters of contour ditches. That's sixty kilometers . . . that's not easy!   —*Gabriel Sánchez, Mexico*

W E REALIZED AT ONE POINT that when we were preparing our proposals to work with alternatives for women, in reality what we were doing was giving them extra work. So the group thought about this again and how we divide work. That is called work equity, right? So we have been working the last couple of years in this way: how to visualize sustainable agriculture from a perspective of gender, looking for equity and not just providing activities that load up one of the partners with a lot of work. It has been a learning process.   —*Rogelio Sánchez, Mexico*

Globalization:
The Struggle for Survival and the Struggle for Land

A monster is bearing down on us. A big problem is coming called globaliza-
tion and GMOs. We have to face it down.   —Gabriel Sánchez, Mexico

The Mexican case is illustrative of how globalization has affected farm communities around the world. Mexicans began to see the effects of globalization in the 1980s when, because of the combination of falling oil prices and
rising interest rates, the nation could not pay its $57 billion foreign debt.
Mexico appealed to the International Monetary Fund (IMF) for short-term
financing to meet its payments. The IMF conditioned the loan on changes
in the country's economic policies. The World Bank also stepped in with
funds and technical assistance, also conditioned on the following structural
adjustments to the Mexican economy:

- Privatization: Mexico sold its state-owned telephone company, its
  state banks, its rail system, and part of its transport industry.

HAS STRUCTURAL ADJUSTMENT WORKED?

For the transnational corporations and the *maquiladoras* (sweat shops),
structural adjustment has been quite lucrative. However, for the majority of Mexicans, it has been a disaster. Average income has dropped by
12 percent. Real salaries are at half of what they were 1980. Twenty
thousand Mexican businesses have gone bankrupt. The national debt
grew to nearly 100 billion dollars. In Mexico today, 40 million people
earn less than 50 pesos (5 dollars) a day. The extreme poor (those who
make less than 20 pesos a day) grew by 4 million people; they now make
up half the population.

Basic grains, the mainstay of campesino agriculture, were hit severely. Maize prices dropped by 45 percent. This was due to foreign maize,
whose imports grew twelvefold. Of course, while the United States
maintained its subsidies to basic grain production, Mexico did not.
With no tariffs at the Mexican border, this subsidized maize entered
Mexico at half the price of Mexican maize—far below its costs of production. Transnational corporations (like Cargill) make huge profits
exporting North American maize. Along the way, they broke Mexican
producers who had no support from their government. In Mexico,
the birthplace of maize, over 25 percent of the maize consumed is now
foreign.

- Deregulation: The state relaxed all of its tariffs protecting national products and allowed 100 percent foreign ownership of national industries.
- Fiscal austerity: The state reduced social services, especially in agriculture.
- Devaluation: The Mexican peso was devalued in order to make Mexican products cheaper to buy in international markers (in order to garner dollars).

These structural adjustments were ostensibly designed to eliminate the foreign debt and open the way for Mexican capitalist development. Recognizing the great sacrifices this strategy would mean for the Mexican people (and anxious to avert social upheaval), the World Bank insisted that the Mexican president, Carlos Salinas de Gortari, implement a series of social agreements, collectively called El Pacto, to persuade the Mexican people to accept the measures.

In 1994 the United States, Canada, and Mexico signed the North American Free Trade Alliance, or NAFTA. NAFTA effectively placed these austerity-free trade reforms beyond the reach of public influence by writing them into international treaty.

In their drive to privatize all state-owned enterprises, the Salinas government managed to change Article 27 of the Mexican Constitution, effectively privatizing the ejido. Since the land reform of the Mexican Revolution at the turn of the last century, the ejido has been the backbone of cultural, economic, and community life in the Mexican countryside. Ejido land could be passed on from parent to child, but could not be sold. The privatization of the ejido has ushered in profound changes to the countryside.

THE STRUGGLE FOR LAND

THEY BROUGHT US "agrarian reform." In 1992 the reform to Article 27 of the Constitution that protected us as campesinos was changed to open a space for a few mercantilist brutes that became owners of half of the ejidos of our community.

From my point of view this is very grave. The land in Mexico used to belong to the hacienda owners. There was a revolution, blood was spilt; there was a violent struggle so that land would belong to those who worked it and not the *patrón*. Today this is in danger because the ejido land and the communal land are concentrating in private hands, even in the hands of people who are not even Mexican. There are absentee landlords in which the authentic owner is a foreigner. On the other hand, the land that used to belong to the haciendas will now return to big business and even go to transnationals. This places our entire patrimony at risk. This is one of our main worries.

The campesino who has a piece of land must take care of it at all costs. The campesino who loses his land will fall into slavery. This is happening in various parts of the country. His farm now belongs to someone else. Now the campesino is an employee of the guava, avocado, or coffee plantation. This is serious because now one depends on the patrón who says, "work or you don't eat." This is a delicate matter. Many campesinos have not thought about this movement and the Mexican Revolution and the struggle for the land, and it is shameful. President Salinas de Gortari sneakily reversed all of this without spilling a drop of blood. Sure, he has *his* land title and can do what *he* wants. He breaks a culture, breaks an organization like the ejido. Now the local ejido commissioner has lost all power on communal land because they took it away. Today I can sell my ejido without taking into consideration the ejidal assembly or the ejidal authority. I can do it automatically with a notary public. So, all of the organization for cooperating, the communal work days, the meetings to decide things, and community development is lost. This is serious. We need to stay sharp because our patrimony will end up in someone else's hands.

Before, the ejido worked more efficiently, and was more organized. There were opportunities to do *faenas*[2] and more community work. After the changes in Article 27 of the Mexican Constitution, the ejidos start to break up. It got to the point that many people are leaving the ejidos because the sale of two or three hectares is good money.

Of all the things that hurt the countryside, in all the communities that we know, and with our own flesh and blood, is the loss of identity. Today we see our relatives going to the United States. Why? Because they think they can live better there with the dollars they make to maintain their families. But this is all because of the low prices we get for our products that we harvest each year. This is why we are losing our identity in our communities. Sometimes our children don't even like being called "campesinos" because they have lost their identity.

What is the concentration of land about? Since most of the things we produce each year are of little market value, one thinks, "The land is unproductive." One sells the land and it ends up in the hands of a few who have money. The Agrarian Law used to protect us as campesinos. Now it gives us the "right" to sell ejido land. It is happening in our state. In 2000 the statistics from the state indicated that from 1994 to 2000, 13 percent of the land sales in the state were from the campesino sector. I think that now it is much more and this is very dangerous for us as campesinos because look at what will happen: We will depend on other countries for our food. This is the result of globalization and unfair competition. We campesinos with one or two hectares and no proper machinery can't compete with the great First World powers like Canada and the United States. We are at a disadvantage because those farmers have support. Globalization makes us poorer.   —*Gabriel Sánchez, Mexico*

W E FEEL THE EFFECTS of migration in all of our communities. I remember that up until the 1990s, no one in my town went to the United States, not the adults, and never the young people. The young stayed in the community helping their families to produce our food. But after the nineties, 8 percent of the people go to the United States. Most of them are young, seventeen years old or so and they send money to support the home. Really, it is sad because that is where the disintegration of the family begins. Some of the young get lost there in drugs and vices. Some have lost their lives crossing the border. There is a town next to mine called San Simeon where 25 percent of the people have gone to the United States. That is a high percentage.

Unemployment is when instead of working our farm, instead of being productive in our community, we no longer have the opportunity. The government used to help out with small business and productive projects. Today, neither the state nor the federal government does . . . this is what globalization has brought.

We feel the transnational corporations establishing themselves in strategic areas. In our region, in the industrial corridors, these transnationals take in the young, those who have a bit of training, but then they exploit them with twelve-hour days and pay them a pittance. That is why these jobs don't lead to any development in the country.

We all know that globalization rode in on our country's debt. We talk of 100,000 million dollars. Because our politicians have no political will, I think we will continue suffering these crises. Globalization brings us death. In 1994 I remember that while the government was signing the North American Free Trade Agreement (NAFTA), a guerrilla fighter here in Mexico [sub-Comandante Marcos of the EZLN] said, "what they are doing now is digging the grave of the campesinos." We let this statement go by unnoticed, but now we realize that what he said was true.

—*Pánfilo Hernández, Mexico*

T HE TECHNOLOGICAL PACKAGES also are a part of globalization. Who makes them? The transnationals! They are everywhere: Monsanto, Bayer, Novartis. . . . The products of these transnationals have hurt, not helped the Mexican countryside. At first we didn't have good information and we adopted the technological packages. Today, instead of benefiting from them, our lands and our families have been ruined. We have become totally dependent. *—Gabriel Sánchez, Mexico*

T HE FACT IS we are immersed in globalization. The problem is that we do not realize the ways it affects us. We don't understand these effects, right? We have to start getting the information out to the groups and the communities. We need to do this the same way we worked with gender issues . . . integrate themes on globalization, or reflections that make us realize, yes, this is what we are facing. We probably imagine it in other countries far away, with rich people. No, that is a lie. Globalization definitely is hurting the people in the countryside the most. We have to integrate the topic of globalization into our movement without wasting any more time. We have to start doing things now that lead us to reflect and understand what is happening with globalization.

—Alicia Sarmientos, Mexico

THE SUICIDE OF THE KOREAN FARMER IN CANCÚN

In September of 2003, thousands of peasants from Mexico joined protesters from around the world to demonstrate at the WTO meeting held in Cancún, Mexico. At one point in the protests, Lee Kyung Hae, a Korean farm leader, climbed to the top of the fence separating protesters from the WTO officials meeting inside. As thousands looked on, he plunged a knife into his own heart to protest the unaccountable decisions taken by the WTO that destroy farmers' livelihoods. The action had a profound impact on farmers around the world.

Personally, I was deeply moved by this news and I feel that, yes, as a leader, it was a form of making a statement. I feel he could have done more things while alive to push this statement. Because, yes, it hit hard to see how he stuck a knife to his own heart. I began to think, these bastards that are in the WTO meeting aren't even bothered, their consciences were not even moved by this. It was impressive to see the scenes that they showed on television of how he climbed the fence, how he held on and plunged the knife deep in his own heart. That is why it would have been important for him to stop and think that he could have done so many more things by living than by dying because those bastards weren't even going to take him into consideration. Of course we campesinos were deeply moved. I was moved. My God! What courage! And what is sad is those S.O.B.s inside— where are they pushing us? To death! *—Gabriel Sánchez, Mexico*

To confront globalization we have to have equitable exchanges, engage in barter, and we need contacts, not just at the local level, but nationally and internationally. In Michoacán they produce a lot of avocado that gets sold cheaply. I think it is the same here. In Tlaxcala we produce a lot of corn and they buy it at one peso-fifty. There, the *cuartilla* (approximately a half-gallon) of wheat is around four pesos, while here, when we get a good price it is only ninety centavos [100 centavos to the peso]. The exchange would be something that would help us campesinos stand up to the globalization that is experienced by even the poorest families.

—*Gabriel Sánchez*

If these "free market" policies continue I think the future is bleak. The so-called free market is dangerous for the small producer because we get eaten by the big ones. The large companies can cut international deals directly. We are forced to associate ourselves with them and then they exploit us. The poor will never stop being poor this way because the rich get rich on our work.   —*Orlando Martínez, Nicaragua*

GENETICALLY MODIFIED CROPS

The state-sponsored demise of Mexican agriculture under NAFTA has opened the way for genetically modified organisms—GMOs. Genetic contamination of Mexican maize varieties by GMOs from the North was documented by Mexican and U.S. researchers even before the Mexican congress authorized its legal entry in 2003. The invasion of GMOs is part of globalization and allows giant corporations like Syngenta and Monsanto to colonize Mexican agriculture by genetically controlling not only seed production but fertilizer, pesticide, and herbicide application. Farmers, already run over by the Green Revolution, are now bracing themselves for the onslaught of the "gene revolution."

What can we do in our daily life against GMOs? First of all, we have to understand the topic, because we know it only superficially. Then, we have to study it well and share our knowledge with the farmers of other places where we are working. We have to share knowledge through workshops, videos, different forms of communication. In one of the communities where we work there are seven farmers who grow only local species, local varieties. Everyone else is planting hybrids, nothing else. This is a problem we have here too, but no one notices. So we have to work on GMOs because little by little they will start invading us.

The other thing is, don't eat food products with GMOs in them. This is a bit difficult because, how are we to know? Another thing is to detect possible plantings of GMOs. The other is to find the tortilla factories that are using GMO corn and try to establish contracts to supply them with only local varieties of corn. What is happening? Are we losing the culture of the tortilla? Trucks pull up in the most remote of communities and sell their tortillas of GMO corn. They introduce this corn because many people work and don't have the time to make tortillas. This affects us economically as well. Right now the tortillas cost six pesos a kilo. Many times a family has to buy up to five kilos a day when with ten pesos they could make fifteen kilos, well made with local corn.

The role of women is going to be very important . . . in the case of the defense of our native maize seeds. I am certain that women are going to defend local seed better than our own compañeros. Why? Because we live with the seed daily. There is a case in which they tried to bring in hybrids to a farm. They planted and harvested, but the woman told her husband, "You know what? Next year I won't accept this corn because it is of bad quality. It is too light, its taste is insipid, it's difficult to cook, and above all, the tortillas are hard to make." And he lost interest in planting the hybrid. Not even the animals would eat the stalks! Who is he growing it for and why? In that community they don't plant hybrid corn. I feel that if we go out to the communities with the other women we are going to reinforce the Campesino a Campesino movement, above all in defense of our local corn. We have an important role to play as women because these are strong arguments.   —*Alicia Sarmientos, Mexico*

WE MUST TRY TO raise consciousness in our local congresses . . . try to make politicians aware so they will prohibit the entry of GMO seeds. Some have already come in. What can we do to get rid of them? We will see. We have to organize. We have to find mechanisms to eliminate these seeds and enact a law that protects our local and regional seeds.
—*Manuel Moran Madrid, Mexico*

I THINK THAT WE can do something at the municipal level, but let's not forget that we need to start with our base—with the communities of our municipality—because if we start there, then we have the support of the campesinos. If we can pull together a group of campesinos in each community then we can go to the municipal councils and lay out the issue. The municipalities are autonomous. They can also do things. I thing we have to work from the bottom up. Because if we think that those on top are going to solve this mess—for example the Congress—they aren't! They aren't even interested. The struggle has to be at the base, in the Campesino a Campesino base and in the communities. That is where we have to start: from the communities to the municipality, to the state congress and from there up. If we are not well organized at the base, they are going to knock us down easily. But if we are well grouped, this will give the building a good foundation that will be difficult for them to knock us down. We must begin and defend this struggle. Our beautiful local varieties given to us by our ancestors have to be defended at all costs! Because if we don't defend this, then we will become dependent on a new variety each year that we will have to buy continually and this will bring us consequences like soil contamination, water contamination, and the contamination of our health.   —*Gabriel Sánchez, Mexico*

LOCAL VARIETIES

There is a sense among many campesinos that their last line of cultural defense is the seed. The Green Revolution brought monoculture and the predominance of hybrids to the Mesoamerican countryside. While many local varieties dropped from sight, many were conserved by campesinos because they preferred them in their own diet. Today they are the bulwark for agrobiodiversity in the face of the Gene Revolution. The specter of both genetic colonization and genetic contamination of farmers' age-old, traditional varieties by giant seed companies has led many campesinos to a renewed awareness of the importance of in situ seed conservation.

THE BIG PROBLEM is the technological package—the seed, the fertilizer, everything comes in a package for us to plant. . . . All because they want to do away with our native seeds. Where is our native tomato? They want to do the same with our corn, and the beans. They want to kill off all our native seeds! And they give us these technological packages. We have to regenerate our own agriculture and maintain our own seed.
                —*Felipe Tomás, Guatemala*

WE HAVE TO BE careful how we campesinos organize and register our local seeds so that no one else takes them, because others will come and if our seeds ore not registered, they will register them as theirs. We have to make sure they are ours, otherwise we run great risks.
                —*Alicia Sarmientos*

THERE SHOULD BE a way that is not so complicated for the farmer. They must protect their seed, but without complications. The register should belong to the producer. This is their seed. Let the farmer say, I have brought my seed and this is my yield and registration. This is one way. If we don't find a way, some seed company will take our native corn. We are working with three varieties. One is for forage, but we are looking for added value. Another is called Monte Alto. Another is darkish and shiny.

JORGE IRAN VASQUEZ, TECHNICIAN, PCAC-UNAG, NICARAGUA

There is a world of things that we can work with, but we have to prioritize. Seeds, for example, are something that leads to other things. We are holding forums for reflection on biodiversity and seeds are part of this. We developed principles based on the biodiversity of the seed. We did a study on local varieties of maize and beans and identified an enormous quantity—120 varieties of maize and 230 of beans! We found communities where people have been cultivating maize varieties for generations. People save them because the seeds are resistant. The people call them *quita-hambre* [hunger-ending] seeds. With the study, producers discovered a lot of seeds they didn't know existed, and now we have a campesino-run program for the recovery and improvement of these varieties. They share experiences and knowledge about planting, storage, and improvement at Campesino a Campesino exchanges and gatherings. Groups come together, like the women's group, that process different foods and are looking for new local varieties to prepare in preserves. They carried out a survey on wild food varieties in their area in order to propagate them.

We are trying to register its characteristics because it has potential for the farmers to give it added value. No, we can't just say that the price of corn is low . . . we have to give it added value. If we don't give it added value, the product can disappear.   —*Panfilo Hernández, Mexico*

THERE HAVE BEEN some interesting developments. Three years ago the NGOs in this area came together to coordinate a recovery effort of native seeds. Since then the NGOs have continued working, each on their own. A municipal fund for seed recovery was created of 12,000 pesos a year. The fund did not gain interest; it was used for buying seeds and distributing them in the communities with the commitment that each farmer that received seed had to give seed as well. There was no money involved. One could buy or one could give the producer a letter of credit in which they promised to give a kilo and a half for each kilo received.

—*Roberto Vega, Mexico*

Agricultural and Agrarian Policies

We are talking about the campesinado and the poor families of Nicaragua. We are talking about los de abajo [those on the bottom]. . . . There are no policies for us. They displace us. In the countryside, one grows up poor and is always migrating. I think that we just don't have the capacity at the local level to break with the injustice of these rules of the game. Campesinos can't compete with other producers like this. Even rich farmers in this country have stopped producing food because it is not profitable. So it is difficult for us to break with poverty because we are held down by a lack of policies from a government that won't help us.
—Nicaraguan campesina

Campesino a Campesino has focused on developing and sharing knowledge about sustainable agriculture rather than changing the policies that discourage sustainable agriculture. This is, in part, because the Movement has relied on NGOs for institutional support. NGOs are primarily institutional vehicles for implementing projects. Very rarely do they engage in dialogue to influence agricultural policies For the most part, these NGOs have been barred by law from political activity, such as lobbying, and concentrate their efforts on the technical and social, but not the political, aspects of agricultural improvement. The more influential farmer organizations, for their part, have tended to lobby for policies to benefit conventional agriculture, e.g., cheaper fuel and chemical inputs, better prices for export crops, etc. So while sustainable agriculture has found acceptance among the campesino sector on the ground, this is not supported by national policies that would promote it structurally. (The widespread adoption of Green Revolution techniques, for example, was supported by extensive public research, government banking, and state extension services.) Sustainable agriculture is faced with a "policy ceiling." Farmers in the Movement can get the techniques in the field right, but the larger economic context still works against them. Influencing agricultural development policies is a new challenge for MCAC.

How can we influence the agencies that determine our development policies? We are knocking on doors we never knocked on before when we were just working at the local level. We have to move into those policy spaces because otherwise they promote the opposite of everything we are doing. In this sense we have to move forward. As a movement we are still weak. We don't have the strength to stop the onslaught of conventional development. This is still very strong, and our Movement is just getting started.   *—Rogelio Sánchez, Mexico*

CLASS INTERESTS?

"What interest do you have in our class? You are a millionaire. Who knows how many warehouses of fertilizer you have so you can keep on poisoning the people? We organic farmers are saving people, but you are a big sinner. . . . Your visit here is useless. I am sure that if you were among those of your own class they would be clapping for you right now, but not us. We have come to share the truth about our experience. Who knows how many people you have poisoned with your chemicals? How many supply stores do you have to keep on poisoning our people? What interest do you have in our class?"

—Orlando Martínez, Nicaraguan promoter, arguing with the vice minister of agriculture regarding the viability of organic agriculture

WORK AT THE MUNICIPAL LEVEL

IN CAMPESINO A CAMPESINO we have the opportunity to interact as a group, to talk about what is happening in the community, of the government programs, of what is happening at all levels, even internationally. We have had the opportunity to work with the municipal councils. In the beginning they ignored us, but now they have seen our work and the value of the groups, at the municipal level, at the state level, and at the federal level. I think the question still is, "How do we bring together political will with social will?"   *—Gabriel Sánchez, Mexico*

FROM 1988 THROUGH THE 1990S the Grupo Vicente Guerrero had the opportunity to go to the presidency of the municipality of Españita and start a program called "Españita Clean and Green." The state of Tlaxcala appropriated it—they just changed it to "Green and Clean." When there is a local vision for development with a focus on sustainable management of resources, one can get something done.

—Rogelio Sánchez, Mexico

PARTY POLITICS

DIFFERENT POLITICAL parties divide the community too much. It affects our work. The problem is that they have grown. There are more parties each day and daily the people are more divided. This leads to paternalism and individualism, or "you give something and I'll support you." This has had a strongly negative impact on our work.

—Alicia Sarmientos, Mexico

A POLITICAL PARTY CAN offer a lot of things . . . but you will never hear them talk of agriculture. That's the truth! I myself have questioned the political party that I support. The candidate is my friend and everything, and I said, "Look, why don't you guys have a government plan for agriculture? Why don't you really try to reach the farmers?" In San Martín there are 19,000 farmers. Do you think there is a program for them? Nothing! Where are we going to get our food? All they talk about is new roads, or a bridge they want to build, or the gravel they will send. . . . We can't eat dirt! What we are doing in Campesino a Campesino is an important step toward our sustainability.   —*Lázaro Aguín, Guatemala*

THE FUTURE OF THE MOVEMENT

THERE IS A LOSS of confidence in country people. Dignity. People have no support for their dignity. They have been lied to so many times by the organizations and by government institutions.

I think one of the biggest problems we have confronted in the past years has been the neoliberal models of development that only see the economic aspect of things. They are really screwing us over because the transnationals are organized, but to make the population more dependent on them, right? Our government allows it to happen, which is tragic. Our system of agricultural extension serves the interests of the transnationals, they do not respond to the interests of the people.

Another thing that the conventional agriculture system does is to educate everyone in urban thinking, not thinking for rural life. This is a difficult situation because our children, our young people, with this education start getting the idea that they are going to live the same as city people. We have had exchanges with academics and we tell them, "Look at how many technicians are trained each year that come out of the universities. What do they do? They leave for the fields with a backpack sprayer and promote the transnationals' toxic agrochemicals." The transnationals are trying to control humanity, turn us into their slaves—take our culture. Whoever loses their culture loses their identity and becomes dependent. They get in from all sides, through the media, through the educational system, through consumerism. This is the great challenge of the Campesino a Campesino movement. It has not been easy. We are isolated in small groups and we have not found the way to articulate our efforts. We are vulnerable.

We have lived this in the flesh. We have a strong proposal for sustainability and we are in a struggle with the state. We have managed to stop a number of government development projects, but at a price. The price was that we lost the spaces for communication that we had gained. Many of the members of our group went to these spaces and shared their experiences with others. In this sense the Movement has been repressed because the system looks for ways to mess with it and with the groups in Tlaxcala. We have had this bitter experience. We are going along well, but the system looks for our vulnerable points and it is quite cruel. This has given us a lesson to reflect upon . . . we have to strengthen ourselves at the local level and regionally, in order to open up this struggle directly and not be so vulnerable in these aspects. These are lessons learned and they mature us and we improve our proposals and look for spaces for articulation with other movements. This does not discourage us. On the contrary, it motivates us to move forward.

I hope this book we are writing helps people in the Movement reflect on what we have done, and the work we are doing. We have a chance to show the world the value of what we share as human beings and the great possibilities. It is a tool. I hope that it motivates people to keep working in the Movement. I hope more compañeros and compañeras join so that they don't feel like they are all alone.

The Movement is getting stronger. It is a slow process, but I see it with a lot of hope. Daily a great phenomenon affects humanity, and the Movement gets stronger. The work is not easy, but neither is it impossible.

The Movement is a perfect space for us to interface with other campesinos. It can propose alternatives in the face of globalization, migration, and GMOs. There is a lot of accumulated experience that is spread all over. In this sense I have a lot of hope for the Movement. It will always have some alternative, some tool to confront these great challenges that we face.
                                        —*Rogelio Sánchez, Mexico*

FIVE

The Political Economy of Campesino a Campesino

Many people need to learn. It will take a lot of resources to reach all of the campesinos. We can see these resources are controlled. Not everyone can access the resources needed to spread these great truths. For these things, there are always limitations. . . . Resources are always denied for the good things. The economic need to reach these great things is great. What is worthwhile is always dear. Those who control these resources should support us. This is what has been missing: the political will of government, of those that have capital, and those that manipulate our people. That is the difficulty. There is no support for this. This is the life experience I have after seventy-seven years of existence on this planet.

—*José Jesús Mendoza, Santa Lucía, Nicaragua*

THIS CHAPTER FOCUSES on the context that gave rise to the Movimiento Campesino a Campesino (MCAC).[1] It explores agriculture's special function in the development strategies implemented in Mesoamerica from 1960 through the 1990s. By describing the pivotal role played by the campesinado in generating the region's wealth, the chapter also shows how the special character of peasant agriculture led to alternative approaches to agricultural development. The aim is to understand why and how sustainable agricultural and rural development (SARD) strategies appeared in the region and to appreciate the challenges campesinos face when they diverge from mainstream development paradigms. The conceptual and historical foundations laid out in this chapter will help the reader assess MCAC's contribution and potential as a movement to resist the economic and environmental crises that plague the Mesoamerican countryside.

The Agrarian Question

Political economists refer to "the difference that agriculture's difference makes" as the *agrarian question*. Originally, the classic agrarian question was concerned with how wealth from the countryside could be used to build up industry and shift society from rural to urban. During the Industrial Revolution, economists assumed that the traditional, land-based peasantry would disappear as more efficient, industrialized farms took over production. The bulk of the peasantry would either become urban industrial workers or farm laborers in agroindustry. Political economists referred to this as the "differentiation" of the peasantry. In capitalist societies, privately owned agribusinesses were expected to take over agriculture, while in socialist countries the state was to own the means of production. These industrial models of development both depended on the cheap food produced by smallholders to keep industrial workers' salaries low. As large-scale agribusinesses were established, both models strove to displace smallholders in order to access their cheap labor.

The differentiation thesis was called into question after the middle peasantry (smallholders who could employ a few workers and engage in limited or "small commodity" production) did not disappear with the introduction of agribusiness. Theoreticians explained this persistence by noting that smallholders were willing to "exploit" themselves by working below the prevailing minimum wage in order to stay competitive in the market. Further, while differentiation did take place, it was not permanent. Peasant farms based on family labor did lose members to industry when the extended family outgrew their land base. However, some families always stayed in farming and reproduced the peasant mode of production.

The socioeconomic shifts from rural- to urban-based production and from traditional to industrialized forms of agriculture was called the *agrarian transition*. The agrarian transition and peasant resistance to this transition are both part of the agrarian question.[2]

Much later, in the wake of the worldwide economic crisis of the 1970s, a new agrarian question surfaced within the advanced industrial countries. Agriculture appeared to present peculiar obstacles for capitalist development. Models of industrial development had suggested that all production would become increasingly deskilled, compartmentalized, and homogenized. Farms would resemble factories. But even under state policies designed to favor agribusiness over small commodity production, smallholders resisted industrial homogenization, even in the most advanced industrial countries. Why?

For one thing, while agribusiness must make a return on capital investments, smallholders are primarily looking to secure livelihoods. Being both owners and workers, smallholders *are* often willing to work at rates below the prevailing minimum wage, thus providing them with a competitive advantage against agribusiness, which must pay the full cost for labor. (This helps explain why agricultural labor on industrialized farms is typically dependent on poorly paid undocumented workers.)

Further, not all land is good for the production of all crops, and investment capital, once tied up in land, can't easily pull up the farm-factory and move it to a better location. If the market drops on their product, rice farmers with clay soils can't just move to a sandier location and start planting peanuts. The ecological, biological, and climatic variability inherent in farming also discourages capitalists by presenting them with risks they would rather not assume.

Finally, investors of capital do not like the return time on agricultural investments. This reflects a critical *disjuncture* between labor time and production time. While an investment in a shoe factory, for example, yields shoes on a daily basis, farmers must wait months after planting to harvest and sell their crops, all the while investing in labor, inputs, and machinery. This delay ties up capital that could have generated returns if invested elsewhere. Coupled with the possibility of crop or market failures, farming presents a dubious direct investment opportunity (Mann and Dickenson 1978; Goodman, Sorj, and Wilkinson 1987; Mann 1990). Under these conditions, it is safer to loan money to farmers than to invest directly in farming itself.

Governments use national farm policies made up of different incentives and safeguards, like crop insurance, guaranteed prices, target prices, and subsidies, to help capital intensive, industrialized agriculture deal with all the risks and limitations inherent in farming. Of course, banks, agri-industry, and the agrifoods complex also profit enormously from the farm sector *indirectly* by loaning money, selling inputs, buying and selling farm products, and otherwise making farmers, the farm workers, or the consumers bear agriculture's delays, costs, and risks.

However, some of these same risky, adverse conditions actually provide special opportunities for smallholder production, resulting in many different "farming styles" (van der Ploeg 1986). Smallholders tend to be more versatile and flexible, managing soils and microclimates to plant a variety of crops. Working in the niches and around the margins of large-scale capitalist production, smallholders carefully craft their production strategies to combine the comparative advantage of family labor and their site-specific knowledge of soils and climate with smaller, flexible technologies and investment strategies. Local agroecological knowledge and the ability to know when and how to apply a wide range of farming skills are capabilities generally learned over lifetimes on the farm itself. This makes smallholders unlikely candidates for the kind of deskilling of labor that accompanies industrial farming.

In the Third World, the rural poor also avail themselves of a mixture of agriculturally based subsistence *and* market strategies in order to survive the disruptions of differentiation and development. When market conditions are favorable, smallholders will produce more for the market. When they are not, these farmers survive by producing for their own consumption.

Today's agrarian questions also focus on the social, economic, and environmental sustainability of agriculture and of rural societies in which smallholders continue to play an important role. Smallholders tend to rely more directly on environmental resources as part of their production and livelihood strategies than do larger, capitalized production units, making their stake in environmental sustainability greater. Because industrialization has failed to provide enough gainful employment to solve the problems of poverty in the Third World, by eliminating many small holdings, industrial agriculture has ended up exacerbating rather than solving the problem of poverty in the countryside. But undercapitalized smallholdings are not just a symptom of this failure, they are an indication of an opportunity for productive employment and a more equitable distribution of wealth in the countryside.

Indeed, the stubborn "persistence of the peasantry" (Edelman 2000) coupled with the rural environmental crises and the failure of agricultural development strategies to meet the needs of the rural poor in the Third World has led many theorists to question conventional assumptions regarding agricultural development. So, what difference can the peasantry's difference make—not in spite of, but *because* of the sector's size, resiliency, and relationship to the environment? In other words, what special potentials do smallholders have for developing equitable, environmentally sustainable ways of producing food and distributing wealth? This chapter explores this question.

Development in Latin America

Both modern industry and modern agriculture in Latin American developed in the shadow of the United States' economic expansion. The ideology of progress was used to push Latin America's entrenched agrarian societies into the northern economic orbit. The political project behind this notion of progress was supported by theories of modernization.

Modernization theory rose to prominence during the Cold War and was based on the assumption that the Third World would follow the First World's path of economic growth and industrialization. This idea came from the experience in postwar Europe in which the United States, in exchange for market access and military bases, loaned money for European reconstruction through the Marshall Plan.[3] The Marshall Plan was very successful in terms of European reconstruction and securing U.S. political-economic dominance post-WWII. This later led policy makers to apply the same strategy to the Third World, where they claimed that "development" would pull these nations out of their postcolonial backwardness, into the capitalist economy, and away from the socialist influence of the Soviet Union. The problem of underdevelopment was framed as a lack of technology, know-how, investment, and entrepreneurial culture. Rostow's *The Stages of Economic Growth: A Non-Communist Manifesto* was the recipe used by development planners (Rostow 1960). The IMF and the International Bank for Reconstruction and Development (World Bank), originally designed to create a fluid and stable trading environment for the reconstruction of Western Europe, were recruited to develop northern capitalism in the Third World (Preston 1996; Rapley 1996).

Latin American economists, however, were skeptical of the First World's economic growth theories. They saw development policies such as the Truman Doctrine (1947) and later John F. Kennedy's Alliance for Progress (1964) as powerful political tools supporting U.S. intervention in weaker economies. For them, underdevelopment was not simply a lack of investment and technological know-how, it was the result of a world divided into powerful *core* economies that produced expensive industrial goods and subordinate *peripheral* economies that supplied them with cheap raw materials. Industrial goods always became progressively dearer in relation to raw materials, forcing primary exporters to export more and more in order to pay for the same industrial imports. And while these nations were encouraged to industrialize, they bought outdated technology from the industrialized countries, so they found it difficult to compete. In this view, underdevelopment and development were actually two sides of the same coin. Poor countries in the Third World could never become rich countries by following in the First World's footsteps because they would always be several steps behind. This was the core of "dependency theory (Furtado 1964; Frank 1967). To achieve greater economic autonomy for peripheral states, they proposed breaking out of the cycle of dependency on the industrialized countries by substituting foreign industrial imports with domestically produced goods. This development strategy was called ISI, Import Substitution Industrialization (Prebisch 1950; Rapley 1996).

In order to build the industrial plants, factories, and infrastructure to develop their productive potential, Third World countries borrowed heavily. During the 1970s, northern banks awash with petrodollars were eager to put their money to work. They were happy to lend money and did so on very easy terms.

Modernization and dependency theory were really both modernist development theories. Both theories rely on the direct intervention of governments and expert-led, top-down management for economic development. Under both of these projects, agriculture was to mobilize a significant social and economic surplus from the countryside to the cities for urban industrial growth. This collection of related theory and development practices, which operated within Latin America throughout the 1960s and into the 1980s, is referred to as the "classic development paradigm" (Blaikie 2000). It is also often called "mainstream" development or "development with a big D." Big D development (hereafter "Development") not only refers to the development of industry, it is the "industry of development," in which large national and international institutions—usually from the global North—staffed by highly paid professionals, implement development programs to influence the socioeconomic and political outcomes of countries in the global South.

AGRICULTURE: THE KEYSTONE OF DEVELOPMENT

Under Development, the modernization of agriculture was equated with its intensive capitalization and large-scale mechanization. Since this was to replace small-scale, labor-intensive campesino agriculture, it required the eventual dissolution of the peasantry. Both modernization and dependency approaches accorded the peasantry an initial role in industry's appropriation of agricultural surplus. However, each thought that the continued presence of the peasantry created an obstacle to the agrarian transition and both explained the persistence of subsistence forms of production as part of the backwardness of underdevelopment. This backwardness was believed to be due either to stubborn peasant traditions and the self-exploitation of family labor or to the difficulty of modernizing agriculture in the global South in the face of northern industrial dominance. No one considered that perhaps modernized agriculture was inherently incapable of undercutting the competitive advantage of the small family labor farm (Goodman, Sorj, and Wilkinson 1987). No one in Development imagined that peasants just might know something about the efficient use of the land, labor, and capital actually existing in the countryside.

State-led development policies created a favorable financial and institutional climate for the Green Revolution, the blueprint for agricultural modernization (Jennings 1988). Led by Nobel Peace Prize–winning scientist Norman Borlaug and initially financed by the Rockefeller and Ford Foundations, the Green Revolution entailed the establishment of a massive research and extension system to develop and disseminate hybrid high-yielding varieties of grain (HYVs). The International Center for the Improvement of Maize and Wheat (CIMMYT) in Mexico was staffed by

First World scientists who developed the HYVs. These hybrids were then adapted to local conditions at national agricultural research stations and disseminated through national agricultural extension in collaboration with government credit programs. The HYVs' yields were dependent on "packages" of credit, fertilizers, pesticides, and timely irrigation. They favored the use of modern agricultural machinery. In Mexico, the Green Revolution raised agricultural productivity on large, mechanized farms with access to agricultural extension, irrigation, and the production credit needed to buy the technological packages.

Initially, the Green Revolution failed to incorporate poor and middle peasants. This tended to accentuate existing socioeconomic disparities in the countryside (Hewitt de Alcántara 1976; Jennings 1988; Pearse 1980). With the help of development institutions, governments implemented integrated rural development projects to address these social problems. In what became known as the "second" Green Revolution, smallholders were offered credit and agricultural extension in order to facilitate widespread adoption of commercial hybrids. It was assumed that early adopters would "make it" in modern agriculture. Nonadopters and late adopters would be forced out of production and into the labor market. Higher efficiencies would make basic grains cheap and bring down urban food prices for industrial expansion (i.e., the agrarian transition).

An unspoken objective of the Green Revolution was to avoid implementing agrarian reform. Rather than raise production through redistribution of land to smallholders, the Green Revolution favored raising production through technological intensification. By pushing the "surplus" peasantry out of agriculture, this concentrated agricultural land in fewer and fewer hands.

THE TRICKLE OF DEVELOPMENT

This strategy was especially successful in kick-starting industrial development and raising GNP in the larger economies of Latin America, leading development experts to talk of the Mexican and Brazilian "miracles." In fact, the 1960s and 1970s in Latin America were characterized by optimism and unprecedented economic growth. The World Bank produced the "World Development Report," which specifically celebrated Latin America's economic progress. But this optimism ignored the negative aspects of capital expansion. By selecting GNP as the sine qua non indicator for development, the World Bank's report masked the contradictions of economic growth without social redistribution and reinforced the idea that Development was simply a linear process of accumulation (Méndez-Quintana 2000).

In fact, even though some countries saw the emergence of a sizable mid-

IARCS, NARS, GOVERNMENT EXTENSION, AND NGOS

As actors in Development, IARCs (International Agricultural Research Centers), NARS (National Agricultural Research Systems), and NGOs (nongovernment organizations) share an institutional lineage. They all originated in the post-WWII institutional renaissance when global institutions were created to represent the interests of the allied powers in the expansion of Western capital and to manage the social, political, and economic tensions this expansion created. This arrangement resulted in the "institutional dualism" between the World Bank/IMF on the one hand and the United Nations on the other. From the beginning, and to this day, the World Bank and IMF, dominated by the United States, have aimed to broker economic growth in the Third World. The United Nations (pitifully funded in comparison) over time has provided a platform for voicing the diverse interests of the Third World in the Development project.

NGOs, the oldest institutional forms of development assistance, first came to prominence as humanitarian organizations during post-WWII reconstruction (e.g., CARE). Later, under the social-democratic umbrella of the United Nations and the initiative of the Development Decades, NGOs were invited to expand their mission from relief to development. For the economically and politically weak United Nations, the recruitment of NGOs was a way of bringing resources from the public sphere into Development, and of establishing welfare states in the Third World, thus strengthening social democracy (de Senarclens 1997).

The IARCs are also part of the institutional boom of the Development Decades, though they owe their existence to the capital-intensive, rather than the welfare wing of development. Jennings (1988) has documented the emergence of CIMMYT, the first Latin American IARC, the result of the Rockefeller Foundation's Mexican Agricultural Project (MAP). The MAP effectively replaced the decentralized Mexican research and extension system designed to develop agriculture within local *ejidos*, with a centralized model of research and development, dominated by foreign scientists and funded by multilateral sources. This was the institutional foundation of the Green Revolution, which, with key start-up funding from the World Bank, quickly metastasized into thirteen, then twenty-seven IARCs in the Third World, all organized within the CGIAR. The international centralization of agricultural research within the IARCs rested on the NARS, which both provided the IARCs with a steady stream of new genetic material and adapted the HYVs to local domains for their subsequent dissemination by government extension services. While CGIAR affirmed its central role in combating world hunger through HYVs, these technologies (generated with public funds) transferred huge economic benefits to private agribusiness in the developed countries. These benefits leveled off over time, leading to a decline in funding from industrialized countries to CGIAR and a financial crisis for the IARCs. The capital foundations of the IARCs became clear when, in 1994, the World Bank bailed out the CGIAR system with massive financial transfers accompanied by the appointment of a World Bank vice president as chairperson of CGIAR.

The political formations of the IARCs, NARS, and NGOs have blurred over time. NGOs and LDOs receive help from the United Nations, the World Bank and AID, as do the ministries of agriculture in the Third World. *The distinctiveness of these institutions resides in their relative positions within the structure of the Development project and in the ways in which each one accumulates and channels the social, political, and economic resources.* These differences help explain the changes in the relationships among IARCs, NARS, and NGOs over time, as the development project itself shifted from neo-Keynesian to neoliberal, to "post-Washington consensus" approaches. As the World Bank/IMF and the United Nations adapted their policies to the changing needs of capital expansion, IARCs, NARS, and NGOs sought out opportunities to consolidate their roles within the Development project. SARD was one of these opportunities. While the neoliberal shift in the Development project was to sound the death knell for NARS, it was also to breathe new life into the IARCs and led to another dramatic expansion of the number and the influence of NGOs.

dle class, poverty and socioeconomic disparity actually intensified. Development theorists responded to critics by claiming that the economic gains obtained by the wealthier classes would eventually "trickle down" to the poor. But the newly generated wealth raised social and economic expectations that were not forthcoming. The dispossession of the peasantry led to landlessness and migration to cities, where industry's inability to absorb surplus labor produced an explosion of city slums. The concentration (rather than the distribution) of Development's new wealth, coupled with extensive government involvement in state-owned industries, fuelled rampant corruption. Rather than progress, Development unleashed widespread political unrest. With the direct or tacit support of the United States, governments frequently exercised brutal political repression to deal with the waves of dissent brought on by Western "progress."

In the early 1970s, embarrassment over the failures of Development's trickle-down strategies prompted mitigation measures by the World Bank. The Bank instituted a "redistribution with growth" strategy, emphasizing the small-medium agricultural sector (Brohman 1996). For their part, Latin American theorists articulated the *basic needs approach* to development, later embraced by the International Labor Organization and the United Nations. To counter the macroeconomic bias of the "World Development Report," the UN produced a "Human Development Report." Rallying international support, the UN declared the 1960s, 1970s, and 1980s the "Development Decades" and advanced the idea of "global interdependence," in which the security and progress of the First World depended on the economic development of the Third World. Calls for a new international economic order (NIEO) and the transfer of resources to the poor to meet basic needs were the key concerns of global interdependence (Preston 1996). In an effort to bypass governments that were seen as corrupt or inefficient, the UN enjoined NGOs to participate in Development, thus opening the door to what later became an explosion of NGOs (Sollis 1995).

The basic-needs approach of the UN was a combination of grassroots activities and orthodox, top-down approaches to economic development. The approach shifted power away from Third World governments and toward development projects closely overseen by First World experts (Preston 1996). The World Bank also shifted its policies toward development projects because this allowed the Bank to claim it was eradicating poverty through targeted programs and took attention away from the more fundamental, structural changes it promoted through its macroeconomic policies in the Third World (Brohman 1996). Throughout this period, northern banks flush with petrodollars loaned lavishly to southern governments for development. The World Bank helped prepare the investment terrain, disbursing billions of dollars in public funds for massive infrastructure projects and bold colonization schemes.

Flaws in ISI, the oil price shocks in the 1970s, and the First World's economic recession sent the Third World into a severe economic crisis in the 1980s. Northern banks began to call in their loans from Third World countries. Unfortunately, debtor countries were asked to pay up precisely at the time their products had lost their value and their market share, sending the Global South into a profound economic crisis that resulted in negative economic growth and an unprecedented, and unpayable, foreign debt (Sonntag, et al. 2000).

Development through "expert intervention" proved incapable of solving the intractable problems plaguing the countries of Latin America. In fact, in many ways, Development actually contributed to poverty, political repression, and the perniciously skewed distribution of wealth. Development had failed "in terms of its own, stated objectives" (Blaikie 2000).

The failure of Development produced an impasse. Free market advocates blamed state-led development strategies for inefficiency and corruption. Others accused Development of elitism and questioned it from an environmental as well as a social perspective (Rapley 1996). Then the dismemberment of the Soviet Union removed Development's geopolitical raison d'être. If Development was not needed to keep the poor from becoming communists, was it even necessary? Joining in the disillusionment, postmodernist interpretations led to "postdevelopment" and "antidevelopment" critiques that called for an end to Development altogether (Esteva 1992; Esteva and Prakash 1998).

Neoliberal economics came to the fore in this period, signifying a dramatic reversal in strategy from planned, state-led change to spontaneous market order. This approach embraced the neoclassical economic model of a pure market system at the center of human development, with minimal interference from the state (Friedman 1968; Balassa 1971; Bauer 1981). Neoliberals focused on trade as the engine for growth and prescribed trade liberalization, privatization, currency devaluation, deregulation, and fiscal austerity. The new neoliberal development paradigm was soon enshrined in what became known as the "Washington Consensus," implemented through the structural adjustment policies applied in the 1980s to the Third World by the World Bank and the IMF. Under the guise of macroeconomic stability, the IMF and the World Bank forced Third World countries to open up their economies to foreign investment by making debt relief and foreign aid contingent upon the liberalization of markets, the deregulation of controls on international finance capital, the privatization of state-held industries and services, and the deregulation of labor (Pieterse 1998; Gore 2000).

THE CONTINUING DISASTER OF DEVELOPMENT: NEOLIBERALISM

In this way, the Third World debt (itself the result of three decades of Development) was used as a lever to force developing countries to accept these structural adjustment policies. When debtor countries faced default on their loans to First World banks, the World Bank and the IMF extended new loans, conditioned on structural adjustment, to keep national economies afloat and to keep First World banks happy.

The structural adjustment programs were a disaster for the peasantry. Trade liberalization opened the door to cheap, subsidized grain from the United States. Priced at less than it cost to produce, imported grain undercut grain grown by local farmers and destroyed regional markets. With the privatization of state-owned rural development banks, agricultural production credit for small producers disappeared. Under the new austerity measures, national agricultural research programs and basic services such as

agricultural extension were drastically reduced, and in some cases completely eliminated. The peasant sector, virtually ignored, was expected to
"get efficient or get out," with the tacit assumption that most would leave
agriculture, thus opening the doors to more lucrative profit-making ven-
tures in the countryside such as resource extraction, tourism, or sweatshops
to take advantage of cheap rural labor.

It took less than a decade for the failings of the neoliberal model to
become evident on the ground: rising unemployment, reductions in general welfare, declining manufacture, large private debt burdens, a balloon-
ing "informal sector" of semiemployed, massive emigration, environmental
damage, and the erosion of fragile democracies. Market-driven strategies
had not been able to lift the Third World out of poverty. This evidence, and
the destabilization of nation-states in the Third World, led to a reformula-
tion of the Washington Consensus and the reintroduction of limited policy
reform in multilateral lending and development aid, known alternately as
the *Post–Washington Consensus* or the *New Policy Agenda* (Fine 1999; Gore
2000).

The New Policy Agenda maintained that the problems did not lie in the
market but in corrupt and inefficient governments. In this view, privatization and the dismantling of the state, undertaken during the heyday of
structural adjustment, was not enough. States not only had to be mini-
mized, they also had to be reformed. The World Bank prescribed programs
for "good governance" as a solution (Boas and McNeill 2003).

The neoliberal strategy of market led development not only continued
to dominate the agenda of the IMF, the World Bank, and the Inter-
American Development Bank, it was championed by the powerful WTO
and became policy for Canada, the United States, and Mexico with the
signing in 1994 of NAFTA.

Alternative Approaches to Development

As state-led Development was being abandoned for free market Development, other economic theories of intergenerational equity and sustainability entered the development discourse. Ecological and environmental
economics incorporated cost-benefit analyses of environmental services and
"future discounting" (Pearce, Barbier, and Markandya 1990). The United
Nations introduced the concept of *sustainable human development*, with a
focus on justice and equity, basic needs, and notions of participation in the
development process by "stakeholders" (UNDP 1991).

A diverse array of development positions and approaches has since
appeared, both in response to the collateral damage resulting from neolib-
eralism and to the crisis of Development more generally. In the mainstream,

Development thinking splits between the performance-oriented Washington Consensus and the normatively oriented Sustainable Human Development approaches. The first is championed by the World Bank and IMF, the latter by the United Nations (Pieterse 1998).

The notion of sustainable agricultural development emerged from the ideological rubble of the fractured Development arena. Some hailed it as a bridge between World Bank and United Nations approaches. Others saw it as an alternative to both. Peasant farmers considered it on the merit of whether or not it would help them survive another decade of Development.

THE EMERGENCE OF SUSTAINABLE AGRICULTURAL DEVELOPMENT

Alternative agricultural development approaches first appeared in Mesoamerica in the late 1970s in response to the agroecological and socioeconomic failures of the Green Revolution's seed and fertilizer packages—the *paquete tecnológico*. The tendency for the Green Revolution to increase social differentiation in the countryside and the low adoption of the paquete tecnológico by peasant farmers led Mexico to introduce "integrated rural development projects," which provided production credit for the purchase of chemical inputs to peasant farmers, even those without irrigation or tractors (de Janvry 1981). This "second" Green Revolution, specifically designed to extend high-yielding varieties to smallholders, was implemented in similar forms in most of Mesoamerica. In terms of adoption, the second Green Revolution was remarkably successful in generalizing the use of hybrids, fertilizers, pesticides, and herbicides throughout the campesinado.

But capitalization and the shift to commercial monocultures put previously diverse subsistence systems at higher risk of failure. Timely access to credit and inputs was unreliable, and extension services were generally thin, resulting in a consistent "yield gap" between trials conducted on agricultural research centers and production in farmers' fields. Later, it became apparent that the external input packages actually masked soil degradation and provoked pest explosions, leading to the now familiar "pesticide treadmill." Yields dropped and environmental criticism began to surface. According to noted agroecologist Stephen Gliessman (1998a, 6), "[In] many areas where [Green Revolution] practices were instituted for growing grain . . . yields [leveled] off and . . . even decreased following the initial spectacular improvements in yield." In Central America, contrary to the conservationist claims of Green Revolution advocates, these changes in agronomic practices often provoked (or did nothing to prevent) deforestation and soil erosion, both major problems for smallholders who were often farming on hillsides.[4] Ecological degradation became a limiting factor to agricultural production, particularly for the campesino sector (Stonich 1993, 1995).

Influenced by "appropriate" and "small-scale" technology movements in the developed countries, NGOs attempted to revive tools from preindustrial northern agriculture to fit the conditions of technology-poor smallholders. But as long as input subsidies were available, Green Revolution packages were widely adopted by smallholders because of the *possibility* of higher yields and less drudgery and because either the credit or the inputs obtained could also be used as currency to solve household cash-flow problems. Further, because peasant holdings were becoming smaller (*minifundización*), they were forced to intensify production in order to remain economically viable. Pumping crops with fertilizers seemed like a quick and easy way to raise production. At first, no one suspected that the *paquete tecnológico* would raise costs even as yields and prices for grain dropped, eventually erasing farmer's profit margins.

Adoption among poor, risk-prone campesinos was still highly uneven, however. In terms of yield, hybrids responded better to the paquete tecnológico than local landraces did, while the landraces responded better to the traditional agroecological practices than did hybrids. The former offered the possibility of higher yields in good years, but the latter was more ecologically resilient, producing lower yields in good years but higher yields in bad years. While farmers attempted to retain traditional landraces in a mixed traditional/modern approach, the agroecological practices that accompanied these seeds (such as cover crops, intercropping, staggered and mixed varietal planting, etc.) were routinely discouraged or even prohibited by extension and credit agencies. The changing mix of Green Revolution and traditional practices led to increases in external inputs and monocultures and a steady decrease in the agroecological practices associated with mixed or polycultures. This shift masked processes of ecological degradation and agricultural "involution" (when productivity declines and the system degrades despite increasing inputs) and pushed these agroecosystems toward ecological and economic collapse: when soils, weeds, and insects became unresponsive to the paquete tecnológico. When subsidies disappeared, farmers discovered that their agroecosystems were so degraded that soil itself, its moisture and its organic matter, were now the basic factors limiting their production.[5]

Alternative agriculture development, at that time practiced by a handful of NGOs, began to shift from tools and "appropriate technology" to soil and water conservation. Low external-input agriculture and embryonic efforts in organic agriculture were promoted, though without the benefit of the credit, markets, or research systems available to the Green Revolution

(Jeavons 1974; Gliessman et al. 1981; Bunch 1985; Richards 1985; Wilken 1988; Altieri 1990).

Unsurprisingly, farmer adoption of these technology-oriented strategies in alternative agricultural development never even remotely approached the massive levels of adoption attained by the Green Revolution. During the 1970s and 1980s, these development projects were alternative pinpoints in a sea of conventional agriculture. This general pattern of widespread "semi-technified"[6] Green Revolution technology, peppered with isolated, NGO led appropriate-technology alternatives, characterized Central American agriculture in the 1980s and into the 1990s.

The Center for the Improvement of Maize and Wheat (CIMMYT) was the home of the Green Revolution's "miracle wheat" and was instrumental in spreading the Green Revolution throughout Mexico and Central America. However, CIMMYT's claims that the region's total food production had increased through the widespread adoption of its paquete tecnológico rang hollow when they also had to admit that, by the 1990s, per capita productivity had stagnated and that the increase in overall production was primarily due to the increase in the *area* under cultivation (Bolaños 1992). In Central America, this expansion of agricultural land was largely a result of the displacement of subsistence smallholders by capitalized agriculture from the rich volcanic soils of the Pacific plain to the central hillsides and the virgin forests of the eastern interior. For Central American governments, peasant colonization of the *frontera agrícola*—the agricultural frontier—was a substitute for redistributive land reform. It also provided a continuous supply of cheap grains and opened vast undeveloped areas to extensive cattle ranching for beef exports (Utting 1993; FUNDESCA 1994). As it turned out, the expansion of both hillside and frontier agriculture was the major cause of both increased production *and* environmental degradation, leading to the disappearance of over a third of the region's tropical forests.[7]

SARD: THE OFFICIAL RESPONSE

The rates and patterns of environmental degradation in Central America and those of the rest of the Third World are disturbingly similar. Global concerns regarding environment and development were first expressed by the Club of Rome's *Limits to Growth* (1972) and at the Stockholm Conference on the Human Environment in 1972. Fifteen years later, *Our Common Future* (1987), the Bruntland Commission's precedent-setting report, established a global environmental mandate to be taken up at regional and local levels and launched the United Nations Environment Program. The publication had a profound discursive effect on agricultural development.

SUSTAINABLE DEVELOPMENT

The Brundtland Commission maintained that economic equity and environmental sustainability were the two primary conditions for sustainable development. However, according to the commission, the export of natural resources by "lesser-developed countries" (LDCs) was increasing relative to the remaining supply. Their acute need for foreign exchange and the predominant dependence on exports drawn from natural resources made it impossible for them to manage natural resources for sustained production. Poverty, population pressure, and bad economic conditions put further pressure on the environment and make problems unmanageable. The world economic decline of the 1980s brought a drop in export prices and a growth in LDCs' debts. This situation led to the exploitation of natural resources primarily for debt servicing, with little left over for investment in development. This emphasis on debt service and the concomitant decline in living standards due to poverty and institution of austerity measures was not sustainable and led to political destabilization (WCED 1987).

Notably, "sustainable agriculture" came to replace "alternative" agriculture in the development lexicon.

However, the Green Revolution's IARCs were not the first out of the gate in the race to develop sustainable agriculture. The Consultative Group on International Agricultural Research (CGIAR) was the coordinating body for what were then sixteen international research centers located in the Vavilov centers of genetic diversity worldwide. Sustainable agricultural and rural development—SARD—reached these formal institutions for agricultural research after financial pressure from the World Bank and political pressure from environmentalists persuaded the CGIAR system to assume responsibility for developing and promoting sustainable agriculture. With financial pressure from above, political pressure from below, and, eventually, internal pressure from a small but articulate handful of its own scientists, the centers were forced to address the issue of agricultural sustainability. New programs for SARD began to appear (Blaikie 2000).

Why was SARD resisted by the Green Revolution's institutional base? The answer is found in the paradigms and the political economy of the CGIAR. First, there was a conceptual problem due to the ambiguous nature of the term *sustainable development*. Some authors claim that the normative definition in *Our Common Future*, "development that meets the needs of the present without compromising the ability of future generations to meet their own needs," is so flexible as to mean almost anything to anyone. "Sustainable development" can mean sustaining *economic growth*, sustaining the *ecological basis* of human life, or sustaining the *social basis* of human life to meet basic needs. While all three aspects are now routinely integrated into the same term, the problem of defining sustainability still depends on just what is being sustained, for how long, for whom, at whose cost, and at what scale or in what area. Further, simply defining "sustainable development" does not necessarily address the controversial *causes* of unsustainable development or environmental destruction (Lélé 1991; Pretty 1995; Dore 1996).

Predictably, at first the CGIAR simply defined sustainability in terms of maintaining growth in production, or "validating conventional production models with simple environmental feedback as an afterthought." In effect, "conventional Green Revolution experts . . . [sold] their old wine in the new bottle of 'sustainable agriculture'" (Lélé 1991, 424).

The "old wine" strategy failed to convince the development community that CGIAR's research and development programs truly addressed sustainable agriculture. NGOs, like International Union for the Conservation of Nature (IUCN) and Oxfam, the UNDP, and even the FAO, had been wrestling with the negative social and environmental effects of the Green Revolution since the UN's second "Development Decade" and the FAO's "Freedom from Hunger" campaign in the 1960s. The UNDP and the NGOs pressed for more substantive technological changes in agricultural development, while the FAO adopted natural resource management (NRM) as a component of food production.

By the time the United Nations held the Earth Summit in Rio de Janeiro, Brazil, in 1992, not only the term, but the mandate for sustainable development had been taken up by most mainstream development agencies, by the World Bank, and, notably, by one of the Bank's major clients—CGIAR. Yet a mandate implied not just rephrasing, but rethinking the way agricultural research was conceived, conducted, and extended. The main agricultural research centers in Central America attempted to incorporate NRM into their research agendas and to shift some of their research from center-driven grain improvement to collaborative farm systems and watershed improvement. This was the essence of the project that came to be described as SARD.

However, SARD was difficult for the IARCs because they generated their technologies from a central point. These technologies were designed to substitute the ecological factors of production with external inputs—irrigation, chemicals, and machinery. By exchanging hybrids for local landraces, irri-

THE WORLD BANK'S GREENING OF CGIAR

"To spruce itself up for the 1992 UN Conference on Environment and Development (UNCED)—the 'Earth Summit'—Consultative Group for International Agricultural Research (CGIAR) expanded itself to eighteen IARCs and added on forests, fish, and bananas to its newfound 'green' agenda. At a time of flagging enthusiasm for aid in general and agriculture in particular, however, the move was a disaster. Within two years donor support plummeted 21 percent (U.S. financing fell 40 percent), 2,000 people were struck off the employment rolls, and four IARCs had to be rolled into two" (*Ecologist* 1996). CGIAR's "green renewal" was introduced by Ismail Serageldin, the vice president for Environmentally Sustainable Development of the World Bank. Serageldin, an engineer and planner by training, was named chairman of CGIAR in 1994. He promptly oversaw the well-publicized eighteen-month renewal (which was clearly orchestrated by the World Bank), announcing that "Agricultural transformation in the world's developing regions will require a thrice green revolution: green for productivity, green for environmental sustainability, and green for increased income as the entry point to improved living conditions, dealing with the access side of food security" (Serageldin 1997).

The fact that CGIAR named the environmental officer of the World Bank as its chair reflected the Group's two main problems: economic stagnation and a bad environmental image. Ironically, the Green Revolution, like so many poor farmers before it, was in danger of going broke. Luckily, unlike poor farmers, the CGIAR had access to the World Bank: "The World Bank stepped in to save CGIAR by offering to match other contributions to CGIAR at a 50 percent rate to a maximum of 20 million over 1994–95. With confidence restored, CGIAR's budget jumped from [$]235 to [$]300 million in 1996" (Ecologist 1996).

However, World Bank support was conditional. The target of effective congressional pressure brought by environmental groups as early as 1983, the Bank itself had initiated environmental assessments of its projects in 1989. Basically, the Bank found "the costs of not appearing green to be too high, and realized it had to keep the green NGOs quiet" (Wade 1997). In 1992 the Bank's "Development and Environment" World Development report stated that Serageldin had made it clear that CGIAR would follow the World Bank's policy imperative and pay attention to "the nexus of agriculture, the environment, and poverty as the basis for nurturing sustainable agriculture for food security . . . renewed emphasis on sustainability issues, including the management of tropical forests, soil and water management, and the productive use of marginal lands inhabited by the poor . . ." (*Ecologist* 1996, 259–70).

The World Bank bailout was analogous to a neoliberal SAP within the Green Revolution, complete with institutional cutbacks and a significant shift in "partnerships" from the public to the private sector, particularly in regard to biotechnology. However, in a balancing act, a number of holistic and less commodity-oriented programmatic trends such as sustainability, resource management, farmer participation, and a focus on marginal lands also came to the discursive fore.

gation for rainfall management, fertilizers for organic matter, pesticides for ecological management, and herbicides for labor and multistory shading, the Green Revolution spread its paquete tecnológico across a wide range of farming systems with relatively little regard to ecological specificity.

The science of agronomy provided a continuous flow of new genetic material from the research centers to selected agronomic "domains" where varieties could be tested in field trials to determine appropriate levels of fertilization, planting and harvesting dates, and so on. From there, national agricultural research centers financed by the national ministry of agriculture used agricultural extensionists and bank credit to spread the use of hybrid seed and fertilizers among farmers (Deo and Swanson 1990).

But sustainable agriculture is fundamentally different in this regard because it does not substitute capital inputs for the ecological factors of production. Rather, it attempts to utilize, enhance, replicate, and otherwise manage the *ecosystem* to raise crops (Gliessman et al. 1981; Altieri 1983, 1987; Conway 1985; Gliessman 1990). The science of *agroecology* and an understanding of specific ecosystems are integral to this knowledge-intensive ecological approach. Further, because agroecosystems and society shape and affect each other, neither agroecology nor sustainable agriculture can be divorced from their specific cultural contexts. Each agroecological system reflects the unique combination of social organization, knowledge, technologies, and values of its particular area (Norgaard 1987). It follows that sustainable agricultural development cannot consist of centralized generation and transfer of homogenous technology packages but must be grounded in local ecology, knowledge, and practices.

Sustainable agricultural development raised the difficult social and technical problem of just how to produce agroecological knowledge at the local level and how to do that across an entire region.

How could a research system designed to extend centrally generated

---

THE LUCRATIVE BUSINESS OF SAVING THE WORLD FROM HUNGER

According to the organization Rural Advancement Foundation International (RAFI):

> Foreign germplasm contributes $10.2 billion annually to the U.S.'s maize and soybean production. . . . [M]ost of this germplasm comes from CGIAR research centres paid for by foreign aid and . . . maize and soybean are just a tiny fraction of overall U.S. benefits reaped from CGIAR. . . . According to a 1996 study by one of CGIAR's IARCs, the International Food Policy Research Institute based in Washington, D.C., germplasm from . . . CIMMYT, which focuses on maize and wheat, can now be found in 58 percent of the U.S. wheat crop, its cash contribution since 1970 to U.S. farmers is not less than $3.4 billion while that to the country's food processing companies is about $13.4 billion. . . . As much as one third of the annual flow of tropical seed samples from CIMMYT now ends up in the hands of transnationals like Pioneer Hi-Bred and Cargill (*Ecologist* 1996).

---

technologies build local capacities for agroecological research and development throughout the socially and ecologically diverse Mesoamerican region?

CGIAR's challenge was to integrate agroecology's spatial scales into their regional project for SARD. First of all, they had absolutely no experience in this. Second, only a few of the scientists associated with the CGIAR system understood or were even interested in ecology or the cultural anthropology of such an undertaking (Blaikie 2000).

There are two more reasons that explain CGIAR's difficulties with SARD. The first is simply that SARD was not very profitable for agribusiness. One of the little-publicized facts about the Green Revolution's publicly funded research is that it is tremendously lucrative for private corporations in the North. SARD's knowledge-intensive agroecological management *decreased* farmers' reliance on external capital inputs (hybrid seeds, fertilizers, pesticides, herbicides, etc.). While poor farmers may have stood to gain from these savings, this was of little use to agri-industry.

The second factor had to do with the global economic crisis and the structural adjustment policies imposed on governments of the region throughout the 1980s. Beginning in the early 1980s, the World Bank and the IMF worked in tandem to privatize state businesses, cut back public spending, and open Third World economies to international capital investment. Most developing nations had borrowed heavily to finance development projects throughout the 1960s and 1970s. Governments were counting on profits from increased production to pay back these loans. However, inefficiency, corruption, and the global economic downturn resulting from the oil shocks of the late 1970s ate up savings, obliging them to borrow heavily. The result was the "Third World Debt Crisis." Developing countries had to borrow money just to pay back loans. Often, they were able to pay only on the interest, not the principal. In order to refinance their debt, they had to agree to fiscally strict monetary policies of the IMF. These SAPs forced governments to privatize government enterprises, lower trade barriers, and devalue their national currency. The SAPs imposed severe fiscal policies that drastically reduced basic government services in health, education, welfare, and agriculture.

During the Green Revolution, the ministries of agriculture in the Meso-american countries had been key in conducting field trials and extending the paquete tecnológico to farmers through government extension services. But with the SAPs, national agricultural research and extension services basically disappeared. Without these government services, IARCs like CIMMYT had no link to farmers. How were these centers to develop sustainable agriculture, itself dependent on extensive relationships with farmers over a diverse range of agroecosystems, when they were no longer even able to extend the paquete technológico?

Some researchers at CIMMYT and other IARCs tried methodologies designed to bring researchers and farmers together: Farmer-back-to-Farmer, Farmer First, and Participatory Rural Appraisal (PRA) were all designed by researchers searching for a substantive relationship between formal agricultural research and smallholders.

While the approaches certainly benefited *some* farmers and provided *some* researchers with a fresh perspective on SARD, without national, ground-level counterparts within the ministries of agriculture, it was expensive and impractical for the top-heavy international research centers to carry out direct extension.

As state-run extension services disappeared under the SAP knife, development programs run by NGOs spilled into the rural services void left by the vanishing state. NGOs developed rich on-the-ground empirical experience in soil conservation, integrated pest management, crop diversification, and agroforestry.

However, from CGIAR's perspective, NGOs were unsuited to properly develop SARD because of their limited scientific and technical capacity, a lack of program continuity, and their geographic fragmentation (Bebbington et al. 1993; Kaimowitz 1993; Bebbington 1997). Nonetheless, they were endowed with complementary qualities the formal research institutions lacked:

NGOs' strength . . . lies in agricultural practices compatible with natural resource conservation and alternatives for farmers unable to compete in agricultural produce markets. NGOs have multiple advantages for using agricultural technology to meet the challenge of low input sustainable agriculture and reducing rural poverty. . . . NGOs are highly motivated . . . [they] have a more holistic approach . . . they can incorporate marketing and credit concerns, [and they] have the advantage of flexibility in institutional structure, human resources, and program.[8]

But importantly for agricultural research institutions, over time the NGOs had produced a host of participatory methodologies designed to enroll campesinos in their projects. In fact, "participation" rather than actual results in production or conservation was commonly used as a measuring stick to evaluate NGO projects. Donors not only determined what development activities to fund (e.g., sustainability, empowerment, and gender), they also conditioned their support on the participation of project beneficiaries. The better an NGO could demonstrate participation in their projects, the better chance they had to continued funding from donors. NGOs were considered the institutional "missing link" to communities, agroecosystems, and farmers.

THE OTHER AGRARIAN TRANSITION: SCALING UP SUSTAINABLE AGRICULTURE

The "other agrarian transition" refers to the transition from conventional, capital-intensive, environmentally unsustainable agriculture to sustainable agriculture and rural development (Sinha 2000). Despite over twenty years of noble declarations, programs, and projects, the "other agrarian transition" has yet to take place on a significant scale in Mesoamerica (with the exception of Cuba). Its social, economic, and environmental failures notwithstanding, Green Revolution agriculture, now with a new, growing emphasis on genetically modified crops, continues to dominate the countryside. It is unlikely that CGIAR's IARCs will make the structural, internal changes needed for them to adequately address SARD, and thus far their "partnerships" with NGOs have yet to make the critical difference. This has led many SARD advocates to put their efforts on "scaling up" SARD through NGOs.

Scaling up or *going to scale* in the NGO sense refers to efforts to increase the impact of grassroots development projects beyond micro or local scales. The desire to scale up comes from the view that despite the explosion of the nongovernmental sector itself, and despite their favorable reputation, NGOs have had a limited impact on development at the global level (Edwards and Hume 1992). In its simplest form, *scaling up* means spreading out benefits to more people over broader, geographical scales, either by multiplying the number of people served or by increasing the number of services offered. However, *going to scale* can also mean the spread of ideas, approaches, and methodologies from the grassroots *into* official development institutions (Bebbington and Farrington 1992; Chambers 1992).

Thus, "going to scale" can imply scaling up, scaling out, scaling in, or even scaling down of such diverse activities as research, investment, training, technologies, and services (across, within, and between institutions) over broad demographic and geographic areas and through time (suggesting some form of sustainability). The debates on going to scale generally range from a certain dissatisfaction with the role of junior partner and social service provider assigned to NGOs to political calls for linking local and global NGOs to influence development policy (Gonsalves 2001). For NGO development projects then, going to scale may not only imply a quantitative increase in size, but also a functional increase in activities, and an increase in organizational strength and political activity from service delivery to empowerment (Uvin, Jain, and Brown 2000).

"Going to scale" without addressing the structural aspects of the "agrarian transition" still relegates SARD to the NGO world of projects and programs. This tends to exclude them from the arena of political and economic policy. While development NGOs may desire a transition to sustainable agriculture, they have no strategy to effect the structural changes needed to provide the political-economic context for that transition.

It remains to be seen whether in the face of global free market capitalism, development can actually be modified to ensure food security and equitable economic distribution, much less environmental sustainability or the well being of the peasantry. Without addressing the structural inequalities inherent in agrarian transitions, it is doubtful that even the "participatory development" approaches now popular will significantly alter the unequal playing field faced by campesino farmers. To what extent is farmer-driven SARD a means to this end? To what extent can it influence the structure as well as the techniques of sustainable agriculture?

The "Post"-Agrarian Question

Over the last decade, neoliberal economic trends toward globalization (Washington Consensus, WTO) and regionalization (NAFTA, Free Trade Agreement of the Americas [FTAA]) have hollowed state agricultural services, driven prices for basic grains below the costs of production, and cleared regulatory controls for the corporate introduction of genetically engineered (GE) crops. These trends reflect deep global shifts in agroindustrial capital toward what some theorists refer to as "postindustrial, flexible, informational, and recombinant forms of production" (Heller 2001; McAfee 2004).

In Latin America, neoliberal restructuring first took the form of IMF/

GOING TO SCALE

Scaling up or *going to scale* refers to efforts by NGOs to increase the impact of grassroots development projects beyond micro or local scales. The desire to scale up grows from the belief that despite the explosion of the nongovernmental sector itself and despite their favorable reputation, NGOs have had a limited impact on development at the global level. In its simplest form, scaling *up* means spreading *out* benefits to more people over broader, geographical scales either by multiplying the number of people served or by increasing the number of services offered. However, scaling up can also imply the spread of ideas, approaches, and methodologies from the grassroots *up* into official development institutions.

This interinstitutional scaling up is referred to by Uvin and Miller (1996) as *integration*. Edwards and Hulme (1992) describe these forms as belonging to *additive* and *multiplicative* strategies, respectively, and refer to a spontaneous, informal spread as *diffuse* scaling up.

A number of workshops held by development groups like the Institute for Development Studies, the International Institute for Rural Reconstruction, the Natural Resources Institute, and the Nongovernmental Organization Committee within the Consultative Group for International Agricultural Research (NGOC-CGIAR) have further developed these ideas to address the scaling *out* of NRM (Harrington 2000), scaling *forward* of sustainability and equity (Taylor 2001), and scaling *up* of participatory research (Gündel, Hancock, and Andeson 2001).

Addressing NGO development projects, Uvin and Muller (2000) suggested four types of scaling up, including *quantitative* (increase in size), *functional* (increase in activities), *political* (from service delivery to empowerment), and *organizational* (increase in organizational strength). These ideas draw from Korten's (1990) first, second, third (and fourth) *generation* strategies of community-based organizations and grassroots-driven social change that emphasizes the central role of NGOs.

Synthesizing the ideas from a four-year workshop series initiated by the NGOC-CGIAR, Gonsalves (2001) claimed that the different levels, spheres, and qualities of influence of going to scale could be understood within a conceptual framework that included temporal, spatial, economic, technological, institutional, and equity aspects of both *horizontal* (additive) and *vertical* (multiplicative) strategies (Gonsalves 2001).

Thus, going to scale can imply scaling up, scaling out, scaling in, or even scaling down of such diverse activities as research, investment, training, and services (across, within, and between institutions) over broad demographic and geographic areas and through time (suggesting some form of sustainability). The range of debates on going to scale generally range from a certain dissatisfaction with the official development role of "junior partner"/social service provider assigned to NGOs to the dangers of bureaucratization of grassroots NGOs to political calls for strategies that link local and global NGOs for effective advocacy and influencing of development policy.

The notion of scaling is itself grounded in the neopopulist policy frameworks of alternative development paradigms in which NGOs are generally considered the institutional operatives of social change. These strategic considerations are part and parcel of neo-Toquevillean notions of civil society, in which the "third sector" (NGOs) is given a central role in promoting democracy and development. Thus, the debate on scaling up invokes the language of social capital, civil society, and conflictless partnerships that link "bottom-up" neopopulist approaches to "top-down" conventional structures (MacDonald 1997; Pearce 2000). For example, Taylor (2001, 15) enumerates the three basic principles for "valid" scaling up processes:

- Three-way partnerships to balance bottom-up and top-down action.
- Action based on locally specific data.
- Changes in community behavior (to) produce sustainable social change.

Because the concept has evolved primarily through conversations in the NGO intellectual community, "going to scale" has tended to be seen as a mechanism for increasing the influence of NGOs within mainstream development institutions, rather than as a strategy for structural, social, or radical political change.

There is considerably more written on how to link participatory approaches to government, business, and multilateral development institutions than about how successful project experiences might link and empower existing and potential social movements to seriously challenge hegemonic political and economic structures. Increasing the range and scope of *local* empowerment is emphasized over strategic forms of structural empowerment or resistance. While there are some case studies that illustrate important lessons of global-local coordination for specific mobilization and resistance (e.g., dams, resettlements), there is little in the scaling up literature to suggest ways to scale up political resistance to liberalization, regionalization, or privatization. Further, the "lessons for scaling up" permeating the narratives of NGO project literature rarely identify or critique the structural barriers encountered when going to scale, i.e., there are very few lessons shared about projects that were *prevented* from going to scale. This analytical separation of structure from scale elides the larger, contextual issues that limit sustainable, equitable, development and gives the entire notion of scaling up a decidedly reformist character.

The suggestion that each of the world's 20,000-plus southern NGOs can scale itself up through some sort of structureless, participatory development fosters competition rather than cooperation, ultimately dividing grassroots organizations from each other. Further, by hiding real structural and social conflicts behind a programmatic veneer of growing "partnerships" and "participation," scaling up fails to address divisions *within* communities and grassroots organizations, certainly one of the major obstacles to scaling up in the first place. As with "sustainability," the notion of going to scale cannot escape the thorny political questions regarding what is being scaled up, why, and, ultimately, for whom.

World Bank SAPs. This was followed by multilateral regionalization, implemented through the NAFTA, signed in 1992 by Canada, the United States, and Mexico; blueprints for a "Plan Puebla-Panamá" (PPP) to reorient productive infrastructure; and a concerted push, primarily from the North, for a continent-wide FTAA.[9] The effect on agriculture has been decisive. Because of heavy subsidies, the costs of cultivating maize in the United States are significantly lower than those for basic grain producers in the region. The case of Mexico, where 2.5 million smallholders make up 68 percent of the agricultural sector and depend largely on maize cultivation, is illustrative: costs of production are double those of farms in the United States. When the Mexican government implemented NAFTA tariff reductions ahead of schedule, imports of maize from the United States increased from 396,000 metric tons/year to 4,854,000 metric tons/year (USDA, cited in McAfee 2004). Liberalization of tariffs, combined with the removal of subsidies and the disappearance of government buying has driven hundreds of thousands of campesinos from agriculture (Zamora 2003b).[10] There were 700,000 migrants the first year of NAFTA alone (Santiago Levy and Sweder van Wijnbergen, in Zamora 2003b). Presently, Mexican migration to the United States stands at approximately 300,000 per year. In Mexico's case, NAFTA has simply institutionalized neoliberal trends in trade and eco-

nomic policies initiated through World Bank/IMF SAPs implemented after
the peso crisis in 1982.[11] The same trends and SAPs have been applied to
Central American countries, with much the same effect on the countryside.
In the face of the structural adjustment of the 1980s, by 1990 more than
one million Guatemalans, Nicaraguans, and Salvadorans had left their
homes (Wise 2003).

The influx of remittances from migrants is immense. In Mexico between
1980 and 1998, the flow of remittances increased eightfold, from $700 mil-
lion to $5.6 billion. Remittances rival tourism as a share of GNP and are
equivalent to 10 percent of total exports and 80 percent of foreign direct
investment (Castro, in Zamora 2003a). Remittances to Central America
went from $1 billion in 1980 to $10 billion a year in 1999 (Orozco 2003).
The Economic Commission on Latin America—ECLA—estimates that
over the next ten years, remittances from the region will reach some $25
billion (Zamora 2003a, 2003b).

Most studies on remittances conclude that they are a positive factor in
economic growth, commerce, and distribution in recipient countries
(Adams 1998; El-Sakka 1999; Ilaf 2000, all in Orozco 2003). Some analysts claim that remittances keep rural economies afloat during the agricultural "transition." But the effects of remittances on agriculture are still
unclear. Remittances tend to be invested in consumption of basic goods,
savings, or productive investment. In the case of investment, they tend to
be directed toward a) fixed capital, b) capital goods, and c) small businesses.
In the poorer countries of Central America (Honduras, Guatemala,
Nicaragua), most remittances are directed to consumption. Unsurprisingly,
given the unfavorable markets, nowhere is agriculture a significant site of
investment (Ascencio 2003).

TABLE 3.6 · MESOAMERICAN REMITTANCES

	MILLIONS U.S.$	PER CAPITA	% EXPORT INCOME
Mexico	5,627.0	35.3	4.5
El Salvador	1,337.5	276.0	54.6
Guatemala	456.5	49.6	16.0
Honduras	220.0	51.8	10.9
Nicaragua	200.0	53.4	34.5
Costa Rica	112.0	45.0	2.0

FMI, 1999, UN State of World Pop 2000, http://www.unfpa.org/SWP/2000/indicators2.html
(Ascencio 2003)

THE BIOLOGICAL COLONIZATION OF AGRICULTURE

The economic crippling of the Mesoamerican countryside has opened new opportunities for international capital and for biotechnology. Though supported by the Agreement on Trade-Related Aspects of Intellectual Property Rights (TRIPS) and the Agreement on Agriculture (AoA) of the WTO, the introduction of GE crops to Latin America has nonetheless met with heavy resistance from environmental, consumer, and peasant groups throughout the region. While environmentalists and consumers tend to criticize the introduction of GE crops because of threats to biodiversity and health risks, peasant unions see GE crops as a direct threat to rural livelihoods. Writing on Mexico, McAfee (2004) contends that

> The introduction of GMO crops will bring about significant changes in agricultural production systems and in hemispheric and international trade . . . because of the pivotal role of GE in international agro-food politics, the full-scale adoption of GE crops in Latin America would accelerate current trends toward greater industrialization and external-input dependency on farming. It would strengthen the comparative advantage of the United States in Latin American and world food and fiber markets and speed the incorporation of Latin American food systems into a global agro-food complex dominated by a small number of powerful conglomerates . . . these political-economic trends are likely to undermine further what remains of Mexico's self-provisioning, corn growing communities, and with them, the repositories of maize germplasm that those communities have created and conserved.

Advocates of agricultural biotechnology assert that by genetically overcoming the limiting factors to production, GE crops will raise yields and reduce the need for external inputs. The belief that high-yielding GE crops will reduce the rate of expansion of agriculture into nonagricultural land (e.g., tropical forests) lead GE proponents to claim that biotechnology is the sustainable answer to world hunger (Leisinger 1999; Perseley and Lantin 1999; Pinstrup-Andersen and Cohen 1999). What is usually not explained is that GE crops permit agri-industry to appropriate key steps in the farming labor process (such as seed selection and propagation, fertilization, weeding, and pest control), thus removing them from the farmer's control, both economically and managerially (Goodman, Sorj, and Wilkinson 1987; Kloppenburg 1988).

Smallholders tend to occupy a diversity of marginal, high-risk agroecological niches (hillsides, drought-ridden areas, etc.) and rely on the flexible micromanagement of production factors to deal with the uncertainties of climate, markets, pest outbreaks, and so on. The GE "one-size-fits-all" approach to production is criticized by many agroecologists who claim that ecosystem-specific management of on-farm ecological functions can achieve similar or better results than those of GE crops while protecting biodiversity (Altieri 1987, 1989, 2001; Gliessman 1998a; Rosset 2002). Agroecology is anathema to GE crops because it is based on autonomous farmer control over the very production factors that biotechnology aims to appropriate into the circuits of agribusiness.[12]

THE AGROECOLOGY OF GENETICALLY MODIFIED ORGANISMS

A GE or transgenic plant is one in which the genes from another plant or animal are inserted into the desired crop through techniques in genetic engineering. By introducing foreign genes into the plant, scientists hope that it will develop certain characteristics from the gene "donor." Farmers and researchers have done the same since agriculture was invented through the cross-pollination between different varieties of corn, for example. But genetic engineering also allows scientists to combine plant and animal genes: bacteria with maize, pig with tomato. Genetic engineering breaks natural biological barriers between species and invents what are essentially new species.

Research has already shown that outside the controlled experimental plots, transgenic crops do not produce more than nontransgenic seeds. Secondly, transgenic crops have not eliminated the need for agrochemicals, they have increased them. For example, Monsanto's Bt-corn has a gene from the *Bacillus thurengensis* (Bt) bacteria. Bt has toxic substances that function as a natural pesticide. Actually, many farmers, especially organic farmers, apply Bt manually to their crops in order to control pests. Corn with Bt genes produces its own pesticide *within* the leaves of the plant, thus eliminating the need for surface application. The idea sounds good, but it ignores how insects develop resistance to pesticides. Bt corn actually facilitates resistance because insects can ingest Bt little by little as they eat the corn leaves. If the Bt corn pollinates other gramineous plants nearby, insects will have even more opportunities to develop resistance. Higher and higher concentrations of Bt will be needed (both transgenic and manually applied) to combat pests. Once resistance has developed, Bt will be useless, both in Bt corn and when applied manually. For organic farmers, this means the loss of one of their primary organic means of controlling insect pests.

Another example is "Roundup Ready" sorghum. This seed has a foreign gene that makes the sorghum plants resistant to Roundup (Monsanto's brand name for the herbicide glyphosate). Farmers can then weed their fields by applying massive doses of Roundup without worrying about affecting the growth of the sorghum crop. The objective is to apply *more* herbicide, not less. . . . While farmers might reduce the number of herbicide applications, costs of production are not necessarily lower and yields are not necessarily higher.

The ecological consequences of introducing GMOs into the environment are very poorly understood. Genes can escape and contaminate wild plants or other crops. The "Roundup Ready" seed can create "superweeds" resistant to herbicide. Bt corn can not only create resistant strains of pests, it can affect the soil's microbiotic life. We don't know the long-term consequences of gene release into ecosystems.

Because GMOs depend on the right to patent life forms, there are serious legal and economic implications for farmers. In Canada, organic canola farmer Percy Schmeiser's crop was contaminated by GMO pollen from a neighboring field. Schmeiser's crop was ruined for organic sale. When he tried to take Monsanto to court for damages he found instead that Monsanto was suing him for using their genetic material without permission! Monsanto won the suit.

Finally, it is simply not true that the problem of world hunger will be solved by increased production from GMO crops. Today farmers produce enough food to feed each person on the planet a kilo of grains, half a kilo of meat, milk, and eggs, and half a kilo of vegetables and fruit, daily. Enough food is produced to feed 8 billion people (the world's population is currently 6 billion). Why is hunger still a problem? People are hungry not because there is a shortage of food, but because they are *poor* and are unable to buy the food being produced (Altieri 2001).

Since a lot of the world's poverty is found in rural areas, the best way to eliminate hunger and poverty would be to distribute land to the landless for food production. This way they would have food and money. But this implies *re*-distributing land—increasing the number of farms and thus reducing the size of large landholdings presently dedicated to industrial agriculture. Governments are reluctant to touch these landholdings. These plantation farms tend to support GMOs because GMOs simplify their gigantic operations and ultimately help to consolidate their power in agriculture. Thus, another reason GMOs are being promoted by governments in the developing world is to attempt to raise food and avoid facing the issue of land reform.

The Challenge

The MCAC faces the formidable challenge of developing sustainable agriculture in the face of powerful global trends that undermine smallholder agriculture economically, reduce the family labor force, and invade the ecological production factors on which they base their strategies for sustainability.

Abandoned by the state, unable to compete with heavily subsidized grain imports from the United States, and seen as an obstacle to modernization and to foreign investment in agriculture, the campesinado has borne the brunt of this agrarian transformation. Yet, despite it all, many campesinos continue stubbornly producing basic grains for subsistence.[13] They persist, despite the removal of government support, despite "free market" dumping, the migration of large parts of family labor, the privatization of communal land, and the threat of a new wave of agroindustrial "colonization" through GE crops. Smallholders have not been driven completely from agriculture. Among the survivors, those making out best are the peasants like the farmers of Campesino a Campesino, who use sustainable agricultural techniques based on agroecology and shared farmer to farmer. What are the possibilities for farmer-led, sustainable agricultural development among this sector? What chance do smallholders have for tipping the balance in favor of sustainability? We will take up these questions in the next, concluding chapter.

SIX

Movimento Campesino a Campesino

From Cultural Resistance to Social Change

I think we should not fall in the trap of seeing the development of
agroecology by just looking at the physical aspects of the farm or just
at the economics. The greatest impact of our work in promoting
sustainable agriculture is precisely the "human farm." We as NGOs
have a problem with our social position in which we are serving as
a dike and often an obstacle to processes of agency within the people
and greater local organization. I think we have to look for processes
because any aid that arrives, whether it is food for work or whatever,
will work if the community is strong and organized. . . . Agroecology is
not just a collection of practices. Agroecology is a way of life—
contrary to the way we are always doing things. We can't have an
agroecological change without a campesino movement. We NGOs
can accompany them, but we can't do it. We promote projects, and
projects have a short life. They are unsustainable. The problems
go farther than whether or not the aid arrived or if the people
implemented different techniques.

—*Nelda Martínez, Nicaragua*

Why Aren't All Farmers Sustainable?

A few years ago, while attending a university seminar, I listened as a group
of graduate students in agroecology presented scientific evidence on the
sustainability of different farming practices to a skeptical group of conservation biologists. Using probabilistic models to compare conventional
farming with agroecological practices, they showed time and again that
smaller, diversified, low-external input farms were much more sustainable
than larger, monocropped, industrial farms. The question-and-answer
period was lively and full of debate over the assumptions built into the mod-

els, their validity, and the applicability of the results. Finally, one biologist just shook his head, "Why aren't all farmers sustainable?" he asked.

The question stopped the agroecologists cold. Why indeed? At the end of the day, unless farmers actually implement sustainable practices, it does little good to talk about their socioeconomic and environmental benefits. The answer is not found in probabilistic models or even in the practices themselves, but in the political economy of agriculture—in the institutions and relations of power among farmers, consumers, agribusiness, and governments.

Campesino a Campesino holds many lessons for those of us concerned with sustainability, food security, the eradication of rural poverty, and the protection of the environment. The promoters of MCAC have shown that, given the chance to generate and share agroecological knowledge freely among themselves, smallholders are perfectly capable of developing sustainable agriculture, even under highly adverse conditions. The capacity to develop agriculture locally is not only the agroecological key to sustainable agricultural development—for campesinos it is a matter of survival. This explains in a very fundamental way why the movement has spread as widely as it has: it works.

However, the Campesino a Campesino experience still leaves us with the question: If sustainable agriculture is so great, why aren't *all* campesinos doing it? What keeps it from scaling up? Why is it still the exception rather than the rule?

The development of sustainable agriculture in Latin America ultimately depends on a combination of efforts between farmers and the countryside's social institutions: the markets, banks, government ministries, agricultural research institutions, farmers' organizations, churches, and NGOs. Each of these institutions—including the market—has its own strengths and weaknesses; and each responds to the political agendas of the actors who are able to use it. Sustainable agricultural development is part of the larger Development arena, where the power of these institutions is accessed, contested, or undermined for different, frequently incompatible ends—such as corporate profit versus the conservation of biodiversity, or exports versus food sovereignty. Scaling up the successes of any experience in sustainable agriculture, including MCAC, is therefore not simply a technical or administrative exercise but a *political project* that will necessarily engage the power of these institutions in one way or another.

Smallholders have relatively little control over the institutions shaping agriculture. If MCAC has provided them any influence at all, it is because the movement's successes expose the glaring failures of Development. Though they may still be just "islands of sustainability," MCAC's farmers have tremendous social and political potential, simply because conventional agriculture has failed to produce anything better—for campesinos, for the environment, or for the food security of the millions of poor rural and urban dwellers in Latin America. However, without structurally enabling conditions, a few hundred thousand agroecological smallholders will not tip the balance from conventional to sustainable agriculture in Meso-america. Advancing farmer-led sustainable agricultural development requires overcoming the structural obstacles to sustainability through the institutions that promote the idea of sustainability, but in practice often hold it back.

This book has attempted to share stories that provide a campesino perspective on the utility of these institutions. This final chapter will briefly sum up the political opportunities and constraints to MCAC in order to then address both the question "Why aren't all farmers sustainable?" and, just as important, "What can we do about it?"

Going to Scale: NGOs, Government Programs, Agricultural Research Institutions, and Farmers' Organizations

As we have seen, many things influence MCAC: personalities, traditions, war, the global economy, even droughts and hurricanes. In order to think about MCAC's potential as a successful alternative, we need to briefly assess the institutional factors facing campesinos in the Development arena. The key institutions in this regard have been NGOs, government ministries, agricultural research institutions, and farmers' organizations. All are in some way a part of Campesino a Campesino and as such represent the potential for "going to scale" or "tipping the balance" in favor of sustainable agriculture.

INSTITUTIONAL STRENGTHS

Nongovernmental organizations have been pioneers in sustainable agriculture and rural development. Thanks to the diverse array of NGOs, farmers in MCAC have been able to put on workshops and travel between villages and countries. They have developed and refined their methodologies for experimentation and knowledge sharing. NGOs have brought in technical experts and have taken MCAC promoters to development forums. They have encouraged campesina women to be promoters and have often opened up local dialogues on equity, pluralism, and integrated development. The somewhat eclectic, rural experiences of NGOs have resulted in creative, village-based alternatives to conventional agriculture. NGOs have "scaled out" sustainable agriculture by increasing the number and size of their programs over more and larger areas.

For their part, *mainstream development institutions* that implement bilateral and multilateral aid programs have attempted to go to scale in sustainable agriculture by availing themselves of farmer-to-farmer techniques to increase local participation in national development projects. Indeed, the Campesino a Campesino methodology is one of many participatory approaches often used to make smallholders feel like "stakeholders" in conservation, reforestation, and other rural development projects.

The International Agricultural Research Centers have applied formal scientific research approaches to sustainable agricultural development similarly to the way science was applied to the generation and transfer of Green Revolution technologies. Some have piloted successful farmer-led approaches, like CIAT's Local Agricultural Research Centers (CIALs), and the Farmer Field Schools of Centro Agronómico Tropical de Investigación y Enseñanza (CATIE), both of which work extensively with MCAC promoters.

Farmers' organizations like the National Farmers and Ranchers Union of Nicaragua played a key leadership role in spreading MCAC through their Campesino a Campesino Program, PCAC. Because of the union's national scope, they reach farmers across the entire country, rather than in just a few villages or municipalities. Other farmers' organizations have followed suit, either in response to demand from members or to funder-driven opportunities for sustainable agriculture projects.

A combination of all these strategies would be ideal. After all, the Green Revolution transformed the Mesoamerican countryside in a couple of decades precisely because it brought governments, research institutions, banks, development agencies, and producer associations together in a concerted effort to modernize agriculture.

Unfortunately, this has not been the case with sustainable agriculture. With some exceptions, on the whole, the sectors working in sustainable agricultural development operate in separate institutional worlds. True, sometimes they overlap geographically or thematically, and occasionally farmers' organizations, NGOs, and research institutions find themselves working alongside each other in the field. Once in a while, everyone meets at a conference on sustainable agricultural development. In general, however, there is little sustained coordination among institutions, a fact painfully obvious to farmers on the ground.

The Campesino a Campesino movement *does* work with NGOs, government development projects, research institutions, and farmers' unions. It also works with local churches and religious groups, parent-teacher associations, and local government. While MCAC has clearly provided these institutions with an alternative approach, an innovative methodology, and a very active and committed constituency of "stakeholders and beneficiaries," it has not played a coordinating function per se between institutions, and for all the talk about farmer-led development certainly does not "lead" the development institutions, the governments, the farmers' organizations, or the NGOs. This is understandable: MCAC has no centralized hierarchy and its leaders are farmers who basically lead other farmers by their own example.

Could MCAC play a catalyzing role between these institutions? Should it? What might it look like? Before answering, it is helpful to review the shortcomings of each institutional actor to try to understand the key factors limiting the integration and coordination of these efforts in the first place.

INSTITUTIONAL LIMITATIONS

The IARCs (International Agricultural Research Centers) continue to play a decisive role in conventional agriculture, but are neither prominent nor central in the development of sustainable agriculture. In part, this is because they have not really abandoned the Green Revolution and treat sustainable agricultural development as an "add-on" research area. Their sustainable research programs are dwarfed by the conventional agricultural research budget, and their support for the development of genetically modified crops does not contribute to their effectiveness in the development of agroecology. In fact, the preference of these institutions to prioritize capital-intensive, industrial-scale "fixes" to the problems of agricultural productivity undermines the scope of the relatively few agroecological projects they *do* have. A further serious structural problem with the international agricultural research institutions is that they tend to centralize research. Agroecology, the science of sustainable agriculture, is based on the understanding of ecosystem functions in agriculture. Because agroecosystems are highly diverse, their study tends to be ecosystem specific. Applied agroecological research flourishes in a *decentralized* research system. Centralized research systems tend to use agronomy and genetics to produce agricultural technologies that substitute for ecosystem functions—like genetically modified seeds and the Green Revolution's technological packages. Decentralized research systems (like those found in Cuba) are able to use the science of agroecology to understand local agroecosystems and raise production by *enhancing* ecosystem functions. This has the added benefit that researchers are in direct contact with farmers and technicians over broad areas, helping to overcome the difficult problem of technology transfer.

Until their basic agroecological research is effectively decentralized (and unless they somehow wean themselves from the power of the transnational corporations pushing GMOs), it is unlikely that the IARCs will ever play the same prominent role in sustainable agricultural as they do in conventional agriculture development.

While UNAG's Campesino a Campesino project literally put the Campesino a Campesino movement on the map, most *farmers' unions,* including UNAG, have yet to politically address sustainable agricultural development. Though not true for all of these organizations, many are run by large-scale farmers who tend to farm conventionally. Though as board members they may make room for sustainable agricultural *projects* for their campesino constituents, they do not pressure for sustainable agricultural *policies* as an organization. The farmers who dominate the boards of directors tend to lobby for cheaper agricultural inputs and subsidies for conventional agricultural production. This actually increases farmers' dependence on the agribusiness-agrifoods complex, making them more vulnerable to the whims of a market dominated by global finance capital and transnational corporations. In these farmer organizations, putting sustainable agriculture on the policy agenda is limited by a "democratic deficit" between small-holders in the rank and file and large farmers in leadership positions. Larger farmers have more time and money to devote to board meetings, lobbying, and political influencing. Smallholders, even though more numerous, thus have less say in what these organizations do. There is more of a chance of sustainable agriculture actually becoming a part of the political agenda in those farmer organization where leadership positions more closely reflect the campesino majority and where power is more equitably distributed between large farmers and smallholders.

Because they primarily concentrate on implementing sustainable agriculture projects, *NGOs* have not paid much attention to policies, and rarely address structural issues like land security or guaranteed prices for sustainably produced agricultural products. Having been so effective at promoting sustainability on the ground, what keeps them from addressing the larger structural issues? For one thing, most NGOs are small and cannot afford to have both professional agroecologists and professional policy advocates on staff. The truly effective development NGOs work deep in the countryside, far from the capital cities were policies are set. These NGOs tend to be funded by Northern foundations, which rightly point out that foreign international organizations have no business influencing national policy. Others either believe in the political and economic assumptions behind the laissez faire, free market approaches, or simply take these structural conditions as given. Developing the methods and techniques for sustainable agriculture in the field has been difficult enough. For most of these organizations, addressing the macroeconomic conditions for sustainability as well is simply too daunting to consider.

Campesino a Campesino methodologies have been easily co-opted by most of the *mainstream development institutions* within their "participatory" development frameworks. Of course, these frameworks do not allow for participation regarding substantive program, budget, or political decisions.

Rather, they are designed to give farmers the sense of belonging, of being "stakeholders" in the project being offered. Having a "stake" in a project, however, is an insufficient condition for the development of sustainable agriculture or for the survival and well-being of the region's peasant farmers. Having a stake means little if it can be given and taken away depending on the whims of a development institution or a fickle international market. A stake in an agricultural development project is clearly not the same as exercising a *controlling share* in agriculture itself.

MCAC and the Globalization of Mesoamerica

Campesino a Campesino has enhanced smallholders' "share" in sustainable agricultural development by helping them to improve agriculture while eliminating their dependence on external inputs. Smallholders have stopped erosion, reclaimed soil, forested hillsides, diversified crops, and raised productivity. This has stabilized the family food system and resulted in a marketable surplus, thus providing most farmers in the Movement with some autonomy from the vicissitudes of the hollowed state and the skewed global market. In many cases it has led to higher levels of local organization for village or municipal development.

Nonetheless, MCAC does not exist in a vacuum. The sad fact is that agrarian and economic policies work against smallholders in Mesoamerica. Because these countries have not protected their agriculture from the heavily subsidized imported grains from the First World, few family farmers are doing well. Southern governments have favored agribusiness and conventional agriculture by letting land concentrate in fewer and fewer hands.

Multilateral development institutions often tout their rural development projects, market-driven land reform programs, and nontraditional export projects designed to integrate farmers into the global market. Unfortunately, the precarious benefits from these programs pale against the juggernaut of structural adjustment, privatization, and trade liberalization that destroys domestic markets, shuts down agricultural services, and privatizes everything from rural credit to drinking water.[1] Currently, the real weight of development assistance in Mesoamerica is for maquiladoras, natural resource extraction, tourism, and large infrastructure projects like hydroelectric dams, waterways, and highways. This development model sees no role for smallholders, does not seriously consider regional food security, and on the heroic assumption that free trade and massive infrastructure will automatically bring about development, views sustainability primarily as a question of sustaining growth in GNP. Although there is no solid evidence that any of these activities will lead to improved rural livelihoods instead of more crushing external debt, the region's development institutions, led by the World Bank and the Inter-American Development Bank, continue to insist on NAFTA, CAFTA, the Initiative for Infratructure Integration of South America (IIRSA), and the Plan Puebla-Panamá. The net effect is to push campesinos off the land, leaving the food system in the hands of the transnational agribusiness-agrifoods complex. The add-on rural development projects directed toward the impoverished rural sector are designed to mitigate this structural damage, not to advance socially, economically, or environmentally sustainable agricultural development.

The differences and inconsistencies between actors and institutions in sustainable agriculture reflect the realities of the global political economy, which is centered on maximum resource extraction and profit, not sustainability and equity. Does this mean that sustainable agriculture is doomed to fail? Couldn't these actors and institutions work together to overcome these shortcomings? What if formal research institutions teamed up with NGOs to decentralize research and reach farmers directly? What if farmers' unions prioritized smallholders' agroecological demands to government policy makers and mainstream development institutions abandoned free market reforms to provide aid for credit, guaranteed prices, agricultural extension, and marketing within a campesino-driven sustainable agriculture policy agenda? What if instead of being viewed as a problem, the peasantry was viewed as a solution? Given the impressive thirty-year track record of Campesino a Campesino, what keeps all this from happening?

If we believe that the global economy itself must be transformed before we can have local conditions for sustainability, then sustainable agriculture will require nothing short of a global revolution. This is unlikely in the short or medium term. But sustainable agriculture in MCAC has always been a strategy of *resistance*, not revolution. And it is not simply another recipe for development. If, despite an adversarial political-economic context, the Movement has still gained a foothold "from below" in Mesoamerica, then instead of waiting for a revolution, perhaps it is better to ask what aspects of the current context are changeable. How can these be changed in a way that strengthens the social and political base of autonomous, farmer-led alternatives? Instead of waiting for social change, how can sustainable agriculture itself become a force for social change?

From Cultural Resistance to Social Change

Campesino a Campesino's extensive knowledge networks have been highly successful in generating and spreading sustainable agricultural practices on the ground. In effect, MCAC has decentralized the practice of agricultural development. This is both a measure of and an explanation for its successes. If agriculture is to be sustainable it must not only be based on the ecology of the specific agroecosystem where it is being practiced, it must evolve from the social structures and cultures in which the system itself is embedded. Campesino a Campesino has built local agroecological capacities. Based on these capacities, smallholders develop their own agriculture, arguably, as sustainably as can be expected. While they are clearly constrained by lopsided global markets, hostile agrarian polices, and the absence of any effective support from the state, they have nonetheless figured out how to farm without damaging the environment or going broke. In short, they have survived.

If sustainable agriculture is to become the norm rather than the exception, then these embedded, agroecological experiences must scale out, geographically; up, into the institutions that shape agriculture's social, economic, and political terrain; and in, into the culture of agriculture itself. To go to scale, Campesino a Campesino must not only be effective on the ground, it needs cultural, social, and political power to affect the structures and policies that *hold back* the development of sustainable agriculture.

As evidenced by the appearance of sustainable projects across Latin America, sustainability, equity, social justice, and the conservation of ecological and cultural diversity have become regular discursive currency for development institutions. However, they are far from replacing the "bottom line" of national, multilateral, or regional development programs. In this context, sustainable development, whether through state intervention, multilateral projects, or the "invisible hand" of the global market, is still fundamentally focused on sustaining permanent economic growth to pay off the permanent foreign debt. By this logic, redistributive strategies that address food security, sustainable livelihoods, social and economic justice, and the conservation of ecological and cultural diversity are at best secondary, mitigating considerations in the face of the massive extraction of wealth from the countryside. Changing the superstructure of economic development to favor sustainable agriculture implies the political, economic, and social transformation of the societies that produce that superstructure. The transition to sustainable agriculture requires social change.

What kind of social change? If history has anything to teach us, it is that fundamental changes come about when an existing order enters into crisis and when social movements create political will through broad-based social pressure. Behind the façade of economic progress, industrial models for agricultural development are clearly in social and environmental crisis. Widespread, and increasingly organized, local and regional resistance to structural adjustment, transnational privatization, genetically modified crops, and debt-heavy infrastructure projects are a reflection of this and are an indication of the potential for social change in Latin America.

While many advocacy groups lobby for sustainable agriculture in national and international forums, campesinos—the men and women actually developing sustainable agriculture on the ground—are relatively silent. Smallholders are disperse and politically weak and have little time and few resources to engage in political activity. The MCAC has spread, not through high-profile, charismatic leaders or by force of lobby or protest, but through hardworking promoters and farmer-to-farmer "capillary action" linking experiences of thousands of smallholders from hundreds of communities.

Though the MCAC-NGO partnership has been highly effective in supporting local projects and developing sustainable practices on the ground, it has had little impact on the policy context for sustainable agriculture. Despite a far-flung network of hundreds of NGOs, these supporting institutions have generally not lobbied, pressured, or otherwise organized around policy issues in a significant way. Lobbying in itself is only effective to the extent that it represents and articulates significant political and social force. In the Mesoamerican countryside, "lobbying" often means mobilizing hundreds or thousands of campesinos in marches, protests, invasions, or occupations. Presently, neither the NGOs nor the advocacy groups promoting sustainable agriculture have the capacity to do this. Some farmer organizations do mobilize around agrarian issues, particularly on access to land. However, once peasants receive land, support for the sustainable use of that land is rarely, if ever, the subject for protest or mobilization.

Ironically, MCAC's strength as a network—i.e., its capacity to generate farmer's agroecological knowledge in a horizontal and decentralized fashion—is also its political weakness as a social movement. On one hand, there is no coordinating body capable of mobilizing MCAC's network for social pressure, advocacy, or political action. On the other hand, MCAC's effectiveness at developing sustainable agriculture at the local level has kept its promoters focused on the agroecological *practices* rather than the socioeconomic *conditions* for sustainable agriculture. A focus on the socioeconomic policies limiting sustainable agriculture, and the ability to create social pressure, are necessary conditions for MCAC to become an effective movement for social change.

For the Movement to overcome these limitations, the campesinos in MCAC will need to become as knowledgeable regarding the structural conditions for sustainable agriculture as they are in the practices of sustainable agriculture itself.

As the testimonies in this book demonstrate, MCAC's promoters are very aware of globalization. Their information, however, is patchy, and their understanding of where and how they might resist is unclear and limited to sustainable farming and migration. There is no reason to assume, however, that promotores in the Movement could not become *structurally literate*. There is every reason to believe that they could and would also incorporate political-economic information about industry, policy, markets, and finance into their existing networks for sharing agroecological knowledge. With thematic and methodological support from NGOs, promoters could incorporate a dialogical suite of farmer-to-farmer methods for sharing structural information into MCAC's body of agroecological knowledge. Structural issues like food sovereignty, agroecological agriculture versus genetically modified crops, intellectual property rights versus farmers' rights, and other themes could be included in MCAC workshops, cross visits, and regional gatherings.

The missing link between practical and structural knowledge could be bridged by linking advocacy groups and farmers unions and federations to sustainable agricultural development NGOs. Advocacy groups could provide training and information regarding structural issues, NGOs could help promoters develop appropriate methodologies, and MCAC's farmer-to-farmer networks could take care of spreading structural knowledge. As was the case with agroecological knowledge, it would probably only be a matter of time before these networks began to *generate* information as well. Experiences in preserving agrobiodiversity in the face of transgenic contamination, resistance to colonization by the soy-beef industry, or the creation of local and regional markets for food sovereignty could all be easily shared alongside the agroecological innovations that constantly emerge and spread within MCAC.

Just as the expansion of farmers' agroecological knowledge created a demand for services in sustainable agriculture, the expansion of structural knowledge among campesinos will create a demand for agroecological advocacy.

How this demand is met will depend largely on smallholders and the possibilities for complementary capacities with farmers' organizations, NGOs, and advocacy groups and will likely vary widely from place to place. For example, promoters might pressure farmer organizations for agroecological policy advocacy or for greater representation on the boards of directors in order to ensure that their agroecological demands form an integral part of the organization's political agenda. Or they might seek more direct linkages with advocacy groups for direct action. Then again, they might demand more political accountability from the funding institutions and NGOs that bring them agricultural projects, pressuring them to take proactive positions on structural reforms for sustainable agriculture. Perhaps peasants might pressure agricultural research institutions for greater accountability and transparency as well (after all, it is smallholders' agrobiodiversity that provides the basic genetic material to these institutions to begin with). Then again, smallholders might decide to organize locally, within their own municipalities, opposing multinational seed companies and research institutions to keep their counties GMO-free. They might demand that government set up programs to channel and match remittances to finance and market sustainably farmed products.

There are many ways that campesinos in MCAC, when armed with structural knowledge, could influence the institutions presently operating within the sphere of sustainable agricultural development. However, MCAC's most important, singular opportunity in this regard is cultural: promoters can create *social awareness* among the smallholder sector in the Mesoamerican countryside. This is the first step in building a strong, broad-based movement for social change.

Integrated Transnational Advocacy Networks

Most campesinos don't fight for water rights, land rights, or for abstract notions of sustainability, justice, or "participation" in development . . . they fight for food, for water, for land, for forests, and for a fair price for their products. They struggle for good healthcare, for decent dwellings, and for education for their children. In short, they fight for their livelihoods, not for causes.

As individuals, campesinos hold on fiercely to their dignity, and they reaffirm their rural and indigenous cultures, not because of the principle of dignity or the ideal of culture, but because cultural integrity ensures their existence—to ignore or deny it is to sabotage the networks of mutual aid and reciprocity recognized as essential to survival in a risky, unpredictable, and often hostile world.

Agroecology and sustainable practices help reduce campesino families' risk of livelihood failure over time by reducing their level of vulnerability to external economic, environmental, or political shocks. In this concrete, straightforward sense, the struggle for sustainability is a struggle for autonomy, for protection of and control over production factors essential to survival.

This is not new. Campesinos have survived this way for centuries. What *is* new is that the Campesino a Campesino movement has used agroecology and horizontal learning networks to link campesino communities across village, municipal, and national boundaries. Also new is that these networks occur in a larger, structural context of national and transnational movements for social justice and environmental sustainability. The MCAC's networks have practice and demographic weight but no political influence. The advocacy networks can exert significant political influence but lack a social base for lasting change. The divide between sustainability as advocated by activists and sustainable agriculture as actually practiced on the ground by MCAC reflects the social and political atomization of both campesinos and activists. Overcoming the divide between alternative politics and the struggles of everyday life in the countryside depends on linking the two. Successful social movements are formed by integrating activism with livelihoods. These integrated movements create the deep, sustained, social pressure that produces political will—the key to changing the financial, governmental, and market structures that presently work against sustainability. Sustainability requires social change, which is in turn dependent on the force of social movements.

If Campesino a Campesino is to become an effective social movement that affects both agricultural practice *and* the structures holding back sustainability, it will need to link its agroecological practice to structural literacy and to the *transnational advocacy networks* that lobby and pressure for structural change worldwide. By the same token, if activists for sustainable agriculture expect to have a social impact on political and economic structures, they will have to integrate their advocacy to ground-level campesino struggles for sustainable livelihoods.

The integration of Campesino a Campesino networks with transnational advocacy networks is the major challenge facing the Movement and facing sustainable agriculture in Latin America.

Establishing integrated transnational advocacy networks for sustainable agriculture will depend less on the farmers of MCAC than on the NGOs and activists supporting and advocating sustainable agricultural development. It is not up to campesinos to bridge the divide between development and advocacy—it is up to NGOs and activists to begin linking activism with practice. The Campesino a Campesino movement offers many opportunities for building a deep and politically effective social movement for agricultural sustainability. Localized, "small-scale experiments" in this kind of integration are already underway. If activists and NGOs can learn to work with MCAC's hands of production and protection and walk with the Movement's legs of innovation and solidarity, these networks may well have a significant impact on the struggle for sustainability in Latin America.

W E CAME TOGETHER to write a book. This is a way of writing a continuing chapter, a chapter that makes us stronger, a chapter that brings us together. In the future I hope that we can all carry out actions together for the good of our land and our self-sufficiency. As farmers we defend what we produce and consume. We have to promote unity among our organizations. The unity between campesinos is the way to defend the Campesino a Campesino movement and we are going to make it stronger each day. Remember, our chapter is open. We have so much to write, so much to continue doing, so much to work for, and above all, so much to contribute.   —*Alicia Sarmientos, Tlaxcala, (Mexico 2004)*

Appendix A
UNAG and Campesino a Campesino

THE CHARACTER OF the PCAC-UNAG relationship during this period reflects the general tendency within UNAG to provide social space for campesino agency while simultaneously reserving political power for larger farmers and party leadership. In their inside accounts of UNAG and of the Nicaraguan Cooperative Movement, respectively, Kees Blokland (1992) and Luis Serra (1991) provide extensive quantitative and analytical evidence to explain UNAG's strategies and structures in the context of the complex political tensions between and within UNAG and the FSLN during the revolutionary period.

The cross-class agrarian alliance within UNAG was essential not only to consolidate the revolution's hold in the countryside but to negotiate a middle road between desarrollistas, colectivistas, and campesinistas. As part of their strategy to appease both the rural bourgeoisie and the peasantry, on one hand UNAG offered "patriotic producers" (pro-FSLN large landholders) power and direct representation within the union's central and departmental boards of directors. On the other hand, to keep the campesinado faithful, UNAG implemented a number of projects whose aim was to allow smallholders "self-representation within separate channels of agency" (*gestión*). The most prominent of these were the cooperative federation (FENACOOP) and ECODEPA, UNAG's national chain of *tiendas campesinas*, or country stores, both heavily financed and supported by international nongovernmental organizations. The Women's Section and Programa Campesino a Campesino (PCAC) were also supported through international NGOs, though their profile within UNAG was considerably lower than FENACOOP or ECODEPA (Blokland 1992). In large part this was because they were not viewed as structurally strategic; i.e., both were considered more as social services than as projects that addressed control over the means of production, price, markets, etc. Further, the outside resources brought in by PCAC (approximately US$50–80,000/yr) were paltry compared with ECODEPA, for example, that brought in approximately US$21 million from 1985 to 1989 (Blokland 1992). While the co-ops, the stores, and the teams of promotores were generally characterized by local-level leadership and democratic decision-making, they all remained subjugated under the protective institutional and financial mantle of UNAG's board of directors, who controlled the purse strings, and ultimately the politics. While both the coordinators of FENACOOP and ECODEPA were members of UNAG's national board of directors, PCAC coordinators were always subordinate to board members. Over the course of its existence, PCAC was shuffled from the International section to the Training section to FENACOOP and back to the Training section. Sometimes the PCAC coordinator reported directly to an UNAG board member, other times to a "responsable de area" who then reported to the board of directors.

Medium- and large-scale farmers and FSLN party cadres dominated UNAG's national and departmental boards of directors. UNAG's powerful public forum, the Consejo Nacional, reflected the political dominance of large-scale farmers: 18 percent of farmers in the Consejo had more than 500 manzanas, 56 percent had 50 to 500 manzanas, 19 percent between 10 and 50 manzanas, and only 7 percent had fewer than 10 manzana (1 manzana = 1.73 acres) (Serra in Blokland 1992, 280). While Blokland argues that the capacity of larger, more eloquent, and more mobile farmers to represent all farmers in policy discussions is more important than the number of large farmers in decision-making positions, he is careful to point out UNAG's notorious weakness in this regard: "Many times these spokespeople for UNAG didn't even refer to the criteria of the organizations they represented and instead spoke in their own name" (1992, 281).

Both Serra and Blokland refer to the military history of the FSLN and the impact of the culture and politics of the revolutionary vanguard on the practice of leadership and the development of democracy within UNAG. According to Serra, the hierarchical nature of the revolutionary politico-military structure, the absence of democratic structures within Nicaraguan civil society, and the need to respond quickly to the volatile conditions of the counterrevolutionary period led to a continuation of the Sandinista's top-down *vanguardista* style of leadership: "The liberation movement's project for a just and democratic society is seriously obstructed by a social logic imposed during a profound, prolonged bellicose conflict. The Sandinista experience . . . shows that that the strategy for the 'taking of power' is not a substitute for the construction of hegemony" (1991, 270).

Returning to Freire's concept of praxis, Serra asserts that the Sandinista revolution suffered a break between political reflection and political practice in which the vanguard took charge of cognitive reflection while the popular sectors were moved to action by appealing to the affective and ethical dimensions of change. Orders came from the top down, while very little information (and fewer decisions) flowed from the bottom up. While he makes this observation in relation to the inability of the farmers in the cooperative movement to affect government, party, and union politics, the same holds true for Campesino a Campesino in the sense of separation of leadership from the base within UNAG.

Thus, while UNAG provided a political and institutional umbrella of agrarian protection and project development for Campesino a Campesino and other "channels of agency," it was careful to keep national decision-making power within an elite, centralized enclave of party members and "patriotic" rural bourgeoisie.

PCAC was never seriously considered as a *production* project by the large farmers and party cadre of UNAG's board of directors. If it had been, it would have been located in the Production Section. Rather, it was viewed as a novel form of agricultural extension for campesinos. Nonetheless, PCAC was politically important to UNAG in several ways. During the Sandinista regime, PCAC provided the union with a high-profile project whose emphasis on farmer-led development appealed to campesinos' sense of autonomy, brought smallholders together within UNAG's sphere of influence, and helped mitigate the disaffection of many peasants with UNAG and the Sandinista Revolution. After the Sandinistas' fall from power, the example of PCAC helped UNAG challenge the neoliberal state regarding its lack of attention to campesinos. And while PCAC did not bring in massive economic resources, during one period of donor-driven expansion in the mid-1990s, UNAG used the program to hire a number of union organizers in its departmental offices as "PCAC promotores" (author's interview, Marcial López, PCAC coordinator, 1997). Perhaps most importantly, PCAC was essential to UNAG's public relations in the development arena because it gave neopopulist donors the impression (not entirely false) that UNAG was a campesino organization working to develop sustainable agriculture from the ground up. For these reasons, UNAG jealously guarded PCAC and the notion of a farmer-to-farmer movement as its own creation and was careful to maintain the project under strict political and institutional control.

However, the Campesino a Campesino movement, through PCAC, also had a significant influence on UNAG. In his section describing UNAG's reaction to structural adjustment, Serra states, "UNAG [argued for] integral and coherent development policies that improved national resources and campesino participation, [they] questioned the technological focus based on mechanization and chemical inputs that were no longer economically viable without subsidies, and proposed . . . strengthening the knowledge and technical creativity of the campesino, [by] scaling out the . . . Campesino a Campesino Program. . . ." (1991, 126).

According to Blokland, in the course of the productive and political failures of the Sandinista land reform, UNAG shifted its strategic framework from individual versus collective forms of production to *extensive* versus *intensive* forms of production: "UNAG relaxed its concept of [cooperatives] as a superior form of production. . . . In the late eighties, there were changes . . . that suggested a tendency towards intensification. . . . UNAG pushed a program dedicated to the exchange of technical knowledge among producers, on-farm experimentation, and more autonomy" (1992, 242).

Blokland extracts the primary elements of UNAG's shift toward intensification by citing their support for the following:

1. stabilizing economic policies (to prevent the deterioration of production factors and a return to traditional practices)
2. incentives for producers to establish their own production costs
3. participatory technical assistance in which the producer is the promotor of technological innovation in the countryside
4. a broad technological offer
5. strengthening campesino organization at the grassroots, farmer-to-farmer exchanges and an organizational framework for participatory technical assistance

Aspects 3, 4, and 5 clearly reflect the influence of the Campesino a Campesino movement on UNAG's thinking, and Blokland points to PCAC as evidence of one way UNAG attempted to pursue these strategies. Blokland admits that PCAC was unable to reverse the national tendency toward extensive (and environmentally destructive) forms of agriculture, attributing its failure to "objective limitations" that prevented UNAG from rapidly extending the Campesino a Campesino program. While he does not elaborate on these limitations, he may well be referring to the lack of project funds for project expansion. I would submit that had the UNAG board of directors pursued farmer-led sustainable agriculture aggressively with its donors, funds for PCAC were probably limitless—subjective political factors within UNAG were at least as important as the "objective limitations" limiting the influence of PCAC.

Perhaps because the institutional framework and focus of both studies is UNAG (not PCAC), neither Blokland nor Serra addresses Campesino a Campesino as a regional movement that originates and continues outside of UNAG. Both treat Campesino a Campesino as a creation of UNAG. In this view, the union's promotion of PCAC is not only evidence of UNAG's commitment to campesino-led sustainable agriculture, it is the result of this commitment. Consequently, neither of these authors explore the ways in which the Campesino a Campesino movement influenced UNAG through PCAC. Given the extensive trajectory of MCAC, whose origins predate and whose geographical and programmatic influence outdistance UNAG, this would appear to be an important area of future study.

Appendix B

Hurricane Mitch: A Case Study
in Farmer-Led Research

FARMER-LED sustainable agricultural development approaches have been criticized in conventional development circles for not "scaling up" (i.e., massive adoption), for their alleged weak economic viability, deficient science, and for the lack of evidence regarding claims of sustainability. These criticisms are not entirely misplaced. Analyzing the economic viability of peasant farming styles with their complex blends of pluriactive, risk-averse mixture of subsistence and marketplace strategies is a daunting task, not easily undertaken by the NGOs and farmers' organizations that have pioneered sustainable agriculture in Mesoamérica. Further, it is difficult to predict the overall sustainability of a given agroecosystem and impossible to prove it beyond the "test of time."[1]

Hurricane Mitch, Central America's "storm of the century," provided MCAC with the opportunity to assess over two decades of farmer-led, sustainable agricultural development and to address questions of scientific validity, economic viability, and scaling up. Nearly 2,000 *campesinos* and from forty farmer organizations and NGOs in Guatemala, Honduras, and Nicaragua codesigned and implemented *Measuring Farmers' Agroecological Resistance to Hurricane Mitch in Central America* (Holt-Giménez 2001). The purpose of the study was to evaluate the relative sustainability of MCAC practices and subsequently to propose participatory strategies for sustainable agricultural reconstruction. The results were remarkable. I present the study here in brief because it illustrates the power of campesino pedagogy when coupled with a farmers' movement.

Hurricane Mitch, like all "natural" disasters, was actually a combination of natural hazard and human *vulnerability* (Wilches-Chaux 1994; Smith 1996). Vulnerability is the level of difficulty to "anticipate, cope with, resist,

Source: Holt-Giménez, Eric, "Measuring farmers' agroecological resistance after Hurricane Mitch in Nicaragua: a case study in participatory, sustainable land management impact monitoring" in *Agriculture, Ecosystems and Environment* 93 (2002), 87–105.

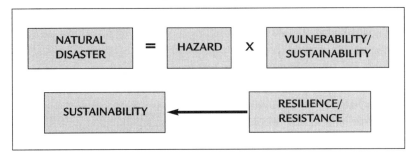

Figure B.1. Theoretical Model for Vulnerability and Sustainability

and recover from the impact of natural hazard" (Blaikie et al. 1994) and can be expressed as an inverse function of the level of sustainability of a model or course of development (Jeffery 1982; Wisner 1993; Duffield 1994; Cardenal 1999).

In this definition, sustainability is a function of resistance and resilience in response to disturbance and stress Increasing the level of resistance or resilience to disturbance will raise the relative level of sustainability (and lower the relative level of vulnerability), mitigating the effects of natural disaster. Using this model, trends toward or away from agroecological sustainability may be assessed by measuring trends in system resistance and/or resilience.[2]

In this study, farmers used paired observations on neighboring farms to measure the relative differences in agroecological resistance between agroecological MCAC farms and their conventional neighbors.

Methodology: Participatory Action Research Design

Farmer-led experimentation (primarily field trials) and farmer-to-farmer field visits have been key practices within MCAC for many years. However, agroenvironmental research at a regional (Central American) scale was untried. The study employed a participatory action research framework, PAR (de Wit and Gianotten 1991; Fals-Borda and Rahman 1991), to guide a research process based on farmers' objectives and their organizational and agroecological capabilities.

In February of 1999, three months after the hurricane, Guatemalan, Honduran, and Nicaraguan farmers' organizations (FOs) and NGOs working in sustainable agriculture were invited to national meetings to discuss the idea of a participatory study on the effects of Hurricane Mitch. There was high interest among organizations that used the Campesino a Campesino approach. Further, FOs and NGOs were keen to evaluate their programs and wanted to influence debates regarding regional reconstruction.

They felt that an objective study comparing sustainable and conventional farms would not only test assumptions regarding sustainability but could contribute to the debate on participatory, sustainable reconstruction. It was hoped that at least twelve FOs/NGOs (four per country) could participate in the research, each with three farmer-technician field research teams. However, as news of the study spread, the number of interested organizations grew. By March, forty FOs/NGOs had joined the study (nineteen from Nicaragua, eleven from Honduras, and ten from Guatemala).

Each NGO organized one to five farmer-technician teams. Once field methods and instruments were developed and field tested, national coordinators held training workshops in all three countries to prepare the teams. Over 100 farmer-technician teams were trained over a three-week period in one-day workshops conducted on farms in potential research areas.

Researchers helped teams select sites from within their own project areas. Teams were trained in field methods and then instructed to identify at least ten farms that they considered had implemented the best set of sustainable practices. To qualify for the study, each sustainable farm also needed a neighboring conventional farm as a control, either bordering or close nearby (100 m), with the same topographical conditions (slope, cardinal orientation, location in the watershed, surrounding topography, and vegetation) to form a paired observation. Small representative plots (~0.5 ha) were selected on each farm for measurements.

Because the number of paired sites was large (nearly 1,000) and because

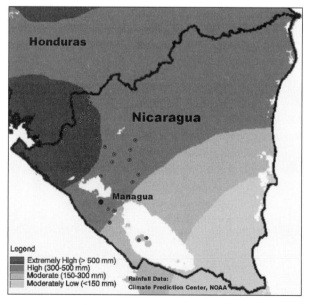

Figure B.2. Map of Research Sites in Nicaragua

these observations covered areas of moderate, high, and extreme storm intensity from southern Nicaragua to eastern Guatemala, the body of observations was a good representation of smallholder practices, ecological conditions, and storm effects in Central America (see map).

The methodological challenge was to sufficiently train a large number of research teams to take consistent, unbiased measurements and observations in highly variable ecological conditions. The importance of precision and unbiased observation was a central theme in team training. To control observational error between teams, technicians were all trained by the same researchers using the same methodology and field manual. To eliminate measurement errors between pairs of farms observed by the same team, each farmer-promoter was trained to make a specific set of measurements and observations. Within each team the same person always made the same measurements. Slope measurements were repeated four times per plot, soil depth, moisture, and erosion measurements three times. As a field check, both farmer-owners (sustainable and conventional) accompanied the research team during the data collection on both farms. Farmers signed off on the field sheet to indicate that in their view, observations and measurements had been done in an unbiased manner (otherwise, the paired observations were either thrown out or done again). Teams carried out ten to twenty paired observations, usually one pair a day. Because the study wanted to isolate the effects of the hurricane, fieldwork was conducted between the end of April and early June, before the onset of the spring rains. Because it would have affected topsoil and moisture measurements, farms that had already begun to prepare fields for planting did not enter into the study. Since most paired observations took place well before farmers began preparing their fields, almost all of the selected farms were able to participate in the study.

Results

There was a consistent pattern of significant differences favoring agroecological plots (A) over conventional plots (C)—see Figure B.3. Despite high ecological variability between paired sites, agroecological plots in all three countries had more topsoil, more field moisture, and more vegetation. Measurements of severe erosion made in Nicaragua showed a similar pattern.

Topsoil, Depth to Humidity, and Vegetation

On average, agroecological plots had 30 to 40 percent more topsoil than conventional plots. While differences of two centimeters may seem small, they are equivalent to 200 m²/ha of topsoil and an approximate erosion rate of 100 tons/ha/yr (Toness, Thurow, and Sierra 1998).[3]

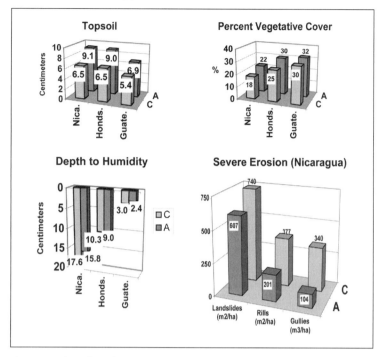

Figure B.3. Physical Results

The indicator used to compare levels of field moisture did not establish field moisture per se, but compared the depth to observable moisture from the dry soil surface. The assumption was that moist soil found closest to the surface indicated greater levels of field moisture. On average, farmers had to dig 3 to 10 percent less on agroecological plots than on conventional plots to reach moisture.

The measure of vegetation was considered both an indication of storm impact and a general indication of on-farm regenerative ecological processes. Agroecological plots had approximately one-fifth more vegetative cover than conventional plots.

Erosion: Landslides, Rills, and Gullies

On average, agroecological plots lost 18 percent less arable land to landslides than conventional plots and had a 49 percent lower incidence of landslides. Agroecological plots averaged 47 percent less rill erosion than conventional plots. The frequency of rill erosion among agroecological farms was 58 percent lower than on conventional farms. Eighty percent of conventional plots were found to have up to 78.1 m²/ha more rill erosion than agroecological plots. Agroecological plots averaged 69 percent less gully erosion compared to conventional farms. Gullies occurred 63 percent less on agroecological plots. Eighty percent of conventional plots had at least 20 m²/ha more volume of land loss to gully erosion than did agroecological plots.

Trends in Agroecological Resistance

A close inspection of the data revealed some important trends:

- Old agroecological farms (ten years and older) had two and three times larger differences in topsoil, soil moisture, and percentage of vegetation with their conventional neighbors than did young agroecological farms (one to two years) with theirs, indicating that resistance increased over time for these indicators.
- However, differences in severe erosion rose in favor of mature agroecological farms (three to five years old) then dropped for old farms, indicating a drop in agroecological resistance. This may be because farmers on older farms with established terraces tend to abandon the use of conservation ditches.
- Differences in severe erosion tended to rise with increasing storm intensity, indicating increasing agroecological resistance with increasing levels of rainfall disturbance.
- However, on 30 to 50 percent slopes, the differences in severe erosion between agroecological and conventional farms tended to fall, indicating the need to deal more effectively with heavy runoff on steep hillsides and/or a "threshold" for the effectiveness of these practices.
- Agroecological farms on very steep slopes and those under extreme storm intensity lost their profit advantage in relation to conventional farms. This loss of relative economic resistance under a combination of extreme stress and disturbance (slope and rainfall) suggests physical limits to the economic viability of present agroecological practices.
- Newly established agroecological farms (one to two years) also had no profit advantage over their conventional neighbors, suggesting that farmers are economically vulnerable early in the transition from conventional to agroecological practices.

Feedback Phase: Reconstruction Policy from the Grassroots

The research employed several post-fieldwork steps to share and enrich the study's findings:

- An initial "feedback" phase in which preliminary findings were first shared by research organizers with the NGO/FO, the farmer-technician research teams, local authorities, and other local NGOs.

- A grassroots phase, in which the farmer-technician teams shared the study with villagers in the communities where the research had been carried out.
- A national presentation phase in which researchers, promotores, and technicians presented findings in a seminar for a broad audience of national and international NGOs, government officials, university researchers, and the national press.
- An extended, public phase in which the study's findings were made available to the development community in Central America through articles, websites, and e-mail.
- A follow-up phase one year after the study in which a one-day workshop was held in Nicaragua. Study participants met to assess the impact that the study had on their reconstruction efforts.

In an effort to explore the determinants of farmer-led, sustainable agriculture, participants were asked why MCAC farmers had adopted agroecological practices and why conventional neighbors had not. Farmers responded that adoption and nonadoption depended on the factors listed in Table B.1.

TABLE B.1 · FACTORS FOR ADOPTION OR NONADOPTION OF SUSTAINABLE PRACTICES

ADOPTION	NONADOPTION
• Need to maximize production on small parcels of land	• Rented or sharecropped land (farmers are unwilling to invest in medium- to long-term improvements)
• Need to reclaim ecologically degraded land to increase production	• Lack of time/family labor (labor-intensive soil & water conservation costs too high, especially for single women)
• Debt avoidance (difficulty in paying off credit for agrochemicals)	
• Need to lower costs	• Lack of knowledge (of SARD/SLM principles, practices and management)
• Desire to reduce vulnerability to recurrent drought and floods	• Too much land (farmers can rotate plots when degradation becomes a problem)
• Desire for greater autonomy (from banks and government conventional agriculture schemes)	• Chemical subsidies (ecological degradation processes are masked by application of cheap fertilizers, pesticides, and herbicides)
• Concern for family health (avoid pesticide poisoning; desire for diverse, balanced diet)	• Lack of environmental awareness (some farmers simply to do not "care" about the environment)
• Access to MCAC training and farmer-to-farmer exchanges	• Tradition (resistance to change, unwillingness to risk new methods)
• Technical assistance from NGO technicians (farmer-led experiments, advice, agronomic knowledge)	
• Incentives (credit, market for organic products, tools, information)	

The consultation with farmers and community members indicated that, in general, the development of sustainable agriculture was directly related to the failures of conventional agricultural on the one hand and to on-the-ground successes of MCAC and institutional support of NGOs on the other. While it was not possible to ascertain the exact reach of MCAC, it was clear that the movement used NGO programs to expand into new areas and to maintain and deepen its presence in farming communities. NGOs provided a supportive vehicle and "policy context" for MCAC by providing transportation and financial support for farmer-to-farmer visits and workshops, support for *campesino* experimentation, access to new information, knowledge, seeds, and technology, and in some cases, credit for sustainable practices and access to organic and international markets. While MCAC's blend of innovation and solidarity were key to the spread of farmer-led sustainable agriculture, adoption did not happen in a vacuum.

Though the agroecological and economic breakdown of conventional agriculture (agronomic involution, disappearance of subsidies, poor extension, etc.) made farmers more receptive to alternative approaches, without access to the human resources in MCAC and to the informational and logistical resources of the NGOs, these farmers might just as easily turn away from farming altogether. Given a favorable policy environment (albeit at the micro level), campesinos had proven themselves capable of developing a form of agriculture that was more sustainable than the conventional agriculture supported by both government agricultural policies and mainstream international/national agricultural research. Farmers pointed out that the criticism leveled at MCAC (primarily from conventional agriculture adherents) regarding its inability to "scale up" sustainable agriculture obviated the fact that to replace traditional agriculture, conventional agriculture itself had relied on extensive support from mainstream agricultural research, cheap credit, and favorable price and market policies.

Community/Researcher Assessment

Campesinos farming in areas where Hurricane Mitch rained hardest claimed that the storm unleashed "ten winters" of rain on their fields in a week. The differences observed between sustainable and conventional farms, they reasoned, were an indication of what might be expected over the next decade. Though erosion processes cannot be extrapolated in such a linear fashion (the impact of Mitch's intensive rains was undoubtedly more severe than ten winters of normal weathering), the study provided farmers and researchers with a compelling picture of agroecological trends and tendencies among and between sustainable and conventional farming styles in Central America. By providing quantifiable evidence of higher agroecological resistance on sustainable farms, the findings validate many years of hard work by farmers in the MCAC, identified key factors driving and limiting sustainable agriculture in Central America, and generated an important list of policy options for "scaling up."

Specifically, the study uncovered problems and possible thresholds to present practices:

- The drop in resistance to severe erosion over time and on very steep slopes indicates that MCAC farmers need to renovate, modify, and maintain conservation structures to deal with excess runoff from extreme rainfall events (e.g., reverse-slope bench terraces, sloped toe drains, etc.).
- The collapse of economic resistance on very steep slopes and at high storm intensity suggests that some conditions are simply too extreme to farm successfully using current agroecological practices. Sustainable agriculture needs to address issues of ecologically based land reform and policies for appropriate land use on hillsides, particularly in upper watershed areas (e.g., payment for soil and water conservation, reforestation, maintenance of biodiversity, etc.).
- Lower economic resistance in the early years of establishing agroecological practices suggests that farmers are making the transition to sustainable agriculture precisely when their farms are most vulnerable, i.e., after the "diminishing returns" agroecological involution have already begun. This points to the need both to provide incentives for transition *before* farms become so vulnerable and for initial subsidies or backstopping during the transition period.

The fact that NGOs and farmers were able to coordinate on a national level to both monitor their own projects and carry out simple but relevant research opens up important opportunities for coordinated, decentralized approaches to sustainable agricultural research. Follow-up studies of this nature could increase both farmers' technical capacity and the scope for scientists' research. Given the complex, diverse, and ecosystem-specific nature of sustainable agricultural development, further broad-based participatory work in the area of agroecological vulnerability could offer new ways of researching agroenvironmental problems. Once agroecological domains and indicators are chosen and field methods are mastered, the model for agroecological resistance could be reapplied to address agroecological resilience as well. New indicators for low-intensity and local, recurrent disasters such as drought, pest outbreaks, and even market crashes could be developed to further measure resistance and resilience.

Notes

Preface

1. Historically, the Tlaxcaltecos, tired of giving heavy tribute to the Aztec empire, had sided with the Spaniards during the conquest of Mexico. They paid a high price for their imperial alliance: Tlaxcala's dense forests were promptly razed for their lumber (allowing Spain to build its famous armada) and turned into pasture for Iberian sheep. The Spanish *hacendados* set aside the worst land for their indigenous *peones*, where the impoverished Tlaxcaltecos grew corn, beans, and squash. By the time the Mexican Revolution finally finished turning the haciendas over to the peasantry in 1938, Tlaxcala, the smallest state in Mexico, had become the most highly populated, the poorest, and the most highly eroded state in the nation.

Introduction

1. *Campesinos* and *campesinas* are the men and women whose livelihoods are based on small-scale agriculture, who generally engage in small commodity production, and who rely primarily on family labor. I use the term interchangeably with *peasant* and *smallholder*. The term *campesinado* refers to the peasantry as a sector.
2. The *Green Revolution* refers to the agricultural transformation of the Third World by CGIAR—the Consultative Group for International Agricultural Research. Originally funded by the Ford and Rockefeller foundations, CGIAR established international research centers around the world. These centers developed high-yielding grain varieties and hybrids (HYVs). The HYVs raised yields, but only with the use of fertilizers, irrigation, and pesticides. Since only larger, capitalized farmers had access to these inputs, the Green Revolution tended to benefit large- rather than small-scale farms.
3. The United Nations Conference on Environment and Development (UNCED) held in Rio de Janeiro, Brazil, in 1992 officially refers to sustainable agriculture and rural development (SARD) in its document, Agenda 21, dedicating Chapter Fourteen to principles and strategies for implementation.
4. *Ejidatarios* are farmers with rights to state-owned communal land called *ejido*. This system of communal landholding, originally legislated during the Mexican agrarian reform, provides for usufruct, but not individual, ownership over agricultural land. Ejidos are run by local assembly through locally elected officers.
5. The terms *promotor*, *promotora*, and *promotores* refer to the peasant men and women who both farm and teach sustainable agriculture.

Chapter One

1. This section draws extensively from Holt-Giménez 1996.
2. *Praxis* is the process of learning and changing the world by integrating theory, practice, and social action.

3. There was a handful of groups experimenting with alternative agricultural techniques: CEMAT (Center for Apropriate Technology Management) in Guatemala, the Mexican Friends Service Committee, Promoción de Desarrollo Popular (Mexico), Oxfam, Heifer Project, World Neighbors. Peace Corps volunteers also looked to small-scale alternatives in remote areas.

4. In particular, the absence of agricultural machinery made incorporating green manures tedious, shortages of water and labor limited composting to home gardens, and the absence of winter freezes (and insect die-off) made many types of seasonal insect control inoperable. There is also a decades-long, continuing history of failure in development projects focusing on penned chickens, rabbits, and goats (following North American and European farm systems of the earlier 1900s) to supplement income and diet.

5. Personal communication with Roland Bunch, 1994.

6. Author's interviews with Guatemalan promotores from Chimaltenango, 1987; Mexico, 1994 and 1995; and Honduras, 1998. Names of promotores withheld upon request.

7. "The basic needs approach to development, stimulated by the World Employment Conference of the International Labor Office in 1976, defines the five main basic needs as food, health, water and sanitation, education, and shelter. By targeting scarce resources on the poorest 40 percent of the population, the basic needs approach aims to eradicate (or lessen) hunger, disease, and illiteracy with fewer resources and sooner than the round-about method of raising incomes" (Streeten 1983).

8. A number of Kato-Ki's leaders fled into the mountains of Guatemala where they joined the guerrilla movement. Apparently, all of these men and women were killed during the bloody insurgency that, falling hardest on the peasantry, cost Guatemala hundreds of thousands of lives.

9. There is some disagreement on the character of the different development tendencies in Nicaragua: Baumeister's *desarrollistas* and *colectivistas* correspond to Maldier and Marchetti's *leninistas* and *desarrollistas*, respectively. The substantive differences between these analytical approaches revolve around the central importance that Maldidier and Marchetti assign the different forms of production and the aggregate agricultural product of Nicaragua's campesinado, while Baumeister focuses on the importance of the campesinado's level of salaried labor.

10. From an interview by the author (Managua 1984). See also Wheelock's accusations that foreign technicians' promoting animal traction and "appropriate" or "intermediate" agricultural technologies as is "institutionalizing underdevelopment" (Wheelock 1985).

11. The Sandinistas consistently misjudged and underestimated the size, importance, and complexity of the peasantry. For an in-depth treatment of the catastrophic blunders resulting from this ideological bias, see Bendaña 1991. For a fine-grained characterization and analysis of the social and productive complexity of the Nicaraguan peasantry and its past and potential contributions to the national economy, see Maldidier and Marchetti 1996.

12. As Scott (1976) put it, "The problem for the peasantry during the capitalist transformation of the Third Word . . . is that of providing for a minimum income."

13. The *Resistencia* (counterrevolutionary forces) reflected the following: the military chain of command mirrored the chain of patronage and power relations in the countryside (Maldidier and Marchetti 1996).

14. Actually, there were historical political differences between MIDINRA and UNAG. The former was run by Jaime Wheelock of the *proletario* tendency, and the latter by *tercerista* Daniel Núñez. MIDINRA reflected the proletario's Leninist orientation, while UNAG reflected the tercerista's eclectic approach. For a discussion of the FSLN's different tendencies and their effect on government, see Booth (1992).

15. This author.

16. On their second visit to Nicaragua, the Mexican team arrived at the Managua airport for a three-week visit, apparently with only carry-on bags. Smiling, they pointed to the conveyor belt as it tumbled their "luggage" into the baggage claim area: each had brought their own moldboard plow from home. Horse- rather than ox-drawn, the Mexican plow permitted the incorporation of organic matter with animal traction.

17. Don Dolores "Lolo" Lanzas, interview with author, 1986.

18. Ramos Sánchez 1998, 73.

19. Ramos Sánchez 1998.

20. From the pedagogical tradition of Paulo Freire, literally "methodologist," a trainer or adult education specialist.

21. Interview with author, 1987.

22. See also Blokland (1992).

23. The Sandinista mass organizations were worker, peasant, and cultural organizations organized and led by members of the Sandinista party (e.g., ATC, the Agricultural Workers Association). They received money from the state as well as direct international aid and were represented in the Nicaraguan Congress.

24. These political encounters worked both ways. Invited to speak at a UNAG rally in Managua, Craig Adams, a small farmer from Wisconsin, said as I translated, "I'm just a small farmer, like you, but I have seen how your government gives farmers land. In my country, the Reagan Administration is using the banks to take the land away from us. He is doing the same here by funding the counterrevolution. He is trying to quash the Agrarian Reform and kill your Revolution. So, I am here today to say, 'your struggle is my struggle'." There was a silent pause while his words were translated, then the plaza erupted as some 20,000 campesinos thrust their machetes and AK-47s in the air shouting, "Poder Popular! Poder Popular!" Adams jumped back from the podium. "What happened? What are they saying?" he asked, truly alarmed. "They like it," I reassured him, "they are saying 'Power to the People'." Soon thereafter, Craig Adams left his farm in the United States and, at UNAG's invitation, moved to a land reform cooperative in Nicaragua with his family.

25. While PCAC did eventually have a handful of full-time, paid promotores, the majority were volunteers or part-time promotores whose primary source of income came from their own farms. NGO-run people-centered approaches also employed campesino-extensionists in this manner, but their institutional range was much more limited than UNAG's.

26. International assistance also had to regroup. For years progressive and social-democratic parties from Europe had convinced their parliaments to support state-run aid programs in Nicaragua because of popular support (both abroad and within Nicaragua) for the Sandinista revolution. Concrete results from this foreign aid were rarely a prerequisite for funding or renewed support. The war, inexperience, and respect for client internal policies and processes were often cited as reasons to fund projects that continually fell short of their goals and objectives. (The programmatic response of the NGO community was to focus evaluations on process and problems rather than product and solutions.) Projects became economic ends in themselves. It is no secret that many foreign NGOs used aid as a nonofficial means of opposing U.S. policy toward Nicaragua and that the Nicaraguan government and the mass organizations (UNAG included) owed their financial existence directly or indirectly to foreign aid. But the Sandinista loss of elections signified loss of state power and implied loss of public support. The effectiveness of foreign aid through Sandinista organizations was seriously questioned abroad. Progressive NGOs were pre-

vailed upon at home to justify their program activities in the face of what was viewed as a political debacle.

27. Merlet (1995) documented this growth from just two municipalities in 1987 to twenty-one in 1991 and thirty-nine in 1993. By 1995, Campesino a Campesino was present (often in several towns at once) in all of Nicaragua's sixty-seven municipalities.

28. These figures do not include the promotores and beneficiaries of the several dozen Nicaraguan NGOs also working in the broader Campesino a Campesino movement in Nicaragua, nor in the rest of Mexico and Central America.

29. Phenologically, because of its ability to transport nutrients to the soil surface and its rapid production and mineralization of massive amounts of organic matter, velvet bean approximated key ecosystem functions of tropical forests. Because of rapid mineralization processes in the tropics, tropical forests store nutrients primarily in the biomass rather than the soil, where high acidity immobilizes phosphorous. Plant roots tend to use soil as an anchor to access nutrients in the decomposing litter. This led Bunch to claim that crops did well when intercropped with velvet bean because they were able to access nitrogen in the rapidly decomposing mulch (Bunch 1995).

30. Interview with author, 1994.

31. When UNAG sent a delegation to Europe in the early 1990s specifically to raise money for their Banco del Campo, or Farmers' Bank, they sent three promotores (all small, individual producers) from Campesino a Campesino along to give presentations in public/NGO forums. The short-lived bank served primarily large- and medium-scale producers and to some extent the co-op sector. The fact that UNAG did not collect membership dues made it completely dependent on heavy infusions of funding, primarily from European NGOs. Campesino a Campesino (which was funded separately through smaller donations) provided an important institutional image that justified NGO funding of UNAG's underlying political project and a public image that gave the impression that UNAG was primarily a smallholders' organization. This was important to UNAG because funders would never have convinced the public that medium and large producers in Nicaragua were in need of their financial assistance.

32. On two different occasions I was contracted to carry out an evaluation of projects in the Rio San Juan region of Nicaragua, each time with a different NGO. On both trips, each NGO led me to the same farmer, introducing him as "their" promotor. While the man was a volunteer, he clearly derived benefits from the NGOs, e.g., travel, access to seeds, training, ideas, etc. When I asked him why he worked for two different agencies, he stated "I am Campesino a Campesino. These NGOs just help me do my work." The "freelance promotor" is common in the movement. Some, like José Jesús Mendoza of Nicaragua, Lázaro Agüin of Guatemala, and others in Honduras, have established training centers on their own farms. Others, like Grupo Vicente Guerrero, formed their own NGO. Still others, like Dolores Lanzas and Catalino Conrado of Nicaragua, travel about informally at the invitation of other campesinos.

33. Cuba was part of the Council for Mutual Economic Assistance (CMEA) which was dominated by the Soviet Union and had as members all the other socialist eastern European countries.

34. Interview with author, Cuba, May 2004.

35. Miguel Dominguez, ANAP.

36. Luis Sánchez, interview with author, June 2004.

37. Héctor Méndez, Cooperativa de Producción Agrícola Julio Pino Machado, Manicaragua.

38. The concept of "capillary nature" is adapted from anthropologist Michael Kearney's concept of "reticular nature," which describes the nonlinear, uneven ways in which immi-

grant cultures penetrate society, following many paths of least resistance at the same time, similar to capillary action. (Kearney 1997, 391)

39. At a workshop session on community development at the thirteenth anniversary of PCAC, several promotores gave reports on the progress of community reconstruction and development efforts after Hurricane Mitch. Proudly, they pointed to their ability to recruit up to twenty government agencies and NGOs per community for the tasks of sustainable recovery and development. Development and social workers present were embarrassed by the obvious institutional overlap and concentration of resources. Campesinos, however, applauded the efficiency with which the promotores were able to bring resources into the community.

Chapter Two

1. A system of centralized political patronage and often corrupt local leadership.

2. This section relies heavily on the work of Anasonia Recinos Montes and her report for the Hurricane Mitch Study, "Las Parcelas Gemelas: Como la agricultura campesina resistió el huracán Mitch" (1999).

3. This and similar quotations are amalgamations of campesino voices from village discussions that took place after the Mitch Study was concluded.

Chapter Three

1. "Men grow physically, they visibly grow, when they learn something, when they come to own it, and when they have done something well." From a Cuban Small Farmers Association report on MCAC.

2. "One of the main things is to do something to be able to teach it. To do something in order to teach others is the best method that exists for moving forward in the countryside."

3. From Paulo Freire's work, *dialogical* refers to a process in which knowledge is created through dialogue and shared experience. *Praxis* is the process of "reflection-action-reflection," also pioneered by Freire.

4 The peer-driven approach to extension goes back further, to the International Institute for Rural Research as established by James Yen in the Philippines in the early 1950s. Prior to this, Yen had pioneered the Chinese "barefoot doctor" approach taken up by the Chinese government. This in turn was adopted and adapted by David Werner (author of *Where There Is No Doctor*) in Mexico and by the Berhorst Clinic in Guatemala during the 1970s.

5. The challenge then became not how to get farmers to participate in development projects, but rather how to get experts to meaningfully participate in village-level processes of agricultural change. This issue has been addressed by Robert Chambers (1994a, 1994b, 1994c) through PRA. However, PRA is not without its critics who claim that its "participatory" agenda is still paternalistic because it assumes experts can "empower" villagers. See Cooke and Kothari (2001).

6. See Freire (1970b, 1973b, 1979).

7. The "preferential option for the poor" describes the social practice of the "liberation theology" wing of the Catholic Church, which sees poverty as an injustice.

8. One well-know promoter who had worked with peasant communities extensively in Nicaragua was involved in a collective land dispute that resulted in the accidental death of one of the parties. He fled to escape incarceration. Disguised, penniless, relying solely on the networks of reciprocity within the Campesino a Campesino movement, he easily eluded authorities for months until his innocence was established, allowing him to return home.

9. This "autonomous informality" (it is not informal for campesinos) in MCAC differs from more institutionalized approaches to farmer-led experimentation. The CIALs (Committee for Local Agricultural Research) promoted by CIAT (Center for Tropical Research) in Cali, Colombia, follow a stepwise methodology in which, often at the behest of CIAT, communities elect local research committees and provide a separate plot for agricultural experiments. The CIALs run self-selected field trials and manage a budget provided by the agricultural research or development institution (see Ashby and Sperling 1995).

10. This diversity in experimental design can lead to some confusion. On the island of Ometepe in Nicaragua, farmers designed experiments to test the adaptability of velvet bean in local farming systems. Farmers tried the bean as an intercrop and cover crop in maize, rice, and plantain. They designed experiments to test velvet bean's usefulness in weed control, fertility, and soil conservation. Test plots were planted in a number of very different soils on hillsides and on the flats in "old" and "new" fields. While farmers did use the "one experiment-one control" in-field design for testing the bean, some measured the plot in meters, others in varas, and others in *tareas* (the area worked in a day); some measured results in weight (kilos), others by volume (*cuartillos,* approximately a half-gallon), others in time worked (*jornales.* or one day's work). While the experiments gave an excellent opportunity to assess the different capabilities and potential of the bean, comparing results became a tower of babble. Luckily, the technician assisting the project had foreseen this difficulty and had quietly converted everyone's measurements to metric.

11. "While it is true that techniques and information are important, without knowledge and wisdom, these are like an ox-team without a plowman...they just go around in circles" (Holt-Giménez 1997).

12. The codification of MCAC's normative principles took place over several years in many farmer-led workshops. Methodologists and promoters interpreted and codified campesinos' thoughts, ideas, and beliefs regarding their movement, drawing widely and from indigenous and populist traditions. The importance of normative values for individuals, families, and communities in farmer-led development was also addressed by Marcos Orozco and by Elias Sánchez. See "La Finca Humana" in IICA (1991) and Smith (1994).

13. Professionals from PRIAG (Program to Reinforce Basic Grain Research in Central America) with extensive ties to MCAC developed the "farmer-experimenter" approach. They later used the approach with the Ministry of Agriculture in Costa Rica to establish links between farmers, researchers, government-extensionists, and promotores in the MCAC network (Hocde et al. 2000). Working with the Inter-American Institute on Agricultural Cooperation (IICA), PRIAG was instrumental in formulating the methodological component of the Honduran-Salvadoran Sustainable Hillside Agriculture project (Miranda 1999).

Chapter Four

1. *Atol* is a drink made of toasted maize. *Pastel* is a type of cupcake.
2. A day of obligatory, nonpaid, community work, usually done on Sunday.

Chapter Five

1. This chapter is based on sections from Holt-Giménez 2002.
2. Originally formulated by Kautsky and addressed by Lenin and Chayanov during the emergence of the Soviet Union, the agrarian question essentially addresses the relationships among politics, agricultural production, and the accumulation of wealth under the changing conditions of capitalist development. It was understood in terms of the condi-

tions for surplus mobilization; urban wage goods (food), industrial labor and exports, as well as the problem of insuring a "home market"; the former to transfer surplus to industry and the latter to find domestic markets for goods produced by industry (Goodman, Sorj, and Wilkinson 1987). For a review and recontextualization of the agrarian question in the Third World, see *Rural Development: Theories of Peasant Economy and Agrarian Change*, John Harriss, Ed., Hutchison University Library, London, 1982 and *The Awkward Class: Political sociology of peasantry in a developing society*, Teodor Shanin, Clarendon Press, Oxford, 1972.

3. During the Depression, economist John Maynard Keynes had convinced government and industry to rely on government borrowing and investment in public works to encourage economic recovery. This "Keynesian consensus" was the basis for the Marshall Plan, designed to rebuild Western Europe and consolidate capitalism in the face of Soviet communism. This rationale then became the basis for the development project in Latin America and much of the Third World (Rapley 1996).

4. Deforestation accelerated during the Green Revolution period, reaching unprecedented levels of 50,000 to 150,000 hectares a year (Utting 1993; FUNDESCA 1994). Not surprisingly, soil erosion was reported as the major environmental problem facing the region's main watersheds.

5. Ecological problems tended to surface more quickly after introduction of the paquete tecnológico in the more tropical regions of Central America than in the Meseta Central of Mexico. In areas of shallow soils, higher mineralization rates led to soil degradation and a rapid decline in fertilizer response within three to five years. I was a rural development worker in Mexico during this period. There were few available resources for alternative agriculture and all were in English. They included sources such as Volunteers in Technical Assistance's *Appropriate Technology Sourcebook*, the *Whole Earth Catalogue*, and John Jeavons's manual on French intensive gardening, *Growing More Vegetables*.

6. Smallholder, rain-fed agriculture using Green Revolution practices were labeled "semi-technified" (*semi-tecnificado*). Basically they used the paquete technológico without agricultural machinery or irrigation.

7. "In the last twenty years there has been a notable deterioration in the natural resource base, and also in the rhythm of deterioration. Between 1970 and 1990, 92 million [hectares] of forest were lost in Latin America and the rate of yearly deforestation rose to 5.4 million [hectares] in 1970 to 6.8 in 1990. Between 1980 and 1990, carbon emissions generated through change in land use rose from 384 million tons to 525 million tons. Eroded, compacted and salinified land expanded" (Kaimowitz 1993, 3).

8. Kaimowitz 1993.

9. The negotiations for FTAA have progressed through three presidential summits—Miami 1994, Santiago 1998, and Quebec 2001—and eight ministerial meetings. Agriculture is one of nine negotiated areas.

10. Corn in Mexico was incorporated into NAFTA in 1992 but protected until 1994 when new policies liberalized markets, changed subsidy policies, and canceled state buying. Help with inputs and interest rates declined drastically with privatization. Fifty percent of maize producers were forced to abandon agriculture (Hubert Carton de Gramont in Zamora 2003a).

11. NAFTA stipulated a gradual phase-out of Mexican tariffs on maize. In its zeal to eliminate smallholder production to make way for larger, capitalized grain production, the Mexican government reduced tariffs below NAFTA stipulated levels. This was coupled with the Article 27 amendment to the Mexican constitution that privatized the collective ejidos, historically the agrarian basis for peasant farmers.

12. "In its several conceptions, agroecology has emerged as a scientific approach used to study, diagnose and propose alternative low-input management of agroecosystems, solving the sustainability problem of agriculture is the primary aim of agroecology. It is maintained here, however, that simply focusing on the technological aspects of the problem, even though promoted technologies are low input, obscures the fundamental problems that lie behind the technology-induced environmental crisis and rural poverty affecting the agricultural regions of the world. Agroecology can provide the ecological guidelines to point technological development in the right direction, but in the process, technological issues must assume their corresponding role within a strategy of rural development that incorporates social and economic problems" (Altieri 1989, 1).

13. In Mexico, importantly, while migration is at an all-time high, the land sales expected from the privatization of the ejidos have not occurred. Peasants appear to be hanging on to land and maize, despite unfavorable conditions (Barkin 2001).

Chapter Six

1. The industrialized agriculture in the First World currently held up as a model of development did not develop under these conditions. Even today, agribusiness in the First World enjoys significant direct and indirect subsidies, thus protecting it from any real competition from Third World farmers.

Appendix B

1. As a property of an agricultural system, sustainability is neither static nor deterministic, but probabilistic. At best, models describe the likelihood that particular management practices will lead to "meeting the needs of the present without compromising the ability of future generations to meet their own needs." Heuristically, probabilistic models and indicators of sustainability have helped researchers identify trends and calculate the possible impacts of specific farming practices on sustainability. Different indices, models, and frameworks (e.g., sustainable land management systems or SLM) for evaluating sustainable land management, as well as the application of basic agroecological principles, can also guide efforts to develop sustainable agriculture. However, environmental stochasticity and the spatial and temporal complexity of farming's constantly changing social and agroecological interactions demand continual redefinition of system goals and the corresponding readjustment of farming practices. There is a constant, widespread, and site-specific need for researchers and farmers to identify those practices leading away from sustainability, as well as to validate those that lead toward more sustainable systems. Participatory Rural Appraisal techniques are now commonly employed by researchers, development professionals, and rural communities to reflect on local socioenvironmental trends. Similarly, Farmer Participatory Research and Participatory Technology Development have been widely used to develop and validate low-external-input technologies to increase yields and lower production costs for small-scale farmers in fragile or degraded agroecosystems. Nevertheless, due to economic constraints, few participatory approaches attempt to evaluate the actual impact of alternative practices. For the most part, sustainable agriculture projects assume that the practices they promote will improve sustainability without ever measuring the results to see if this is actually the case. The development of reliable indicators of sustainability for project managers and farmer-stakeholders is a central concern of impact monitoring in sustainable agriculture.

2. These concepts are compatible with the agroecosystem framework for sustainable agriculture. At an ecological level, sustainability is the ability of an agroecosystem to maintain its productivity when subject to "stress" (a relatively small, regular, continuous

perturbation) and "perturbation" (a relatively large, irregular, and unpredictable disturbance) (Conway 1985). The ability of the farm systems' ecological functions to resist and recover from the stresses of cultivation and harvest parallels the successional tendency of natural ecosystems to return to a similar but modified state after a disturbance known as "dynamic equilibrium" (Gliessman 1998b). The intensity, frequency, and scale of disturbance, either from stress or perturbations, can affect the level of dynamic equilibrium in an agroecosystem, as can the management (or lack thereof) of ecosystem functions. If the agroecosystem is not managed with practices that ensure the maintenance of agroecological functions, the system can lose its capacity for ecological resistance and resilience and become unstable, unproductive, and unsustainable.

3. Differences encountered in topsoil are an especially important finding because they suggest that the regional estimates of erosion damage from Hurricane Mitch based on satellite imagery (that only detected landslides and large areas of bare subsoil) were probably much too low. Ironically, peasants working with shovels and tape measures detected laminar soil erosion satellites missed.

Glossary

abonera — compost heap

agrónomo — agronomist

aparato A — a simple A-frame device for laying out contour lines

biodynamic gardening — an agroecological method of gardening that uses copious amounts of organic matter and deep, raised beds for intensive cultivation. Pioneered by John Jeavons of Ecology Action

campesino/a — peasant, smallholder

campesinado — the peasantry; smallholder sector

compromiso moral — a moral commitment

compañero/a — friend, comrade, partner, companion, spouse

concientización — raising of awareness, usually political

contour ditch — a ditch dug on the level contour of a field to trap runoff

dialogical — characterized by discovery and learning through problem-solving dialogue

ejido — the Mexican system of communal landholding, originally legislated during the Mexican agrarian reform, which provides for usufruct but not individual ownership over agricultural land. Ejidos are run by local assembly through locally elected officers.

encuentro — gathering or large meeting

frijol abono — velvet bean, *Mucuna pruriens, Stizolobium deeringianum*; a plant used as a green mulch in many agroecological systems in Mesoamerica

hectare — 0.7 acres, 100 × 100 meters

huipil — embroidered blouse worn by indigenous women in Mesoamerica

intercambio — exchange of experience; cross visits between farmers

kuchubal — indigenous team system of mutual aid

latifundia/o — large plantation with paid and unpaid peasant labor

manzana — 1.73 acres

municipio — municipality, county

paquete tecnológico — fertilizer, pesticide, herbicide, and high yielding variety/ hybrid seed

praxis — the process of learning and changing the world by integrating theory and practice

promotor/a — a campesino who teaches others based on his or her own praxis

quetzal — Guatemalan currency (named after the country's national bird)

taller — a workshop
técnico — agricultural extension agent
tepetate — hard, weathered, mineral, clayey soil
vara — approximately one yard

Acronyms

ANAP — National Association of Small Farmers (Cuba)
AoA — Agreement on Agriculture (of the WTO)
CAS — Sandinista Agricultural Cooperatives
CCS — credit and service cooperatives
CIAL — Committee for Local Agricultural Research
CIAT — Center for Tropical Research
CIDICCO — Centro Internacional de Información Sobre Cultivos de Cobertura (International Center for Information on Cover Crops)
CGIAR — Consultative Group for International Agricultural Research
CIMMYT — International Center for the Improvement of Maize and Wheat
CMEA — Council for Mutual Economic Assistance
COSECHA — Association of Consultants for a Sustainable, Ecological, and People-Centered Agriculture
ECLA — Economic Commission on Latin America
EZLN — Ejército Zapatista de Liberación Nacional (Zapatista Army For National Liberation)
FAO — Food and Agriculture Organization of the United Nations
FENACOOP — Federación Nacional de Cooperativas (National Cooperative Federation)
FO — farmers' organization
FSLN — Frente Sandinista de Liberación Nacional (Sandinista National Liberation Front)
FSR — research approach that looks at the farm system as a whole, not just at individual crops.
FTAA — Free Trade Area of the Americas
GE — genetically engineered
GMOs — genetically modified organisms
GNP — gross national product
HYVs — high-yield varieties (of crops)
IARCs — International Agricultural Research Centers
IICA — Inter-American Institute for Cooperation on Agriculture
IIRSA — Initiative for the Integration of Regional Infrastructure in South America
IMF — International Monetary Fund
ISI — Import Substitution Industrialization
IUCN — International Union for the Conservation of Nature
LDCs — lesser-developed countries
MAP — Mexican Agricultural Project
MCAC — Movimiento Campesino a Campesino (Farmer-to-Farmer Movement)

MFSC — Mexican Friends Service Committee

MIDINRA — Ministry of Agriculture and Agrarian Reform (Nicaragua)

NAFTA — North American Free Trade Alliance

NARS — National Agricultural Research Systems

NGO — nongovernmental organization

NGOC-CGIAR — Nongovernmental Organization Committee within the Consultative Group for International Agricultural Research

NIEO — new international economic order

NRM — natural resource management

PAR — participatory action research

PCAC — Programa Campesino a Campesino (farmer-to-farmer project)

PPP — Plan Puebla-Panamá

PRA — Participatory Rural Appraisal

PRIAG — Program to Reinforce Basic Grain Research in Central America

RAFI — Rural Advancement Foundation International

SAP — structural adjustment program

SARD — sustainable agricultural and rural development

SEDEPAC — Servicio de Desarrollo y Paz, Asociación Civil (the Peace and Development Service, a Mexican NGO founded by the ex-director of the MFSC program)

SLM — sustainable land management

TRIPS — Trade-Related Aspects of Intellectual Property Rights

UNAG — Unión Nacional de Agricultores y Ganaderos (National Farmers and Ranchers Union)

UNDP — United Nations Development Programme

WTO — World Trade Organization

References

Altieri, M. A. 1983. *Agroecology.* Berkeley: University of California Press.

Altieri, M. A. 1987. *Agroecology: The scientific basis of sustainable agriculture.* Boulder, CO: Westview Press.

Altieri, M. A. 1989. Agroecology: A new research and development paradigm for world agriculture. *Agriculture, Ecosystems and Environment* 27(1–4): 37–46.

Altieri, M. A. 1990. Why study traditional agriculture? In *Agroecology*, ed. P. Rosset et al., 551–564. New York: McGraw-Hill.

Altieri, M. A. 2001. *Genetic engineering in agriculture: The myths, environmental risks and alternatives.* Oakland, CA: Food First.

Amir, S. 1976. *Unequal development.* New York: Monthly Review Press.

Annis, S., ed. 1992. *Poverty, natural resources, and public policy in Central America.* New Brunswick, NJ: Transaction Publishers.

Ascencio, F. L. 2003. Experiencias internacionales en el envio y uso de remesas. In *Migracion Mexico-Estados Unidos. Opciones de politica*, ed. R. Tuiran, 147–166. Col. del Valle, Mexico: Consejo Nacional de Poblacion.

Ashby, J. A., and L. Sperling. 1995. Institutionalizing participatory, client-driven research and technology development in agriculture. *Development and Change* 26: 753–770.

Balassa, B. A. 1971. *The structure of protection in developing countries.* Baltimore:Johns Hopkins Press.

Barkin, David "The Reconstruction of a Modern Mexican Peasantry," *The Journal of Peasant Studies*, Vol. 30:1 (2002), 73–90.

Barreto, H. 1994. Evaluation and utilization of different mulches and cover crops for maize production in Central America. In *Tapado slash/mulch: How farmers use it and what researchers know about it*, ed., D. Thurston et al., 157–168. Ithaca, NY: Cornell International Institute for Food, Agriculture and Development.

Bauer, P. T. 1981. *Equality, the third world, and economic delusion.* Cambridge, MA: Harvard University Press.

Baumeister, E. 1995. Farmers' organizations and agrarian transformation in Nicaragua. In *The new politics of survival: Grassroots movements in Central America*, ed. M. Sinclair, 239–263. New York: Monthly Review Press.

Baumeister, E. 1998. *Estructura y reforma agraria en Nicaragua (1979–1989).* Managua, Nicaragua: Instituto Nacional de Investigaciones y Estudios Socioeconómicos—INIES.

Bebbington, A. 1997. New states, new NGOs? Crisis and transitions among rural development NGOs in the Andean region. *World Development* 25(11):1755–1765.

Bebbington, A., and J. Farrington. 1992. NGO-government interaction in agricultural technology development. In *Making a difference*, eds. M. Edwards and D. Hume, 49–59. London: Earthscan.

Bebbington, A., and G. Thiele, et al. 1993. *Non-governmental organizations and the state in Latin America.* London: Routledge.

Bendaña, A. 1991. *La tragedia campesina.* Managua: CEI.

Blaikie, P. 2000. Development, post-, anti-, and populist: A critical review. *Environment and Planning A* 32(6):1033–1050.

Blaikie, P., T. Cannon, I. Davis, and B. Wisner. 1994. *At risk: Natural hazards, people's vulnerability, and disasters.* London: Routledge.

Blokland, K. 1992. *Participación campesina en el desarrollo económico.* Doetinchem, Holland: Paulo Freire Foundation.

Boas, M., and D. McNeill. 2003. *Multilateral institutions: A critical introduction.* London: Pluto Press.

Bolaños, J. 1992. *Generación y transferencia en América central.* Encuentro Anual de Investigación PCCMA Sobre la Generación y Transferencia Agrícola, Managua, Nicaragua, Programa Cooperativo Centroamericano el Mejoramiento de Cultivos Alimentarios y Ganadería.

Booth, J. A. 1992. *The end and the beginning: The Nicaraguan revolution.* Boulder, CO: Westview Press.

Brohman, J. 1996. *Popular development.* Oxford: Blackwell.

Buckles, D. 1994a. Cowardly land becomes brave: The use and diffusion of fertilizer bean (*Mucuna deeringianum*) on the hillsides of Atlantic Honduras. In *Tapado slash/mulch: how farmers use it and what researchers know about it,* ed. D. Thurston, 249–262. Ithaca, NY: Cornell International Institute for Food, Agriculture and Development (CIIFAD).

Buckles, D. 1994b. *Velvet bean, a "new" plant with a history.* Mexico City: CIMMYT.

Bunch, R. 1985. *Two ears of corn: A guide to people-centered agricultural improvement.* Oklahoma City: World Neighbors.

Bunch, R. 1990. *Low input soil restoration in Honduras: The Cantarranas farmer-to-farmer extension programme.* London: International Institute for Environment and Development.

Bunch, R. 1995. *An odyssey of discovery: Principles of agriculture for the humid tropics.* Tegucigalpa, Honduras: COSECHA.

Bunch, R. 1996. *People-centered agricultural development: Principles of extension for achieving long-term impact.* London: Overseas Development Institute. 11–18.

Cardenal, L. 1999. De la vulnerabilidad a la sostenibilidad: Ejes de transformacion para una sociedad en condiciones cronicas de riesgo. Managua, Nicaragua: United Nations Development Programme.

Cardoso, F. H., and E. H. Faletto. 1979. *Dependency and development in Latin America.* Berkeley: University of California Press.

CCAD. 1994. *Alianza Centroamericana para el Desarrollo Sostenible.* San José, Costa Rica: Comisión Centroamericana de Ambiente y Desarrollo.

Chambers, R. 1992. Spreading and self-improving: A strategy for scaling up. In *Making a difference,* eds. M. Edwards and D. Hume, 40–48. London: Earthscan.

Chambers, R. 1994a. The origins and practice of participatory rural appraisal. *World Development* 22(7):953–969.

Chambers, R. 1994b. Participatory rural appraisal (PRA)—Challenges, potentials and paradigm. *World Development* 22(10):1437–1454.

Chambers, R. 1994c. Participatory rural appraisal (PRA)—Analysis of experience. *World Development* 22(n2):1253–1268.

Chambers, R., A. Pacey, and L. A. Thrupp. 1989. *Farmer first: Farmer innovation and agricultural research.* London: Intermediate Technology Publications.

Colburn, F. D., ed. 1989. *Everyday forms of peasant resistance.* London: M. E. Sharpe, Inc.

Conway, G. 1985. Agroecosystems analysis. *Agricultural Administration* 20:31–35.

Conway, G. R., and E. B. Barbier. 1990. *After the green revolution: Sustainable agriculture for development.* London: Earthscan.

Cooke, B., and U. Kothari, eds. 2001. *Participation: The new tyranny?* London: Zed Books.

de Janvry, A. 1981. *The agrarian question and reformism in Latin America.* Baltimore and London: John Hopkins University Press.

de Senarclens, P. 1997. How the United Nations promotes development through technical assistance. In *The Post Development Reader,* ed. V. Bawtree and M. Rahnema, 190–201. London: Zed Books.

de Wit, T., and V. Gianotten. 1991. Action and participatory research: A case of peasant organization. In *Action and knowledge: Breaking the monopoly with participatory-action research,* ed. O. Fals-Borda and M. A. Rahman, 64–83. Bogotá and London: Intermediate Technology Publications.

Deo, S., and L. Swanson. 1990. Structure of agricultural research in the third world. In *Agroecology,* ed. Peter Rosset et al., 583–612. New York: McGraw-Hill.

Dore, E. 1996. Capitalism and ecological crisis: Legacy of the 1980s. In *Green guerrillas: Environmental conflict and initiatives in Latin America and the Caribbean,* ed. H. Collinson, 8–19. London: Latin American Bureau.

Duffield, M. 1994. Complex emergencies and the crisis of developmentalism. *Institute of Development Studies Bulletin* 25(4):37–45.

The Ecologist. 1996. CGIAR: Agricultural research for whom? *The Ecologist* 26:259–270.

Edelman, M. 2000. The persistence of the peasantry. *North American Congress on Latin America* XXXIII(5):14–19.

Edwards, M., and D. Hume, eds. 1992. *Making a difference: NGOs and development in a changing world.* London: Earthscan.

Enriquez, L. 1991. *Harvesting change: Labor and agrarian reform in Nicaragua, 1979–1990.* Chapel Hill: University of North Carolina Press.

Esteva, G. 1992. Development. In *The development dictionary,* ed. W. Sachs, 6–25. London and New York: Zed Books.

Esteva, G., and M. S. Prakash. 1998. *Grassroots post-modernism.* London and New York: Zed Books.

Faber, D. 1993. *Environment under fire: Imperialism and the ecological crisis in Central America.* New York: Monthly Review Press.

Fals-Borda, O., and M. A. Rahman, eds. 1991. *Action and knowledge: Breaking the monopoly with participatory action-research.* London: Intermediate Technology Publications.

Fine, B. 1999. The development state is dead—Long live social capital? *Development and Change* 30:1–19.

Flores, M., and N. Estrada. 1992. El estudio de caso: La utilización del frijol abono (*Mucuna spp.*) como alternativa viable para el sostenimiento productivo de los sistemas agrícolas del litoral Atlántico (thesis). Amsterdam: Center for Development Studies, Free University of Amsterdam.

Frank, A. G. 1967. *Capitalism and underdevelopment in Latin America.* New York: Monthly Review Press.

Frank, A. G. 1975. *On capitalist underdevelopment.* Oxford: Oxford University Press.

Freire, P. 1968. *Contribución al proceso de concientización en América Latina.* Montevideo, Uruguay: Junta Latino Americana de Iglesia y Sociedad.

Freire, P. 1970a. *Cultural action for freedom.* Cambridge: Harvard Educational Review.

Freire, P. 1970b. *Pedagogy of the oppressed.* New York: Herder and Herder.

Freire, P. 1973a. *Education for critical consciousness.* New York: Seabury Press.

Freire, P. 1973b. *Extensión o comunicación? La concientización en el medio rural.* Mexico City, D.F.: Siglo Veintiuno Editores.

Freire, P., Catholic Institute for International Relations, et al. 1975. *Conscientization*. Geneva: World Council of Churches.

Friedman, M. 1968. The role of monetary policy. *American Economic Review* 58:1–17.

FUNDESCA, ed. 1994. *El último despale … La frontera agrícola Centroamericana*. San José, Costa Rica: Fundación para el Desarrollo Económico y Social de Centro América.

Furtado, C. 1964. *Development and underdevelopment*. Berkeley and Los Angeles: University of California Press.

Gliessman, S. R. 1990. *Agroecology: Researching the ecological basis for sustainable agriculture*. New York: Springer-Verlag.

Gliessman, S. R. 1998a. *Agroecology: Ecological processes in sustainable agriculture*. Chelsea, MI: Ann Arbor Press.

Gliessman, S. R. 1998b. Agroecology: Researching the ecological processes in sustainable agriculture. In *Frontiers in biology: The challenges of biodiversity, biotechnology and sustainable agriculture*, ed. S. Chou. Taipei: Academia Sinica.

Gliessman, S. R., et al. 1981. The ecological basis for the application of traditional agricultural technology in the management of tropical agroecosystems. *Agro-Ecosystems* 50:24–31.

Gonsalves, J. 2001. Going to scale: What we have garnered from recent workshops. *LIESA* 17:6–10.

Goodman, D., B. Sorj, and J. Wilkinson. 1987. *From farming to biotechnology: A theory of agro-industrial development*. Oxford: Blackwell.

Gore, C. 2000. The rise and fall of the Washington consensus as a paradigm for developing countries. *World Development* 28(5):789–804.

Gündel, S., J. Hancock, and S. Andeson. 2001. A project design framework for scaling up NRM research. *LIESA* 17:11–12.

Harrington, L. 2000. *Delivering the goods: Generalising and propagating NRM research results through "scaling out."* Washington, D.C.: NGOC-CGIAR.

Harriss, J., ed. 1982. *Rural development: Theories of peasant economy and agrarian change*. London: Hutchinson University Library.

Haverkort, B., J. Vanderkamp, and A. Waters-Bayer, eds. 1991. *Joining farmers' experiments: Experiences in participatory technology development*. London: Intermediate Technology Publications.

Heller, C. 2001. McDonalds, MTV and Monsanto: Resisting biotechnology in the age of informational capital. In *Redesigning Life? The worldwide challenge to genetic engineering*. ed. B. Tokar. London and New York: Zed Books.

Hewitt de Alcántara, C. 1976. *Modernizing Mexican agriculture*. Geneva: United Nations Research Institute for Social Development.

Hocde, H., et al. 2000. Toward a social movement of farmer innovation: Campesino a Campesino. *LEISA*, 16: 26–30.

Holt-Giménez, E. 1989. De Campesino a Campesino: Una nueva relacion. In *El Extensionista Rural*, ed. Orlando Núñez, Managua, Nicaragua: Centro de Investigacion de Reforma Agraria.

Holt-Giménez, E. 1992. *Campesino a Campesino en Nicaragua*. Encuentro Anual de Investigación PCCMA Sobre la Generación y Transferencia Agrícola, Managua, Nicaragua, Programa Cooperativo Centroamericano el Mejoramiento de Cultivos Alimentarios y Ganadería.

Holt-Giménez, E. 1996. The Campesino a Campesino movement: Farmer-led sustainable agriculture in Central America and Mexico. *Food First Development Report No. 10*. Oakland, CA: Institute for Food and Development Policy.

Holt-Giménez, E. 1997. La canasta metodológica: Metodologías campesinas para la enseñanza agroecológica y el desarrollo de la agricultura sostenible. Managua, SIMAS: 19.

Holt-Giménez, E. 2001. *Measuring farmers' agroecological resistance to Hurricane Mitch in Central America.* London: International Institute for Environment and Development.

Holt-Giménez, E. 2002. Movimiento Campesino a Campesino: The political ecology of a farmer's movement for sustainable agriculture in Mesoamérica (dissertation). Santa Cruz: Department of Environmental Studies, University of California. 268.

Hynnemeyer, A.-J., R. de Camino, and S. Muller. 1997. *Análisis del desarrollo sostenible en Centroamérica.* San José, Costa Rica: Instituto Interamericano de Cooperación para la Agricultura.

IICA. 1991. *Agricultura sostenible en las laderas Centroamericanas: Oportunidades de colaboración interinstitucional.* Coronado, Costa Rica: Instituto Interamericano de Cooperación para la Agricultura.

Jeavons, J. 1974. *How to grow more vegetables than you ever thought possible on less land than you can imagine.* Palo Alto, CA: Ecology Action of the Midpeninsula.

Jeffery, S. E. 1982. The creation of vulnerability to natural disaster: Case studies from the Dominican Republic. *Disasters* 6(1):38–43.

Jennings, B. 1988. *Foundations of international agricultural research: Science and politics in Mexican agriculture.* Boulder and London: Westview Press.

Kaimowitz, D. 1993. The role of non-governmental organizations in agricultural research and technology transfer in Latin America. *World Development* 21(7):1139–1150.

Kearney, M. 1997. *Reconceptualizing the peasant: Anthropology in global perspective.* Boulder, Oxford: Westview Press.

Kennedy, J. F. 1961. The alliance for progress. In *The Central American crisis reader,* ed. R. S. Leiken and B. Rubin, 119–123. New York: Summit Books.

Kloppenburg, J. R. 1988. *First the seed: The political economy of plant biotechnology, 1492–2000.* Cambridge: Cambridge University Press.

Korten, D. 1990. *Getting to the 21st century: Voluntary action and the global agenda.* West Hartford, CT: Kumarian Press.

Korten, D. C., and R. Klauss, eds. 1984. *People-centered development: Contributions toward theory and planning frameworks.* West Hartford, CT: Kumarian Press.

Leisinger, K. 1999. Ethical challenges of agricultural biotechnology for developing countries. Paper given at conference *Agricultural Biotechnology and the Poor,* Washington, D.C.: Consultative Group on International Agricultural Research.

Lélé, S. 1991. Sustainable development: A critical review. *World Development* 19(6):607–621.

Long, N., J. van der Ploeg, et al. 1986. *The commoditization debate: Labour process, strategy and social network.* Wageningen, The Netherlands: University of Wageningen.

Lopez, G. 1996. *The villager extensionist in developing nations.* London: Overseas Development Institute. 36–44.

MacDonald, L. 1997. *Supporting civil society: The political role of non-governmental organizations in Central America.* New York: St. Martin's.

Maldidier, C., and P. Marchetti. 1996. *El campesino-finquero y el potencial económico del campesinado nicaragüense.* Managua, Nicaragua: Nitlapán.

Mann, S. A. 1990. *Agrarian capitalism in theory and practice.* Chapel Hill: University of North Carolina Press.

Mann, S. A., and J. M. Dickenson. 1978. Obstacles to the development of a capitalist agriculture. *Journal of Peasant Studies* 5(4):466–481.

McAfee, K. 2004. Corn culture and dangerous DNA: Real and imagined consequences of maize gene flow in Oaxaca. *Journal of Latin American Geography* 2:11–42.

Meadows, Donella H. 1977. *Limits to Growth: A Report for the Club of Rome's Project on the Predicament of Mankind*, New American Library.

Méndez-Quintana, D. 2000. *Una mirada al concepto desarrollo*. Managua: PNUD/UNDP.

Merlet, M. 1995. *Consolidacion y ampliacion del programa Campesino a Campesino*. Managua, Nicaragua: Unión Nacional de Agricultores y Ganaderos.

Miranda, B. 1999. *Proyecto regional: Desarrollo Institucional para la Producción Agrícola Sostenible en las laderas de América Central, 1988–2002*. Coronado, Cost Rica: IICA. 75.

Netting, R. M. 1993. *Smallholders, householders: Farm families and the ecology of intensive sustainable agriculture*. Stanford, CA: Stanford University Press.

Norgaard, R. 1987. The epistomological basis of agroecology. In *Agroecology*, ed. M. Altieri, 21–27. Boulder and London: Westview.

Norgaard, R., and T. Sikor. 1995. *Agroecology: The science of sustainable agriculture*. Boulder, CO: Westview Press.

Orozco, M. 2003. *The impact of migration in the Caribbean and Central American region*. Ottawa: FOCAL.

PCAC. 2000. *De Campesino a Campesino: Producimos conservando los recursos naturales para un futuro autosostenible*. Managua, Nicaragua: Unión Nacional de Agricultores y Ganaderos. 26.

PCAC. 2001. *De Campesino a Campesino*: Comenzamos despacito y estamos caminando. Managua, Nicaragua: Unión Nacional de Agricultores y Ganaderos. 4.

Pearce, D., E. Barbier, and A. Markandya. 1990. *Sustainable development: Economics and environment in the third world*. London: Earthscan.

Pearce, J. 2000. *Development, NGOs, and Civil Society*. Oxford: Oxfam. 15–43.

Pearse, A. 1980. *Seeds of plenty, seeds of want: Social and economic implications of the green revolution*. Oxford: Clarendon Press.

Perera, A. 2002. Evaluación de la metodología "de Campesino a Campesino" utilizada para la promoción de la agricultura agroecológica. *Centro de Estudios de Agricultura Sostenible*. Havana, Cuba: Universidad Agraria de la Habana. 95.

Perseley, G. J., and M. M. Lantin. 1999. *Agricultural biotechnology and the poor*. Washington, D.C.: Consultative Group on International Agricultural Research.

Pieterse, J. N. 1998. My paradigm or yours? Alternative development, post-development, reflexive development. *Development and Change* 29:343–373.

Pinstrup-Andersen, P., and M. Cohen. 1999. Modern biotechnology for food and agriculture: Risks and opportunities for the poor. *Evolving Role of the Public and Private Sector in Agricultural Biotechnology for Developing Countries*. Washington, D.C.: Consultative Group on International Agricultural Research.

Prebisch, R. 1950. *The economic development of Latin America and its principal problems*. New York: United Nations Publications.

Preston, P. W. 1996. *Development Theory*. Oxford: Blackwell.

Pretty, J. 1995. Participatory learning for sustainable agriculture. *World Development* 23(8):1247–1263.

Rapley, J. 1996. *Understanding development: Theory and practice in the third world*. London and Boulder, CO: Lynne Rienner Publishers, Inc.

Ramos Sánchez, F. 1998. *Grupo Vicente Guerrero de Españita, Tlaxcala*. Mexico: Rockefeller Foundation.

Recinos Montes, A. 1999. Las Parcelas Gemelas: Como la agricultura campesina resistío el huracán Mitch. World Neighbors, Managua.

Rhoades, R., and R. Booth. 1982. Farmer-back-to-farmer: A model for generating acceptable agricultural technology. *Agricultural Administration* 11:127–137.

Richards, P. 1985. *Indigenous agricultural revolution: Ecology and food production in West Africa.* London: Hutchison.

Rogers, E. 1962. *Diffusion of innovations.* New York: Free Press.

Rogers, E. 1969. *Modernization among peasants: The impact of communication.* New York: Holt, Rinehart, Winston.

Rosset, P. 2002. *Genetic engineering of food crops for the third world: An appropriate response to poverty, hunger and lagging productivity?* Oakland, CA: Food First/Institute for Food and Development Policy.

Rosset, P., and M. Benjamin. 1994. Cuba's nationwide conversion to organic agriculture. *Capitalism, Nature, Socialism* 5(3):79–97.

Rostow, W. W. 1960. *The stages of economic growth: A non-communist manifesto.* Cambridge: Cambridge University Press.

Sain, G., et al. 1994. Profitability of the Abonera system practiced by farmers on the Atlantic coast of Honduras. In *Tapado slash/mulch: How farmers use it and what researchers know about it,* ed. D. Thurston, et al., 273–282. Ithaca, NY: CIIFAD.

Scoones, I., J. Thompson, and R. Chambers, eds. 1994. *Beyond farmer first.* London: ITDG.

Scott, J. 1976. *The moral economy of the peasant.* New Haven and London: Yale University Press.

Scott, J. C. 1989. Everyday forms of resistance. In *Everyday forms of peasant resistance,* ed. F. D. Colburn, 3–33. New York: M. E. Sharpe.

Serageldin, I. 1997. The CGIAR at twenty-five: Into the future. Paper given at CGIAR conference, International Centers Week, October 28–November 1, Washington, D.C.

Serra, L. 1991. *El Movimiento Campesino: Su participación política durante la revolución sandinista 1979–1989.* Managua: Imprenta Universidad Centroamericana.

Shanin, T. 1972. *The awkward class: Political sociology of peasantry in a developing society.* Oxford: Clarendon Press.

Sinclair, M., and J. Nash, eds. 1995. *The new politics of survival: Grassroots movements in Central America.* New York: Monthly Review Press.

Sinha, S. 2000. The "other" agrarian transition? Structure, institutions and agency in sustainable rural development. *The Journal of Peasant Studies* 27(2):169–204.

Smith, K. 1994. *The human farm: A tale of changing lives and changing lands.* West Hartford, CT: Kumarian Press.

Smith, K. 1996. *Environmental hazards: Assessing risk and reducing disaster.* London and New York: Routledge.

Sollis, P. 1995. Partners in development? The state, nongovernmental organizations and the UN in Central America. *Third World Quarterly* 16(3):525–542.

Sonntag, H. et al. 2000. Modernism, development and modernization. *Pensamiento Propio* 11(Jan–Jun):3–30.

Stonich, S. 1993. *"I am destroying the land!" The political ecology of poverty and environmental destruction in Honduras.* Boulder, CO: Westview.

Stonich, S. 1995. Development, rural impoverishment, and environmental destruction in Honduras. In *The Social Causes of Environmental Destruction in Latin America,* ed. P. Durham, 63–100. Ann Arbor: University of Michigan Press.

Streeten, P. 1983. Rule one: Aim at the poorest. *The New Internationalist* August: 126.

Taylor, C. E. 2001. Scaling up social development. *LEISA: Magazine on Low External Input and Sustainable Agriculture* 17:14–17.

Toness, A., T. Thurow, and H. Sierra. 1998. Sustainable management of tropical steeplands: An assessment of terraces as a soil and water conservation technology (report). College Station, TX: Texas A&M University/USAID. 52.

UNDP. 1991. *Report on human development.* New York: United Nations Development Programme.

Utting, P. 1993. *Trees, People and Power.* London: Earthscan.

Uvin and Muller. 2000.

Uvin, P., and D. Miller. 1996. Paths to scaling-up: Alternative strategies for local nongovernmental organizations. *Human Organization* 55(3):344-354.

Uvin, P., P. S. Jain, and D. Brown. 2000. Think large and act small: Toward a new paradigm for NGO scaling up. *World Development* 28(8):1409–1419.

van der Ploeg, J. D. 1986. The agricultural labor process and commoditization. In *The commoditization debate. Labour process, strategy and social network*, ed. N. Long et al., Wageningen, The Netherlands: Wageningen Agricultural University.

Wade, R. 1997. *The greening of the world bank.* Presentation to Board of Sociology. University of California, Santa Cruz.

WCED. 1987. *Our common future.* New York: Oxford University Press.

Wheelock, J. R. 1985. *Entre la crisis y la agresión, la Reforma Agraria Sandinista.* Managua, Nicaragua: Editorial Nueva Nicaragua.

Wilches-Chaux, G. 1994. La vulnerabilidad global. In *Los desastres no son naturales*, ed. A. Marskey. Bogotá, Colombia: LA RED.

Wilken, G. 1988. *Good farmers: Traditional agricultural resource management in Mexico and Central America.* Berkeley: University of California Press.

Winn, P. 1997. *Americas.* Berkeley: University of California Press.

Wise, R. D. 2003. *NAFTA's untold stories: Mexico's grassroots responses to the North American integration program.* Interhemispheric Resource Center, Silver City, NM.

Wisner, B. 1993. Disaster vulnerability: Scale, power and daily life. *GeoJournal* 30(2):127–40.

World Commission on Environment and Development, 1987. *Our Common Future.* Oxford University Press.

Zamora, R. G. 2003a. *Crisis agricola, tratado de libre comercio y migracion internacional en Mexico.* Zacatecas: Red Internacional de Migracion y Desarrollo.

Zamora, R. G. 2003b. *Los retos actuales de la teoria del desarrollo.* Zacatecas: Red Internacional de Migracion y Desarrollo.

Zurita, F., and E. Holt-Giménez. 1991. *Campesino a campesino.* Managua, Nicaragua: Unión Nacional de Agricultores y Ganaderos, UNAG.

Index

About Food First

FOOD FIRST, also known as the Institute for Food and Development Policy, is a nonprofit research and education-for-action center dedicated to investigating and exposing the root causes of hunger in a world of plenty. It was founded in 1975 by Frances Moore Lappé, author of the bestseller *Diet for a Small Planet*, and food policy analyst Dr. Joseph Collins. Food First research has revealed that hunger is created by concentrated economic and political power, not by scarcity. Resources and decision-making are in the hands of a wealthy few, depriving the majority of land and jobs, and therefore of food.

Hailed by *The New York Times* as "one of the most established food think tanks in the country," Food First has grown to profoundly shape the debate about hunger and development.

But Food First is more than a think tank. Through books, reports, videos, media appearances, and speaking engagements, Food First experts not only reveal the often hidden roots of hunger, they show how individuals can get involved in bringing an end to the problem. Food First inspires action by bringing to light the courageous efforts of people around the world who are creating farming and food systems that truly meet people's needs.

More Books from Food First

Alternatives to the Peace Corps: A Guide to Global Volunteer Opportunities,
Eleventh Edition. **Edited by Paul Backhurst**
   Newly expaned and updated, this easy-to-use guidebook is the original resource
   for finding community-based, grassroots volunteer work—the kind of work that
   changes the world, one person at a time.
   PAPERBACK, $11.95

To Inherit the Earth: The Landless Movement and the Struggle for a New Brazil
Angus Wright and Wendy Wolford
   To Inherit the Earth tells the dramatic story of Brazil's Landless Workers' Movement,
   or MST, wherein many thousands of desperately poor, landless, jobless men and
   women have through their own nonviolent efforts secured rights to more than 20
   million acres of unused farmland.
   PAPERBACK, $15.95

Genetic Engineering in Agriculture: The Myths, Environmental Risks, and Alternatives,
Second Edition. **Miguel A. Altieri**
   Noted agroecologist Miguel Altieri demystifies the hype around genetically modi-
   fied (GM) crops and makes a case for a future based on sustainable agriculture and
   social justice.
   PAPERBACK, $11.95

Breakfast of Biodiversity: The Truth about Rain Forest Destruction
John Vandermeer and Ivette Perfecto
   Why biodiversity is in such jeopardy around the world and what steps must be
   taken to slow the ravaging of rain forests.
   PAPERBACK, $16.95

Earthsummit.biz: The Corporate Takeover of Sustainable Development
Kenny Bruno and Joshua Karliner
   The story of the corporate cooptation of the rhetoric of social and environmental
   responsibility, with 18 muckraking case studies of the ways corporate behavior
   contradicts corporate PR.
   PAPERBACK, $12.95

Sustainable Agriculture and Development: Transforming Food Production in Cuba
Fernando Funes, Luis García, Martin Bourque, Nilda Pérez, and Peter Rosset
   Unable to import food or farm chemicals and machines in the wake of the Soviet
   bloc's collapse and a tightening U.S. embargo, Cuba turned toward sustainable
   agriculture, organic farming, urban gardens, and other techniques to secure its food
   supply. This book gives details of that remarkable achievement.
   PAPERBACK, $18.95

The Future in the Balance: Essays on Globalization and Resistance
Walden Bello. Edited with a preface by Anuradha Mittal
> A new collection of essays by third world activist and scholar Walden Bello on the myths of development as prescribed by the World Trade Organization and other institutions, and the possibility of another world based on fairness and justice.
> PAPERBACK, $13.95

Views from the South: The Effects of Globalization and the WTO on Third World Countries
Foreword by Jerry Mander. Afterword by Anuradha Mittal. Edited by Sarah Anderson
> This rare collection of essays by third world activists and scholars describes in pointed detail the effects of the WTO and other Bretton Woods institutions.
> PAPERBACK, $12.95

Basta! Land and the Zapatista Rebellion in Chiapas, Third Edition
George A. Collier with Elizabeth Lowery Quaratiello. Foreword by Peter Rosset
> The classic on the Zapatistas in its third edition, including a preface by Roldolfo Stavenhagen.
> PAPERBACK, $16.95

America Needs Human Rights
Edited by Anuradha Mittal and Peter Rosset
> This new anthology includes writings on understanding human rights, poverty in America, and welfare reform and human rights.
> PAPERBACK, $13.95

The Paradox of Plenty: Hunger in a Bountiful World
> Excerpts from Food First's best writings on world hunger and what we can do to change it.
> PAPERBACK, $18.95

Education for Action: Graduate Studies with a Focus on Social Change,
Fourth Edition. **Edited by Joan Powell**
> A newly updated authoritative and easy-to-use guidebook that provides information on progressive programs in a wide variety of fields.
> PAPERBACK, $12.95

We encourage you to buy Food First Books from your local independent bookseller: if they don't have them in stock, they can usually order them for you fast. To find an independent bookseller in your area, go to **www.booksense.com**. Food First books are also available through the major online booksellers (Powell's, Amazon, and Barnes and Noble), and through the Food First website, **www.foodfirst.org**. You can also order direct from our distributor, CDS, at (800) 343-4499. If you have trouble locating a Food First title, write, call, or e-mail us:

FOOD FIRST
398 60th Street, Oakland, CA 94618, USA
Tel: (510) 654-4400 • Fax: (510) 654-4551
E-mail: foodfirst@foodfirst.org • Web: www.foodfirst.org

If you are a bookseller or other reseller, contact our distributor, CDS, at (800) 343-4499 to order.

How to Become a Member or Intern of Food First

Become a Member of Food First

Private contributions and membership gifts form the financial base of Food First/
Institute for Food and Development Policy. The success of the Institute's programs
depends not only on its dedicated volunteers and staff, but on financial activists as
well. Each member strengthens Food First's efforts to change a hungry world. We
invite you to join Food First. As a member you will receive a 20 percent discount on
all Food First books. You will also receive our quarterly publication, Food First News
and Views, and timely Backgrounders that provide information and suggestions for
action on current food and hunger crises in the United States and around the world.
If you want to subscribe to our Internet newsletters, Food Rights Watch and We Are
Fighting Back, send us an e-mail at foodfirst@foodfirst.org. All contributions are tax
deductible.

Become an Intern for Food First

There are opportunities for interns in research, advocacy, campaigning, publishing,
computers, media, and publicity at Food First. Our interns come from around the
world. They are a vital part of our organization and make our work possible.

To become a member or apply to become an intern, just call, visit our website, or
clip and return the attached coupon to:

FOOD FIRST
398 60th Street,
Oakland, CA 94618, USA
Tel: (510) 654-4400
Fax: (510) 654-4551
E-mail: foodfirst@foodfirst.org
Web: www.foodfirst.org

You are also invited to give a gift membership to others interested in the fight to end
hunger.

Joining Food First

❏ I want to join Food First and receive a 20% discount on this and all subsequent orders. Enclosed is my tax-deductible contribution of:

❏ $35   ❏ $50   ❏ $100   ❏ $1,000   ❏ OTHER

NAME _____

ADDRESS _____

CITY/STATE/ZIP _____

DAYTIME PHONE (_____) _____

E-MAIL _____

ORDERING FOOD FIRST MATERIALS

ITEM DESCRIPTION	QTY	UNIT COST	TOTAL

MEMBER DISCOUNT 20%	$ _____
CA RESIDENTS SALES TAX 8.75%	$ _____
SUBTOTAL	$ _____
POSTAGE 15% • UPS 20% ($2 MIN.)	$ _____
MEMBERSHIP(S)	$ _____
ADDITIONAL CONTRIBUTION	$ _____
TOTAL ENCLOSED	$ _____

PAYMENT METHOD:

❏ CHECK

❏ MONEY ORDER

❏ MASTERCARD

❏ VISA

NAME ON CARD _____

CARD NUMBER _____ EXP. DATE _____

SIGNATURE _____

MAKE CHECK OR MONEY ORDER PAYABLE TO:
FOOD FIRST • 398 60TH STREET, OAKLAND, CA 94618

For gift memberships and mailings, please see coupon on reverse side.

Food First Gift Books

Please send a gift book to (order form on reverse side):

NAME _____

ADDRESS _____

CITY/STATE/ZIP _____

FROM _____

Food First Publications Catalogs

Please send a publications catalog to:

NAME _____

ADDRESS _____

CITY/STATE/ZIP _____

FROM _____

NAME _____

ADDRESS _____

CITY/STATE/ZIP _____

NAME _____

ADDRESS _____

CITY/STATE/ZIP _____

Food First Gift Memberships

❐ Enclosed is my tax-deductible contribution of:

❐ $35   ❐ $50   ❐ $100   ❐ $1,000   ❐ OTHER

Please send a Food First membership to:

NAME _____

ADDRESS _____

CITY/STATE/ZIP _____

FROM _____